WHAT WAS
I THINKING

a memoir

PAUL HENRY

WITH Paul Little

WHAT WAS I THINKING
a memoir

RANDOM HOUSE
NEW ZEALAND

A RANDOM HOUSE BOOK published by Random House New Zealand
18 Poland Road, Glenfield, Auckland, New Zealand

For more information about our titles go to www.randomhouse.co.nz

A catalogue record for this book is available from the National Library
of New Zealand

Random House New Zealand is part of the Random House Group
New York   London   Sydney   Auckland   Delhi   Johannesburg

First published 2011. Reprinted 2011.

ISBN 978 1 86979 566 5

Cover design: Paul Henry and Carla Sy
Cover photographs: Jane Ussher
Text design: Carla Sy
Printed in New Zealand by Printlink

A NOTE ABOUT THE ILLUSTRATOR

Paul's mum, Olive.

MY MOTHER'S ARTISTIC PROWESS is displayed in this book at its absolute finest.

" I'VE KNOWN FOR QUITE A NUMBER OF YEARS WHAT
THE MEANING OF LIFE IS AND BECAUSE THAT'S THE
POINT OF THE WHOLE THING, I DEDICATE THIS BOOK
TO THE MEANING OF MY LIFE: "

LUCY ROSE
SOPHIE OLIVE HENRIETTA
BELLA SUSANNAH

A NOTE TO THE READER

> "FINDING MYSELF SOMEWHAT UNEXPECTEDLY WITH A BIT OF SPARE TIME — 'THANK YOU, NEW ZEALAND ON AIR' — AND BEING APPROACHED BY PAUL LITTLE AND RANDOM HOUSE TO WRITE MY MEMOIRS, I THOUGHT HOW HARD CAN IT BE? . . . WHAT ARE MEMOIRS?"

I NEVER IMAGINED I would ever have the time, energy, patience or inclination to write a book. In short, the heartbeats. Over the years, on numerous occasions, people have said, you should write a book. I always openly mocked the suggestion. However, finding myself somewhat unexpectedly with a bit of spare time — 'thank you, New Zealand On Air' — and being approached by Paul Little and Random House to write my memoirs, I thought, how hard can it be? . . . What are memoirs?

For the sake of clarification, in my book, memoirs are nothing more than memories: the memories I hold of my life at this point in time. As such they are 100 per cent accurate. I give my personal guarantee that everything in this book is exactly as I remember it. It may have never happened, but this is, I promise you, how I recall my life and circumstances. It's by no means a complete picture for a number of reasons. First, I have found that even remembering things is quite hard work; second, if I remembered it all, the book would be just too long; and third, I have decided to keep two areas of my life private and so not remember anything about either of them. Those two areas are philanthropy and romance.

As for what remains, I have made absolutely no effort to check or in any way clarify names, dates, places or any of the tedious things often referred to as facts. I'm just far too busy with all my philanthropy and romance. I would just say this though: knowing me, as I do, there is just as much chance the fish in this book were bigger than I remember them as there is they were smaller. Indeed over the years, recounting my stories to people, I have often pedalled back on some of the true detail because of its unbelievability.

CONTENTS

Paul in the water

PROLOGUE: HOW I LEARNT TO SWIM

> **WHAT I WANT YOU TO REMEMBER WHEN I THROW YOU IN IS, ESSENTIALLY, IF YOU DO NOTHING YOU WILL FLOAT. SWIMMING HAS NOTHING TO DO WITH STAYING ALIVE. FLOATING WILL KEEP YOU ALIVE. I'M NOT INTERESTED IN QUALITY. WE'RE TALKING ABOUT SAVING YOUR LIFE.**

MY FATHER NEVER CAME home in a bad mood. He would almost always arrive excited to tell my mother and me about something amazing that had happened in his day.

I had just started at Cockle Bay School in Auckland when he came home one day to find me talking to my mother about swimming lessons we were going to have. He was surprised to learn that his son couldn't already swim.

'Go and put your togs on,' he said. 'We are going down to the sea and I'm going to teach you to swim.'

It was late in the day and I sometimes used to get scared going to the beach if it was getting dark because it was quite a long walk through the bush from our house to the water. But I wasn't at all scared this time. I thought it was cool — my dad and me, doing man stuff together.

We clambered up on some rocks at the water's edge.

'Here's the thing,' he said, bending down to me. 'People float. The thing that stops people from floating and the reason people drown is they panic and they flay their arms around and push themselves down under the water, which is where you'll die. What I want you to remember when I throw you in is, essentially, if you do nothing you will float. Swimming has nothing to do with staying alive. Floating will keep you alive. I'm not interested in quality. We're talking about saving your life.'

He was very good at taking things that could be quite complex and making them simple. Then he picked me up and threw me out off the rocks into the sea.

I hit the water and not one part of me thought I wouldn't be able to swim. I didn't have to do anything. I was gasping a bit, but I was floating. Then I started to move a little. Water was going in my mouth and I was spluttering a bit.

'You see?' he called out. 'Now, you're moving slightly so you're swimming. You're doing very, very well. When you finally get to shore here, we'll go up and you can tell your mother that tomorrow you're going to school to tell everyone that you can swim.'

Then he started explaining to me about moving my arms and when I got to shore I didn't get out. I turned around and swam back out, swam in, swam out, swam in again. By the time I went home I was a swimmer.

Gypsy caravan with horse

CHAPTER 1
BRIAN AND OLIVE

> **THE FACT MY FATHER'S MOTHER WAS A GYPSY HAD BEEN A FAMILY SECRET — SECRET BECAUSE IN ENGLAND THE GYPSIES ARE THE LOWEST OF THE LOW . . . APPARENTLY, MY GRANDFATHER STOLE HER FROM A GYPSY CAMP WHEN SHE WAS VERY YOUNG. SO, PREDICTABLY, THERE HADN'T BEEN MUCH CONTACT WITH THAT SIDE OF THE FAMILY SUBSEQUENTLY.**

THE FACT MY FATHER'S mother was a gypsy had been a family secret — secret because in England the gypsies are the lowest of the low. They still are. My mother, Olive, was told, well after she and my father had moved to New Zealand, by one of the family friends: 'Well, of course, Gladys was a gypsy.' Apparently, my grandfather stole her from a gypsy camp when she was very young. So, predictably, there hadn't been much contact with that side of the family subsequently. Looking back — the earrings, the plastic jewellery, all that hair — how could anyone not have known? And if you look at my father, Brian, you can see it with the complexion and the dark hair. But it had been a secret and my mother decided to keep it a secret because she thought everyone else would be as appalled as the people who had told her.

We weren't great communicators as a family. When my mother finally told me, I thought it was fantastic — I finally had something interesting in my background. Not long after that, I was driving over the Rimutaka hills with my father and I said, 'I've heard that we're gypsies.' I didn't know whether he had been told himself, and I couldn't tell from his non-committal reaction whether or not he already knew.

'There'll never be a battle over land if you're a gypsy,' was all he said.

He was Brian Henry Hopes. It was decided all of the men in our direct line would be called Henry or their middle name would be Henry. I was Paul Henry Hopes but I dropped the Hopes officially when I was standing for Parliament. I thought it might be a problem because everyone knew me as Paul Henry, which is what I called myself on the radio. You have to have your full legal name on the ballot form, so I changed it officially.

Both my parents were born in England. My mother was lower working class and worked at Imperial Tobacco in Bristol. All she knew was the one street where she lived and worked. She had no father, which meant she was regarded as a bastard, and in those days that actually mattered. My father's family were a bit better off, probably upper working class, but the family lost a lot of money during the war. They lost quite a bit when Granddad went to the war, as a lot of people did. My father finished school and used to spend all his time at the library teaching himself about engineering. He worked as an engineer on the railway. He was a bad father and a bad husband but he saved my mother from a life of abject mediocrity by bringing her out to New Zealand and by making her step well outside her comfort zone.

The move to New Zealand came after they got married and would have been all his doing. The journey was the important thing. I don't know that he'd worked out what was going to happen when he arrived. The plan was for him to come out and establish a base and for her to follow. He made sure the

DAD - SECOND TO RIGHT!

journey would take the longest possible time by deciding to travel overland in a Bedford van. He bought the vehicle and found some people to pay for the privilege of making the journey with him. It was quite innovative and even got newspaper coverage. It wasn't an easy trip and there were several near-death experiences on the way. When they got to Nairobi, two of the guys decided they had had enough and they booked their passage from the port to carry on by train. On their last night together they were in a market where there was a fortune teller and they decided to get their fortunes told.

The first guy went in, sat down and showed the woman his palm. She told him all the usual vague stuff that anyone could have made up. When the next guy went in and held out his hand the woman closed it up.

'I can't tell you your future,' she said. 'I can't see your future.' She wouldn't take any money from him.

My father was third and again got the vague generalisations we're used to from *Sensing Murder*. But when the last of the group went in she folded his hand up and again said she could not tell him his future. He was a bit more persistent than the other guy.

'What do you mean?' he said. 'Why can't you tell me my future?' He kept on at her.

'Because you don't have a future,' she finally said.

Later they realised that the two guys who didn't get their futures told were the two who were leaving the group. Two days later, the train they were on slipped down a bank into a river and Dad and his remaining passenger had to go and identify their bloated bodies.

I think Dad was an atheist, and certainly the least gullible man alive. He really wrestled with this whole incident. He tried to calculate what the odds were that the fortune teller would refuse to tell the fortune of the two going on the train, then of them dying so soon after her saying they had no future. He was a man who needed answers to questions and it haunted him for years that he could not explain this.

Eventually my mother came out too and there was tension there because she desperately wanted children and my father almost equally desperately didn't. He didn't want anything that would tie him down. I was an only child. My mother got pregnant again, but the child was stillborn. I was 15 months old. My mother had planned to call him Andrew. It was one of those terrible cases where the new baby had died but she had to deliver it normally and endure weeks of people asking her when the baby was due.

As a result of his attitude, my father didn't care for me when I was very young although I became slightly interesting later on, when I was less needy. I used to clash with his perfectionism. He found me difficult because I had a very short attention span when I was young — and an even shorter one when I was older, for that matter. He would try to slow me down to get things perfect and in so doing he could suck all the fun out of a day.

Once I found the old plastic hull of a toy boat and decided to paint it. I showed it to my father when he came home, and he couldn't understand I could be so stupid as not to realise the drag that the paint would impose on the hull. I had to scrape the paint off. Doing that, of course, I scratched the hull and the drag was now extraordinary. But he was happy because the paint was off.

He once made a Meccano cable car which totally enchanted me. But I wasn't allowed to touch it or any of his Meccano bits and pieces in case I damaged them.

He was a marine engineer and spent a lot of time travelling the world, making things work when other people stuffed up. I idolised him, I still do. I loved him desperately and missed him when he was away. He was a true adventurer and when he came back he would fill my mind with amazing stories, some of which may not have been true or were embellishments of the truth. I saw him do enough amazing things myself to believe they probably were.

He was interested in conservation and the way things grew, but if nature's interests came into conflict with man's, man always came first. If there were people who needed water and bush had to be cut down to get it to them, then the bush was cut down. This happened on one occasion overseas where environmentalists were trying to stop his project going ahead.

In the end he said to them, 'Obviously we're going nowhere here with this project, we're at a stalemate. Why don't I take you for a drive and show you how beautiful this bloody island really is.' He hired buses for the environmentalists and while they were around the other side of the island his men cleared the part that needed to be cleared to get the pipes through with explosives.

If he hit a possum he would stop to make sure there weren't any babies that needed looking after. If there were he brought them home in the boot and usually managed to nurse them back to life. One day he found a baby octopus and brought it home in a milk bottle filled with seawater. The intention was to keep it for a few days and then throw it back out to sea. My mother put the milk bottle in the sink, surrounded by water to keep it cool, and of course the damn thing crawled out of the bottle and into the fresh water and died. He got very annoyed with my mother if he left her to look after something and it perished.

Once he had just finished a long day's work and was getting ready to leave the site when someone heard mooing. They found a cow that had got stuck in mud and, tired as he was, he climbed in and spent the night holding its head above water until he could work out and organise how to get the cow out.

He used to marvel in the smallest of things, plus the most complex of things, and obviously imparted that to me. He also loved gelignite, which he used in his work, and had several gelignite storage sheds that he rented on farms in the middle of nowhere. They looked like farm sheds, but really they were arsenals.

'I'll take you for a drive,' he said to my mother and me one day, which was unusual in itself. We were heading for the coast when he stopped at a farm gate.

'I'm just going to pop in here and grab something quickly.' He headed over to a shed and I ran after him.

'Don't come in here,' he said. 'You'll get a headache. It's full of jelly.'

I wondered why jelly would give me a headache but apparently gelignite does. Eventually he emerged with a box of detonators and a box of gelignite and put them in the boot and we drove to the beach.

'We'll go for a wander down to the beach,' he said. 'There's just something I want to have a look at.'

This was at the beginning of the iron-sands project in New Zealand, a search for ways of extracting the iron content from sand, and he was calculating which type of gelignite, buried at what level, would shift the most sand. As we were walking to the beach we had to climb over a stile. My mother grabbed hold of an old piece of wood as she was climbing over and it snapped. And so did my father: 'Marvellous isn't it? God knows how long that bit of stick has been there. God knows how many people have climbed over that stile. None of them snapping that piece of wood and now no one will be able to hold on to it again.' Within an hour of him saying that he would be blowing huge holes in God's beach.

Mum sat down with a magazine and Dad and I laid the gelignite. Then we had to stand well back.

'Where should we stand, Dad?' I asked.

'I don't know where we should stand, do I?' said my father. 'Would I be here experimenting with gelignite if I knew where to stand? That's the whole point.'

So we stood right back at the car and watched these phenomenal explosions. I couldn't wait to get on the beach and ran towards one of these holes to see how big it was. 'Don't get too close or you'll be consumed by sand,' my father called out. And at that point I was sucked under. Everything went black but he managed to haul me out without too much trouble.

Predictably, he hated bureaucrats and unnecessary rules

and regulations, another trait I've inherited from him. On one occasion we had to take a boat he had designed down a river to drop something off. It became grounded at the side because the channel had moved since the chart he was using had been made and because the boat was sitting so low in the water. Someone pulled over in a small boat.

'Do you want to dig it out?' he called. 'People get stuck here all the time.'

'I don't think you'd be able to dig it out,' said my father.

'Oh, people get stuck here all the time,' said the other sailor.

'No, no, no, it's a pretty heavy boat.'

'Why don't we try and dig it out?' I said, as I thought it was very odd. Dad was the kind of person who would climb in the water and fucking dig it out.

'This boat is full of very heavy stuff that we shouldn't have on it,' hissed my father. 'There is no way we're going to be digging this out with a spade. We are in real trouble here, boy. We're going to need a big boat here to get rid of this.'

It turned out our boat was full of gelignite, which is really heavy. Sitting under a tarp in the baking sun would've been tonnes and tonnes of gelignite. That was so exciting for me.

I think I was a terrible disappointment to him, but he had standards that were impossible to meet. And while I wanted him to be proud of me, I never particularly wanted to meet those standards because I was interested in other things. I don't imagine that he saw the arts as important, so when I wanted to be an actor he would have been greatly unimpressed. He used to talk about there being doers and talkers, and we are both doers — but I think he used to worry that I was just a talker.

He was sceptical of university, but not of study. If he didn't understand something, he went to the library and got books out. He taught himself engineering and everything else he knew, based on a pretty skimpy education.

He was impatient with my mother too. She was very sick with diabetes. When I was young I could tell when there was a minor alteration to her blood sugar level, often when she couldn't. She collapsed once because my father was pre-occupied with a project and refused to believe she needed help. I got very panicked once when we were on a bus and she started to fade and I didn't know if we would get home in time to get her something to eat. She and I formed a very close bond over that.

My mother was enthusiastic about everything I did and she especially fostered any signs of creative ability. Once when I showed her a drawing I had done of a car she looked at it very closely. 'Would you like me to show you how to make the car move?' she said. And with that she drew three little speed lines. I was amazed that anyone could do something so magical.

There were very few restrictions on me. My father was of the opinion that if it was an adventure, anything went. He was an adventurer. My mother, on the other hand, was and is quite timid, but it never seemed to occur to her that anything bad would befall me. She didn't worry about me but she depended on me. She wasn't keen on me going to kindergarten. I went for one day to see if I liked it and I was in two minds about it apparently, but she wanted me around. There were days she wanted to keep me home from school because we were a team and my father wasn't around.

However, I was allowed a dinghy, which I could barely carry, that I took down to the ocean and rowed about in for hours, in the days before anyone thought about lifejackets. I imagined all kinds of things in that boat. I imagined it was much bigger than it was. I imagined I was leaving harbours to get to foreign countries. I imagined I had a job checking on moorings. I went out at the crack of dawn and came home at night struggling with the dinghy in the dark. I took food from home if I thought of it, but life was too exciting to worry about stopping for food. I was a bit of a loner, although I had plenty of friends in our street. I used to like going into the garage and pottering, being away with my thoughts.

We used to visit Waiheke regularly because my father bought a large number of sections and we used to go there to cut the scrub. 'Son, one day half of this island is going to be worth a lot of money,' he said to me on one visit, 'and I'm picking it's this half.' Years later I went back there and his half was still covered in scrub. He had been half right.

Not long after I started school my father got work at Marsden Point and we relocated to a house on sand dunes at Ruakaka. It was just like outback New Zealand. I walked to school in the morning over sand dunes, through marshes and a bit of bush. Even then, it was like New Zealand 30 years earlier. There was still this pioneering spirit. A Maori family was building the first motel, there was one dairy and a scattering of houses. It was a nice little spot which now would cost millions. You went into the water, and it was ocean straight away. There was no fear. It was fantastic.

Combined with my risk-taking side, I had an absolute need for security through permanence. I had a bookcase behind my bed with lots of books. But I only had a relationship with the books with staples, because I imagined as I was reading the books that I was wearing the paper out. 'If the worst comes to the worst,' I thought, 'I could save the staples.' I only wanted things that I thought would last forever. Logic was telling me I wouldn't live forever, but it was important to me.

I'm still like that. My house, which I had designed and built, is completely over-specced. It's got steel beams that run from one end to the other. There's not one tree growing up against it. I like houses that stand proud in the environment. It's solid brick and concrete — concrete is my favourite product — and then all around it are asphalt or concrete or stones. Then I have a little bit of slightly manicured garden and then Jesus looks after 10 acres of bush, which is enduring too, because it replaces itself.

My mother used saccharine that came in oval containers. You slid the top around and one saccharine came out. She gave me her saccharine container with one saccharine left in it. I developed a relationship with this saccharine which focused on my desire to live forever.

'If you are really careful,' I said to my mother, 'if you never smoked, if you never did anything bad, could you live forever?'

'Oh, people just don't live forever,' she said.

But I was obsessed with the idea that if you were unreasonably careful, if you *really* looked after yourself, then you could. In the end I persuaded my mother to say that if you lived an entirely wholesome and impossible-to-live life, you could live forever. And the saccharine represented that to me. It was so secure in its container.

When we lived in Howick, I would be bundled into the car in my pyjamas on the occasional Friday night for a trip into Farmers department store. It was incredibly exciting. I took my saccharine with me one night. Walking from the car park to the store, it was dark and I slid my saccharine so it was sitting in the open area of the container. If someone had knocked my hand, it would have fallen out and been lost. I walked quite a distance with the saccharine at risk like that before sliding it around so it was safe forever.

I was one of the kids brought up with Hector the Farmers cockatoo. It always seemed to be Hector's birthday sale or Hector's Christmas sale, with balloons and decorations everywhere. At the time I thought, 'This is as wondrous as it must get.' I'd sneak into the ballroom and look around at these quite fancy people sitting there and think, 'These people must be so rich.' It was so simple in those days.

I could only love things that would last. People sometimes gave me wonderful toys and I could see they wouldn't last. I played with them a bit but I didn't love them. That has never disappeared. I'm a bit obsessive-compulsive — and finding that out doesn't usually come as a surprise to people. I read meanings into things that other people wouldn't even have noticed.

We used to buy sherry, which my father was partial to, and my mother used the flagons to make lemonade from the Meyer lemons on our tree. Getting a bottle of lemonade was just a phenomenal treat — having the bottle and opening it and listening to it. One very hot summer there was a water shortage and a truck delivered water to Howick. My mother decanted the lemonade and took the flagon down to the truck. I stood there as she was holding the lemonade flagon under the back of the truck and it slipped from her hands and smashed on the ground.

'Well, that's childhood fucked,' I thought to myself. 'Time to grow up now, the flagon's gone.'

OCD and ME

It's my opinion that everyone fits somewhere on
the obsessive-compulsive scale; just like how with
sexuality, no one's 100 per cent male or female.
My psychiatric state has been called into question
by a number of people over the years. I was
described by a leading Auckland psychologist only
a couple of years ago as the most highly functioning
dysfunctional human being he had ever met. In most
cases I wear my personal circumstances as a badge
of honour. Being gypsy, dyslexic, obsessive and in
other ways generally dysfunctional are merely parts
of the rich tapestry of life. These are some of the
OC issues I carry with me daily:

1. The number three.
2. Most permutations of the number three.
3. There it is.
4. Switches left in the on position on sockets with
   nothing plugged into them. Even though logic
   dictates electricity is not pouring out of them onto
   the floor, in my mind it's spooling uncontrollably
   around my legs.
5. Dual climate controls in cars set at different
   temperatures. Clearly this is the point of dual
   climate control, I don't like it one little bit — one
   half of the environment constantly in conflict with
   the other.

6. Knobs, dials, buttons, switches and levers that don't clearly lock into position. I don't like to think there's any possibility something isn't fully on or fully off.
7. Windows, doors, hatches etc as per number six.
8. Toilet paper must not run down the wall side of the roll. That is incorrect and cannot be tolerated. I do accept the one advantage of this is that it's marginally less likely to spool off the tube and heap on the floor.
9. Sand. It's tolerable on the beach, but how do you keep it there?
10. Unfinished business. It hangs like a bloodied dagger by the most frayed of threads above your head, at all times.

Only a few weeks ago on a visit to Annabelle White's house, I used the toilet and discovered in that one small room she was committing two offences from the above list. Very annoying!

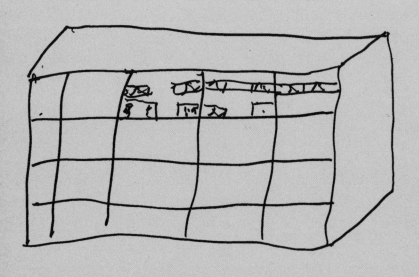

Council flats

CHAPTER 2
PAUL AND OLIVE

66 EVEN WHEN HE WAS MARRIED TO HER, HE WASN'T INTERESTED IN MARRIAGE. HIS MOTHER HAD SAID TO MY MOTHER, 'HE'S NOT THE MARRYING KIND', BEFORE THEY MARRIED. HE TURNED OUT TO BE NOT THE DIVORCING KIND, EITHER. AND HE NEVER WANTED CHILDREN — HE WASN'T INTERESTED IN HAVING CHILDREN. 99

I DIDN'T KNOW FOR ages that my parents had separated. There was no formal conversation where anyone sat me down and explained it and even now I don't know the exact details. My father was away so much and gradually he was coming home less and less and I think my mother found out he had a mistress overseas.

It was obviously very hard for my mother because she had to make all the decisions. They never got divorced. My mother offered my father a divorce after they had been separated for years and he said, 'I don't need a divorce.' He had no intention of coming back to live with her but he wasn't interested in another marriage. Even when he was married to her, he wasn't interested in marriage. His mother had said to my mother, 'He's not the marrying kind', before they married. He turned out to be not the divorcing kind, either. And he never wanted children — he wasn't interested in having children.

So my mother decided to go back to England permanently when I was 11. I was told that we were going there for six months, but I don't think we went on a return ticket. Ironically we moved in with my father's parents as my mother had no family left there apart from a couple of aunts who were quite batty.

The communication around the whole thing was very bad. Once I was in a van with my Uncle Terry and Aunty Edna, my father's older sister. I'd just recently worked out or found out that we weren't going back.

'I'm being kept here under false pretences,' I complained. 'I was told this would just be a holiday.' Edna got very annoyed. I was told I was selfish and I should think about other people.

Going back was an odd move. My mother had only a few friends left in Bristol from the old days. She would have been far better off materially to stay in New Zealand, but she was probably lonely and maybe with the realisation that the marriage was over she thought she needed to change her life and start anew. I've got huge respect for my mother because she isn't endowed with extraordinary ability but she is a terrifically hard worker. My father was endowed with extraordinary ability, which he coupled with intuition and a capacity for hard work. Arriving in England we went from being quite well off to suddenly very poor, and my mother needed all her capacity for hard work. She was doing treble shifts — sometimes working 24 hours in a row — in a plastic bag factory.

After staying with my father's parents, we applied for and got a council flat in Redcliffe, Bristol. Our new home was next to the cut, a smelly river dug by prisoners. Number 19 was on the second floor of a tenement block called Frankcom House, one of three blocks that enclosed a concrete playground with rusty swings and a car park that was a sea of concrete. It was very different from Cockle Bay in Howick.

The kids I went to school with had very low expectations. They dreamt about things that would have been barely tolerable for me. They lived all their lives in the streets they were born into. After school they got jobs at the Imperial Tobacco factory. Bristol was an Imperial Tobacco city, dominated by huge brick nicotine-stained factories. Almost all the boys were signed on to the pension plan at Imperial Tobacco before they left school. The future was discount cigarettes and a job for life, unless you were caught thieving.

But I knew about the rest of the world. I had seen this other life and I knew I had to get out of this one. I developed grand ideas of being a famous actor. From my early teens I used to think of three outcomes — rich, famous and infamous. I tried to decide which would be best if you had to choose one and decided that obviously the answer was rich, because you could buy either fame or infamy. Somewhere along the way I dropped my ambition to become infamous. Which is ironic.

I didn't understand the culture in Bristol, and at intermediate school the culture was really important. It was important what pop stars you liked — the girls all liked David Cassidy — because you spent all your time in your room listening to music. There weren't any options. In my mind you spent all your time running home from school and getting down to the beach with your dinghy.

Southville School was a hole in the ground with big steel bars like a prison on the windows. I turned up in my shorts and sandals, for which offence I was immediately named 'Jesus Boots'. I was teased mercilessly at the start. That was a personality builder for me, and I already had quite a personality. I used to beg my mother to get me proper shoes but we had no money for them. The months wore on, it was winter and I was still wearing my Jesus boots. Eventually they got to the point where they had actually broken and couldn't be worn any more. But by then, if I had got shoes, everyone would have pointed and said, 'Ooooh, look. Jesus Boots has got shoes.' They would have thought they'd won. So I made my poor mother hunt high and low in an English winter to find me another pair of sandals.

Meanwhile, she was struggling to pay the bills and it was hard going for lots of reasons. We had to put coins in the gas and electricity boxes for our power and our flat was broken into a couple of times and coins stolen from them, which wasn't uncommon. People were so poor they would break into their own boxes to get money for bread and say they had been robbed. The double whammy when you were the victim was that not only was your stuff wrecked, but you also had to refund all the money that was taken before you could get your power going again.

It didn't have as much effect on my mother as it did on me. She could render her life down easily. It was a small life and one she had been used to so it wasn't that hard to return to it, even though my father had taken her out into the wide world and she has ended up back in Bristol/Shitsville. Even today, a lot of her friends there are still in the same street they have always lived in.

I went back there for TVNZ, 27 years after I had left, when the British elections were on. My producer went and knocked on the door and explained who she was.

'The programme's host is out in the car and he used to live here with his mother in this flat.'

'Oh,' said the tenant, 'was she that old woman who was going to New Zealand?' So she remembered one conversation she had when she came with the council to look at the flat when my mother was coming to join me in New Zealand. My mother had told her that her son was taking her out to New Zealand to live and the woman obviously hadn't believed her.

I went in. It was even smaller than I remembered it. There was this woman and her husband, sitting in this tiny living room. I could barely comprehend it. They had lived in this shithole overlooking other shitholes for 27 years and they're watching *Avatar* on a giant plasma screen. How could they not know there's a bigger world out there, that there are spaces that aren't the flat, the pub and the factory? Nothing had changed.

My father had two sisters, one in Bristol who we used to visit regularly, in one of those oppressive houses whose inhabitants have covered the walls with photographs of themselves. They spent all their time watching game shows and *Coronation Street*. But they also had a big tropical fish tank that captivated me. They used to joke that I would wear out the fish tank from watching it so much, but there was more exciting stuff happening in that glass box than anywhere else in that entire city.

I had been at school in England for a month when I was pronounced dyslexic and told I also needed glasses. Perhaps I needed them because I had squinted so much with my dyslexia. On the National Health you could get wire-framed glasses for free or, for a very small amount of money, black plastic frames. I knew everyone with wire glasses at school was really poor. 'Can we get the expensive ones?' I asked Mum. These were the cheapest glasses you could buy, but they weren't free. She got them for me and, of course, I wore them for a little while and then couldn't be bothered with them any more.

I wasn't a slow learner, but I was a slow reader and still am. Anyone reading this book will almost certainly finish it in less time than me. Although I never became a lover of reading, I was a lover of information, so I read for that reason. I read even though it meant having to read. Reading always held me back at school, but perversely I have always put myself in positions where I have to read — whether at acting school or in radio and TV.

I was always interested in drama and was able to study it at Ashton Park Secondary School. With scripts, you learn to jump ahead and work out your words before it's your turn. This was a big school on something called 'Lady Smyth's Estate' which included a crumbling stately home. There were grand entrance gates and most of the property was parkland, but everything else was a disappointment. It's been restored since.

In class, people wanted me in their groups because I came up with great ideas. I became very good at delegating tasks and saying 'We need someone who's really good at this because I'll be too busy doing something else', but actually it was because I couldn't read. You learn great skills to cover up inadequacies.

Most dyslexics excel in sometimes unexplained areas. Dyslexics are like Scientologists in that they love making lists of famous people with dyslexia. It amuses me greatly because they tend to reel off a few names and then say, 'And that's just four.' And I think: 'Four's not that fucking many.' Or: 'Einstein was dyslexic and he was a genius.' And I think, 'Yeah but there have been plenty of geniuses who didn't have dyslexia.' You can always find someone who fits into your category but it doesn't follow that you have an ounce of their greatness because you share one trait.

In the end, I did all right with exams — partly because I worked hard, partly because they weren't very challenging. That's the only explanation I can come up with for doing well.

Conscious that we were short of money I was always trying to generate some income of my own. I did what I thought lots of kids did, going door to door asking if people needed odd jobs done. But English kids didn't do that and I never found out why. Perhaps it was their natural English reserve.

On the other side of the cut from our tenement blocks there was a completely different setting — terraced houses with Bedminster Bridge at one end. These were extremely grand houses with substantial sections. Naturally I thought this was where we should be living, being to the manor born as I was. I genuinely thought at that age I had some direct link to the throne. I just *knew* that I was better than everybody else. These houses were quite run down because, although they were grand, they were also the perfect example of the best street in the worst area. I looked at them and imagined which one I would choose and how I would do it up to look even grander. And these were the houses where I used to doorknock.

At one house an old woman answered the door. 'There's a bit of work in the yard out the back,' she said. So I went out the back and it was fantastic. There was a barn-sized stone garage there that I instantly knew was perfect for the recording studio I was going to establish as the foundation of the music industry empire I had just realised I was going to build.

The woman lived on her own in this house, which I am sure was at least five storeys — six or seven if you added in the basement or extras. I knew immediately that she was going to leave me this house when she died, which wouldn't be very far away, she being at least 50. She couldn't afford to maintain the house and certainly couldn't afford to pay me, so we agreed that I would do odd jobs in return for use of the garage. What can a 12-year-old do with a garage? I used to go in there with a notebook and draw plans and scheme. There was going to be a mezzanine and a big sign out the front saying Metropolitan House or something grander if I could think of it. Of course, nothing was ever done. I didn't have time to clean it let alone do anything else to it. Unfortunately, that involvement came to an end as I really needed to find something that paid.

Not far from where my grandparents lived was a pet shop,

My favourite movies

When I was four and a half my mother took me by bus on the long journey from Cockle Bay to Queen Street in Auckland for something she had sold to me as a magical experience. She filled my mind with wonderment as she described what I was about to witness. A room bigger than I'd ever been in before with hundreds and hundreds of people, huge curtains, lions with flashing eyes, stars on the ceiling and ice-cream. She said in this room the lights would go out, people would become suddenly very, very quiet, the curtains would slowly open and I would be taken on a magical journey.

The Civic Theatre was no disappointment and the first movie I ever saw, the first movie to be made in colour is number one on my list of favourite films. So wonderful was that first experience, so excited was I that I begged and begged my mother to take me again straight away. After two weeks of constant pleading, we made the long journey back to the theatre. I was bursting with excitement as the curtains opened and the film started, and then inconsolable as it was explained to me that when you went to the movies you didn't see the same film every time. I didn't even understand The Beatles' Yellow Submarine and kept shouting, 'Where's Dorothy?' My mother and I left after half an hour. What was she thinking?

- The Wizard of Oz
- The Great Race (the one with Tony Curtis)
- Those Magnificent Men and Their Flying Machines
- Chitty Chitty Bang Bang
- The Night of the Hunter (the original)
- The Flight of the Phoenix (the original)
- The Poseidon Adventure (the original)
- Love Story (not so good decades later)
- The Towering Inferno (also not so good decades later)
- The Big Lebowski
- The Castle
- The Constant Gardener
- The Last King of Scotland
- Notting Hill
- Love Actually

As a genre I love horror movies but no specific one makes the list.

sitting in the middle of these little run-down terraces. Fish were very popular pets in England because you could keep them in small spaces. This shop sold daphne, a little creature that's used as live fish food. I saw the daphne in the shop and realised there was a large amount of it down at the docks, which were miles and miles from our home and the shop. I went in and asked to speak to the manager.

'I breed daphne in a controlled environment,' I lied. 'Who's your supplier? Where do you get your daphne from?'

We eventually came to an agreement whereby he would buy daphne from me. So I bought a supply of plastic bags and ties and went down to the dock with a couple of buckets, collected the stuff, falling over and over again into this filthy water as I tried to snare as much as I could. Then I took it home on the bus — it was so thick I didn't have to worry about it spilling — sieved it out in the bath and packed it up for the shop. This was repeated many times.

Another scheme was my film-developing business. I told people at school I could develop film with a kit I had at home. In reality, I had gone to a camera shop and offered to bring them huge quantities of film if they gave me a discount. I kept the difference between what I paid the shop and what teachers and other pupils at school paid me. Photography was a popular hobby and there was always some film to be processed. The trouble was that the prints came back with the branding of the shop, so I had to get paper in and print my own packets, which ate into my profits.

With all these activities I was seldom at home. I spent a lot of time at the docks. When I wasn't collecting daphne, I collected anything else that didn't move and wasn't nailed down. Sometimes I'd have to hide things in different places on the way home because I wasn't strong enough to carry everything all the way in one go. Everything was scavenged with a view to making money out of it in some as yet to be determined way. I could make giant leaps of imagination with minimal prompting. Once I found a huge road spotlight. As I was humping it home, with bits falling off it, thus decreasing its value at every step, I was imagining a grand business where I had a fleet of trucks and did contract lighting for events.

School was an interruption to my life really. I've always had a lot of things going on in my mind; I've always had plans and projects to think about. Sometimes there would be three or four life-changing schemes in a single day. I'd find something else and discard what I was carrying and all of a sudden the empire I was going to have was a completely different one.

I used to wander through the semi-rural posh areas of Bristol and on the edge of Clifton. You crossed the mighty Bristol suspension bridge and suddenly there were beautiful homes with formal gardens on half an acre of land. On the other side were my relations, who were unbelievably unsuccessful but perfectly contented. Buying a second-hand Bedford van and converting it into a semi-campervan, with a week in Spain every five years, was the giddy height of their ambition.

I was hugely aware of class. It was so evident to me in the way we were living that we were lower class, but I saw opportunity in every direction. Looking at those big houses, I knew that I could be there if I wanted and I knew I wanted, so I knew I'd be there. I had absolutely no doubt that I could be anything I wanted to be. So I just didn't see my current environment, which was pretty bloody grim at times; I didn't see it in any way as an impediment. I had more confidence than you could imagine — what I didn't have was a plan.

Entrance to the BBC

CHAPTER 3
TAKING
DIRECTION

> ## " FAME WAS DEFINITELY THE GOAL. DURING THE WEEK, I WAS AT SCHOOL DOING ALL MY COMPULSORY SUBJECTS PLUS STUDYING DRAMA. AND ALL WEEKEND I WAS AT THE BBC WHERE IN THE END THEY STARTED PAYING ME A SMALL AMOUNT FOR HELPING TO ROLL OUT CABLES. "

LIKE SO MANY PEOPLE I lived my childhood dreams vicariously through celebrities. I couldn't afford to go to the movies so my idols were television and radio stars. That looked and sounded like fun but there also seemed to be an opportunity there to become quite famous and wealthy. I went to the BBC to see if there was any work and they shuffled me off to BBC Radio Bristol. There wasn't any really, but the programme director took pity on a 15-year-old schoolboy.

'If you just want to knock around with one of the producers on the weekend, maybe help out rolling cables or something like that, you're very welcome,' he said, little realising what he was setting in motion.

So I took up the invitation and I absolutely loved it. Fame was definitely the goal. During the week, I was at school doing all my compulsory subjects plus studying drama. And all weekend I was at the BBC where in the end they started paying me a small amount for helping to roll out cables. My mother was very enthusiastic about all of it, if only because I was doing it.

My first official job was as cable boy and gofer for *See You Saturday* with Arthur Parkman. He was an extraordinarily un-healthy, obviously overweight, heavy-drinking, heavy-smoking all-round entertainer, and I idolised him. Every Saturday I would leave my shithole of a council flat, walk the miles to Clifton and relish walking through the big gates with grand pillars and big lamps on each side and 'BBC' in bronze above.

It was a music show and a full-scale production. Arthur could play anything on any piano and every Saturday we would take a recording desk out to a pub or club and a live programme would be performed with technicians, music producers, Arthur and his band of equally unhealthy, overweight stars and me. They played between 12 and one while the programme that had been recorded the week before was broadcast.

We had a Hillman Hunter Estate with a hydraulic transmission mast in the middle. On the dash — which being a Hillman Hunter was already as spectacular as you can imagine — there was a sliding panel with proper radio control faders built in. The BBC did things properly in those days. Standards have only fallen in subsequent years. I had a couple of days' worth of work a week, going to recce the locations for the next show, putting up posters, rolling out cables. I couldn't understand how anyone could not want to do that job.

My best subject at school was drama and I won a scholarship to a drama school in Clifton which was not far from home. It was a highly structured subject — you had to study the production areas as well as performing and I loved the whole lot. I loved the technical areas — I loved lighting, and I still do. I also got a place in the Children's Youth Theatre, which did a production in London's West End, but I didn't go to that. Even though you were paid what was then a huge amount to take part — something like £20 — the costs of being away from home were even more, so I couldn't afford to go.

Drama school was also tricky because all the scholarship covered was the fees. I had planned to carry on doing the bits and pieces I had going to cover my costs but that was frowned upon because you were supposed to give your all to your art. But the thing that finished my brilliant drama career before it even started was a visit from the Actors' Equity rep. I had barely started when he turned up. Acting was highly unionised. There were two relevant unions: Equity and another which was tailored slightly more to broadcasters. You could be a member of both, but you definitely had to be a member of one. You could not utter one line, you could not do a voiceover, you could not do anything that came near the definition of acting unless you were paid up.

The Equity rep came to school to sign people up. The classes were small — only eight people or so. He was brought in and introduced to us and addressed the class. Instead of telling us why we needed to belong to the union, he asked us a question.

'Do you know anyone in the business?' he said.

We all looked back at him vaguely.

'Do you know anyone in the business who can help you,' he said, 'because talent won't cut it. As a union we have the highest number of unemployed members of any union in the world. We don't want more. You have to be talented or you wouldn't be sitting in this room but talent is a very small component of whether you're successful or not. But the biggest component by far is who you know.'

Of course, I knew no one. He was trying to talk me out of it, and it worked. I suppose the dream wasn't great enough, because in the back of my mind I felt I could have been a huge success as an actor but I didn't want it quite enough. I did want what I thought that success would bring me, though, so I decided to look for another way of getting it. Since I was mucking around at the BBC anyway, maybe if I focused on getting a full-time job there I would make the sort of contacts you needed to succeed.

I realised that the way to get more work at the BBC was to make myself indispensible. I volunteered to do stuff that probably didn't need doing at all. However, after I had been doing it a couple of weeks, people found they couldn't live without it being done. I was paid irregularly and in small amounts, but I kept all my pay slips for a long time because I thought it was so cool that the BBC was paying *me* — a guy who lived in a council flat.

'Filling in' became my key role. I did all of the jobs that were not done, weren't done properly because no one wanted to do them or were done very reluctantly by the next up in the pecking order. When they realised they didn't have to do them again, they decided they should never do them again, which is where my job was created. For instance, I filled in at the gramophone library. It's unthinkable today — a whole gramophone library at a local radio station. This was just prior to the explosion of private radio. And the library had a receptionist who had a lunch break, so I would fill in while she got her sandwich. Then I started filling in on shifts when people were away on leave and I learnt how to operate the equipment really well. It might sound like a great master plan with job security as the goal but all the jobs I got good at don't even exist now.

Then I started doing continuity. I thought everyone would recognise me when I walked down the street now because I introduced the radio soap *The Archers*. The discipline was exceptional. Nothing could crash the time signals and no music could be faded — you had to hear the beginning and the end of every piece of music that was played. You didn't talk over music, and it didn't go over the time signals. If *The Archers* finished 10 seconds early then you had to have something ready to fill the 10 seconds: 'This evening on BBC Radio Bristol an interesting programme for farmers . . .'

At night I did the fat stock market report for farmers — 'Pork is sold for 13.5, that's a rise of 7.9'. You had sheets and sheets of it and you had to do it right or the farmers would complain. That's something that hasn't changed.

No one was cut any slack but at the same time, we were fully resourced. We had a 15-minute news programme that went out before the news from BBC Radio that we re-broadcast. For this little programme there were at least four readers sitting around a large oval table and you didn't have just one microphone. Each of those buggers had their own microphone and their own cue light and their scripts. And there would be at least one live interview in another part of the studio with *another* host, along with at least two phone interviews and a link to one of the radio cars out at some site.

You had to play individual sound inserts for the news and they were on reel to reel, not cartridges or a computer. You had a stack of reel-to-reel tapes, each with its own cue sheet, a 15-second bite on it and nothing else. So as well as getting telephone links up and making sure the right person was there, you had to run these tapes. You got good at spooling, with three tape machines on the go at the same time.

If you got anything wrong, you were called a cunt by someone who was sweating streams and trembling with rage. If you made a small mistake, the producers would assault you verbally until you started crying and if you didn't, they would hit you. Most days, you were shitting yourself before the programme even started.

ITS A NIGHTMARE JUST THINKING ABOUT IT NOW!

I used to get in there at half past 12, and the programme started at quarter to one. Sometimes, by 17 minutes to one you were still the only person in the studio and you were thinking, wouldn't it be nice even if they gave me just the first tape to load up. Then the doors would crash open, sometimes with 30 seconds to go before the programme, and they'd slam down a tower of tapes on the desk and a pile of paper whose contents you had to ingest while loading up the machines. And all anybody said was, 'Fucking fuck fuck!' because they all had their own nightmares going on. It was fantastic theatre and it was brilliant to be part of.

No one ever said, 'Shit, that was well done.' If you did something perfectly, that was actually no more than the minimum expected of you so why should anyone comment on it? The BBC view was: why would you thank anyone for doing their job. If you interviewed a policeman on air about a case, you thanked him at the end. But if you had crossed to your reporter, why would you thank him? He was being paid; he didn't need to be thanked.

I picked up a lot of things there that I've taken through in my career. And pretty soon I became one of those people who started to care about whether you could hear a click on air. If I stammered over a word doing continuity, I would beat myself up about it. We didn't have compressors or equalisers to smooth out the sounds to the right level — we had to do it all manually. Before putting a caller on air, a technician would talk to them, gauge the level of their hiss and adjust that level, so when you put to them air it was just seamless.

Bill Salisbury, the programme director, had a huge VU meter on the wall in his office that tracked the levels of everything going over the air. And if the dial flicked into the red zone he came thundering down the steps to the studio. 'What the fuck is going on?' he'd bellow. 'That went into the red.' Now, everything bounces around in the red all the time but the transmitters have automatic ways to take care of it.

I LOOKED LIKE A 'BAY CITY ROLLER'.

Bill Salisbury was always to the point. One afternoon on a music show we had a guest coming in. Nothing unusual about that. Not long before we went to air, the presenter came to me. 'This next guy's here,' he said. 'I just went to say hello to him in the green room and he's wearing a fucking pixie outfit.' So this guest was welcomed into the studio in his full pixie glory and the interview took place. I thought it was a good, straight-forward interview about a show he had coming up in town.

Afterwards I was walking out with the presenter and we bumped into Bill Salisbury, who stopped to talk to us on the grand BBC stairway.

'Did you hear any of the show today?' asked the host.

'Yes, I did. Yes.'

'Did you hear our guest? My God! You should have seen him. He was wearing a pixie outfit. It was extraordinary.'

'I did see him, I watched from reception. I saw him wearing a pixie outfit and I was quite interested to listen to him. However, not one of your fucking listeners would have known he was wearing a green pixie outfit, which would have been a much more interesting topic than any of the fucking questions you asked him.' By now he was warmed up. 'What you did is you let every single listener down and you let, potentially, the most interesting interview of your life slip out the door in his green fucking pixie outfit. How could you sit there and not ask the most obvious question? You will die an old man doing this shift if you don't get your act together.'

And I've kept that idea with me throughout my career: when you go into an interview with a list of questions, you've probably got a list of answers as well. As a result, you can overlook the obvious. You should never go into an interview with more than three questions, which are just guidelines. On the other hand, you don't want to become so interested in the conversation you're having that you start to exclude the listeners. At any stage you should be prepared to go in a different direction if a more interesting direction becomes obvious, such as, why are you wearing a pixie outfit? To this day, I still wonder why that man was wearing that outfit. And he probably walked away very disappointed: 'Well, that pixie fucking outfit worked well.'

I was working every hour I could find to fill in at the BBC but eventually I realised that there wasn't a permanent job for me. I would have to change direction again. Somewhat to my surprise, I realised my best option was to go back to New Zealand.

To all the girls I never loved before

I was a very attractive young man in the prime
of my sexuality with, if I was dishonest about it,
a very high-ranking and fascinating job at the
BBC. I should have been a chick magnet. To be
fair, I had a lot of first dates! I was fascinating, but
only for a few hours. The fact is, as I understand it
now, I was just a bit too preoccupied with myself.
I displayed an air of unbridled wankery, frequently
I wore a trilby. I smoked a pipe. I oftentimes sported
a waistcoat with fob watch and sealed all my letters
with wax. If it could be loosely described as mine,
I rubber stamped it multiple times with my full
name. In short I was on my way up and branding
was my trailblazer. I even commissioned a quantity
of colourful cardboard matchboxes with my name
emblazoned on them in gold lettering.

'Do you have a light, young man?' (influential guest
at the BBC)
'As a matter of fact I do . . . Please, keep the packet.'
(me)

I never actually met anyone who I deemed worthy
of striking one of my precious matches for, let alone
giving away the packet.

'Do you have a light, young man?' (someone I
didn't like the look of)
'No.' (me)

Suffice to say, the picture is well and truly painted.

So to the standard first date, using an exact example:
Italian restaurant I couldn't quite afford, sitting opposite a pretty girl whose name I couldn't quite remember, being directed through the intricacies of my magnificence in a packed restaurant of 20–30 tables.
All of a sudden the lovely girl, whose name I never actually knew, interrupted me to tell me she could smell burning. At this point she didn't know, and I was only just finding out, that her date was on fire. A large quantity of matches like a small rodent's Guy Fawkes' event were exploding in the right pocket of my checked jacket. I thought fast: how will I get out of this restaurant with my dignity intact? I excused myself from the table and manouevred, with style, sophistication and haste, between the diners to the restroom, followed by a not insubstantial trail of billowing smoke. By the time I got to the bathroom my jacket was ablaze and I imagine good times were being had at my expense throughout the restaurant, by all except possibly my date, whichever one she was. I returned to the table disguised as a scorched version of The Man from Atlantis. Whoever she was, she refused my offer to escort her home or for that matter, anywhere. My date was over, I never saw her again.

'How was your date, darling?' (her mother)
'He caught fire.' (whoever)

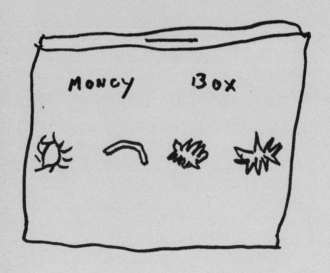

MONEY BOX

Self-explanatory

CHAPTER 4
SELLING OUT

> **I KNEW THEN THAT SELLING ANYTHING MEANT SELLING A DREAM . . . I TALKED MY WAY INTO THE POTENTIAL CUSTOMER'S HOUSE, SAT IN THE MIDDLE OF THE LIVING ROOM FLOOR WITH MY KIT, OPENED OUT THE POSTERS AND LET THE DREAMS FLOAT OFF THE PAGES AND FILL THE ROOM. THE SCRIPT WAS OUTRAGEOUS.**

NATURALLY, WITH THE WEALTH of knowledge I had acquired from my vast experience at the BBC I was able to put together a magnificent CV — such as I was sure no one in New Zealand had seen before — that would propel me straight into the director-general of broadcasting's job at the age of 18.

I stayed with some friends of the family in Auckland, and given there seemed to be some problem persuading the incumbent DG to step down, I applied for a cadetship at the NZBC to get my foot in the door. While waiting for that to come through I got a job selling Lexington encyclopaedias door to door. Many people haven't heard of Lexington encyclopaedias — then or

now — but they were much better than Britannica, especially when I was trying to sell a set.

I knew then that selling anything meant selling a dream. I had a little zip-up satchel with sections from the encyclopaedia and I talked my way into the potential customer's house, sat in the middle of the living room floor with my kit, opened out the posters and let the dreams float off the pages and fill the room. The script was outrageous.

'I'll show you something now,' I said and opened the book to the see-through pages with the cross-sections of the human body.

'Hold the book up by that page,' I said to the husband. 'Now shake it around. Lift it up and shake it around. Now, that is a well-bound book.'

'God, that's amazing.'

'Yes it is,' I said, 'and every page is like that.' They weren't; only the one I showed them was.

'It's only 80 cents a day for the world on a bookshelf in your living room, and you get the bookshelf for free. Eighty cents a day. Look, it's just small change in a money box.' I had a money box with me. It was a thing of wonder with a date display. 'Look at this money box here. When you put the money in, it changes the date, so you get the date as well. For 80 cents you're not only paying for the world but you're getting the current date.'

'Oh, could I have that?' they inevitably said.

'No, not this money box, but I tell you what, I could probably get you one of these. In fact, if I was to write this order down now, I could probably get you one of these for free.'

'Oh, and will it tell the date like that?'

'Yes, it's just like this one.'

Often, I didn't even need to talk about future-proofing their investment by signing up for the yearbooks.

I was not a perfect salesperson by any means. Once I called

at a house where the owners had friends around and I found this off-putting. The perfect salesperson would think, 'It doesn't matter, I'll make the best of it', but I needed to hold court without any distractions. The family insisted I stay, however, so I began my presentation and I still regard what happened as a career highlight. I sold the homeowners a set, I sold their friends a set, and if I had driven myself there, instead of being dropped off outside by my manager, I could probably have sold them my car as well.

Finally my cadetship came through. It was based in Wellington, so I bought a car on hire purchase to get me down there. It didn't sound very good when I set off and the noises it made grew progressively worse until it finally shat itself and broke down at Pokeno. I hadn't had a lot of experience with cars up to that point and didn't know you needed to put oil in them. I hitchhiked to Hamilton and got a bus to Wellington. I was put up in a hotel where everyone in my position stayed and was given exposure to various aspects of radio. Of course, there was nothing anyone needed to teach me, but I humoured the likes of Dick Weir, who was given the superfluous task of mentoring me for a while.

One problem that was immediately clear was that the cadet's remuneration was slightly less than the hotel's tariff. I had a shortfall every week of about $10. I couldn't afford much in the way of food or transport. I was walking everywhere on an empty stomach. So I went to see Human Resources.

'Look, I'm just in shitter's ditch here,' I said — or words to that effect. 'You're not paying me enough to cover my hotel.'

'We never said that your hotel was covered.'

'I know that,' I said, 'but what was I going to say? "I can't come and do your job because I can't afford the hotel?" It wasn't like I was going to say that, was I? Now I've got a broken-down car in Pokeno. God knows how much that's going to cost to fix, and I can't even go and pick it up.'

In the meantime, people in Pokeno were trying to contact me about the car. There was a person at National Radio who I had never met but who had a name similar to mine. They were dealing with him despite his insistence that he didn't have a car at all, let alone one in Pokeno. In the end the powers that be decided to bond me in return for paying the hotel bill.

It became apparent very soon that I should work for the National Programme, as it was called then, because that was the sort of radio I was used to. I got a job working with Relda Familton, compiling the all-night programme, which she presented on alternate weeks. She was impossible to contact in her weeks off although I sometimes had to call her. I knew to wait until the afternoon at least.

'What time is it, Paul?'

'It's two o'clock in the afternoon.'

'Two o'clock? Why am I not up?'

'I'm not sure. Do you want me to phone you back later?'

'No, try not to.'

I was always trying to persuade her to do extra things I thought would be good for the show. And she was always reluctant. When Peter Ustinov came to town, to promote his autobiography, *Dear Me*, I got very excited. 'He's perfect for us,' I told her, 'because we've got the luxury of time. We could do half an hour with Peter Ustinov. We can cut in clips from albums where he's telling stories.'

I had to up-sell it hugely, and may have given the impression my family had been friends of the Ustinovs for ages. On the odd occasion, Relda reluctantly agreed to my plans, and this was one of them. So now I had this huge task ahead of me because the chance of getting an exclusive interview with Peter Ustinov for a programme that aired after midnight was quite slight.

He was staying at the James Cook Hotel and I knew he was giving a press conference one morning at ten o'clock. I also knew there was no way we would get anything decent for our show in a crowd like that. Relda would probably still be in her pyjamas.

'We've got a pre-press conference one on one at nine,' I lied to her. My plan was to turn up, pretend the nine o'clock was arranged and just see where we went from there.

'It's pretty amazing you getting this one on one,' Relda said to me on the way there, 'because I found out there's a press conference at 10.'

'I know,' I agreed. 'We've got a whole hour, I suppose. I mean, he might want a few minutes to prepare for the press conference, but that leaves us at least 45 minutes.'

We managed to get up to his floor and, as luck would have it, his breakfast was being delivered at precisely the time we got there. When the door opened for his breakfast, we shuffled in behind the room service. A woman, presumably his manager, looked us up and down without saying anything.

'Oh, is it inconvenient now?' I said. 'We're here for the nine o'clock one on one with Mr Ustinov. Is it appropriate?'

'The nine o'clock?' she said.

'Yes. Pre-arranged.'

'There is a press conference at ten o'clock,' she said. 'That is when Mr Ustinov will be appearing, long after his breakfast is finished.'

'Is the nine o'clock off, then?'

Suddenly, we heard a familiar voice booming from the bathroom.

'Who is it? What conversation are you having out there? Should I be a part of it?'

'Oh, Mr Ustinov, it's Paul Henry,' I called out. 'I'm here for the nine o'clock with Relda Familton, a very famous New Zealand broadcaster, as arranged by one of your staff members earlier.'

He came out wearing a bathrobe, still dripping wet, saw his breakfast and without even looking at us walked over to the table and started lifting the covers off the plates.

'Well, you'd better sit down, hadn't you?' he said. He divided up breakfast between me, Relda and himself and started telling us wonderful stories, doing brilliant imitations of the likes of Humphrey Bogart and John Huston.

After a while, people began arriving to set up for the press conference and he got slightly irritated with them.

'Please could you make a little less noise,' he said. 'I'm in the middle of a story.'

Since then, basically, my career has been about bullshitting. I think a lot of journalists would say that, but I've done it to get meetings not just with actors, but with guerrillas and prime ministers. For the most part, however, my work with Relda involved not much more than picking music and running series.

During this time I thought a lot about my mother, who was still back in England, not enjoying good health and working too hard. I wasn't happy being so far away from her and decided to head back to the UK. In between leaving National and heading back I somehow ended up working at Radio I.

The station had just moved into a beautiful building on Great North Road in Auckland, and I did midnight to dawn for a couple of months. It had the most bizarre format you could possibly imagine. They called it beautiful music but they made that up, there was no such genre.

The most important qualification for the job was the ability to count to two silently. You played four songs in a row and between them you had to say, 'The beautiful music that is (one . . . two) Radio I.' We had to pause and count every time we said anything. 'You've been listening (one . . . two) to Pepe Arameo and his orchestra (one . . . two) and the duelling pianos of Henry Mancini (one . . . two). It's now (one . . . two) 13 minutes past three (one . . . two) and now (one . . . two) the beautiful music continues.' It was appalling.

I was in the building on my own at that hour. At the front was an alcove in which prostitutes used to congregate. It had an intercom through which the beautiful music that was Radio I was piped. I don't know how they stood it, but there was also a light, so they would wait for clients there and talk to me while they were waiting. It was the only interaction I had with real people and on reflection they may have been the only people who heard the music I was playing.

Graham Someone came over from Australia to organise things, which meant getting rid of a lot of people. Radio I changed staff almost as often as it changed formats in those days. In my time, the format was fine but apparently I was wrong, even though I could count to two with my eyes closed.

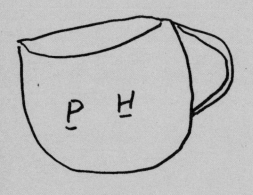

Coffee mug

CHAPTER 5
THE INKLEY
DOOVERY
EMPORIUM

> **ON ONE HAND, BEING DYSLEXIC, THE JOB OF SORTING AND DELIVERING MAIL WAS A TOTAL NIGHTMARE FOR ME. ON THE OTHER HAND, THE JOB SERVED RADIO 2, RADIO 3, RADIO 4, BBC 1 AND 2 TELEVISION, SO I WAS AT THE CENTRE OF EVERYTHING.**

AS I PLANNED MY return to England, my thoughts followed a similar pattern — once they saw me, management would beg me to take over the running of the BBC.

I got a job in the mail room.

On one hand, being dyslexic, the job of sorting and delivering mail was a total nightmare for me. On the other hand, the job served Radio 2, Radio 3, Radio 4, BBC 1 and 2 television, so I was at the centre of everything. I legitimately got to go into every office. Different cities specialised in different areas of production for the BBC. Birmingham, for instance, was drama. Bristol was natural history and responsible for some incredibly popular programmes. Geoffrey Boswell, who produced *The World Around Us*, was based there. Johnny Morris, who did a wonderful children's TV show called *Animal Magic*, was based there and so was David Attenborough. I delivered mail to them and many other giants of television. These people had gilded offices with hospitality cabinets and people to fill the hospitality cabinets with liquor for them. They didn't have a BBC cafe, they had BBC restaurants and bars.

As well as doing the mail, I gained experience by getting attachments — short-term appointments in different roles. I got one as a projectionist for the Natural History Unit. It was quite complicated because it wasn't just a matter of getting the rushes and whacking them on. Curtains were opened, lights were dimmed — they didn't get switched off, they had to be dimmed — and there would be fresh water and cocktails and nibbles on a little tray.

When important visitors came and wanted to view old film — which they often did — the pressure could be intense. First, you prayed to God the item had a combined track — meaning sound and image were on the one piece of film and in sync. This never happened, one of many proofs this book will suggest for the non-existence of God. I had to put the soundtrack on one side of the projector and try to line it up with the images on the other. The more important a project, the more likely it was to have separate tracks because the quality was admittedly better that way.

I had to screen some of *The Iron Age Project* once. This was a wonderful early reality series. I think we called them documentaries then because they often had quite a substantial factual component. For *The Iron Age Project* people were trained and then sent to live in Iron Age conditions for a couple of years. They had it rough but only slightly rougher than I did trying to screen the thing.

In the very beginning of the film there was a man hitting a post with a mallet. When I screened it, you saw him hit it, then four seconds later you heard him. I waited for the inevitable command: 'Let's start a-fucking-gain, shall we? This is going well, isn't it?'

Once a bigwig turned up to see a particularly significant piece of historic film. I opened the tape canister and the last person who screened it had put bits of paper in the film as markers. I knew if these went through the projector they would jam it, so while it was screening I stood there ready to whip them out just before they went through.

Suddenly, someone barked at me from his seat: 'Could you just lift the light on that a little bit?'

'Certainly,' I said and in the moment it took me, a piece of paper went through the projector and, of course, flashed up on the screen.

'Projectionist, what was that?'

'I'm not entirely sure, sir, but it seems to have come good.'

But as the piece of paper went around it jammed the spool, so the film started to roll out onto the floor. I just stood there looking at this incredibly valuable film unravelling all over the room. It was a revelation how long it got in a short space of time. When it's not wound tight, film is like water — it finds a natural level. Pretty soon I couldn't budge because the film was around my ankles and if I moved I would have damaged it. So I decided — with, in hindsight, questionable wisdom — to let it go. As long as no one came into the projection booth — and why would they? — they would never know and I could get the film wound up nicely and back in its can when the screening was over.

My one bit of luck was that they didn't want to sit through the whole thing.

'I think I've seen enough,' said the bigwig about halfway

through. I breathed a sigh of relief and reached over so I could turn the lights back on without moving my feet.

'Thank you very much, projectionist.'

'Thank you, sir.'

'Can you just come in and clear up these glasses and what have you?'

'Yes, I'll do that.' *Just as soon as you've gone.*

But as he was leaving he opened the door to the projection booth, to reveal me paddling in valuable, historic film, some of which now took the opportunity to roll through the door and out of the booth.

'What a fucking embarrassment,' said the bigwig.

'I didn't want to disturb your viewing pleasure, but there was a slight problem because someone had left markers in it, sir. But I thought it was better that, you know, your time is valuable, it's better that you can watch and get on and I'll just sort this out.'

'Do you want to know what's valuable?' he said. 'This fucking mess here is valuable. Sort it.' And he closed the door and walked off. I hope by now they've finished converting all those films to digital.

Eventually I got to be involved in other aspects of the organisation. The BBC was very traditional, but also ready to take chances. They made programmes no one would do now, like *A Year in the Life of a Tree*. They had a tree growing in the middle of the BBC grounds with cameras bolted to it that they kept running for 12 months to see what happened.

We did an outside broadcast for a year with a family of badgers. We parked a spare outside broadcast truck up in a badger sett and at around 10.15 every night it went live for 15 minutes. You could watch the badgers for a quarter of an hour. When they looked at the ratings, which they hardly ever did because they were the BBC, they realised people were checking on the badgers just before they went to bed. Some nights nothing would happen for minutes and those episodes were among the best rating because people stayed tuned in until they had laid eyes on the badgers. When the OB truck was needed for other duties, people wrote in.

I became one of several hosts for *Any Answers*, which was done at Bush House, the BBC headquarters in London. Questions would be read out on air in a show called *Any Questions* and then other people would write in with answers and we would read the best ones. The shows are still running. I was chosen possibly because I had an obvious affinity for mail, but mainly because I had been doing a bit of hosting on local radio and still hadn't turned 20.

'You've got a younger voice, so we'll get you to do the younger letters for *Any Answers*,' the producer told me. I got a first-class train ticket once a week to go to London.

Doing that made me think that the BBC would take any excuse for a radio programme, so I decided to come up with one and took it to one of my bosses.

'I've had this idea and I've done a rough budget on it,' I said. 'We go to the most far-flung, most isolated parts of England and we just talk to the people that live and work there.' There was a little bit more to it but essentially that was the guts of it. It was no surprise to me at all that this producer came back to me after a week and said he liked my idea.

'Here's what we'll do. I'll give you an office and a secretary, and you do the production. You turn it into something that we can then turn around and do.'

So for a while I had an office. I had visions of myself getting plants from the nursery and furnishing the thing and then mail people would come around and I'd be this mysterious character tippy-tapping away or dictating. The best thing about it, as far as I was concerned, was that someone would be delivering me mail. Stationery has always been an enthusiasm and I got a stamp made with my full name on it — Paul Henry Hopes — so that I could stamp any documents I thought needed it.

Of course, I never got around to making the programme. As with so many of my ambitions, I was much more interested in getting the gig than in doing it. Also, it didn't pay any money, which was one of the reasons the producer had been so happy to let me do it, but it was a big disincentive as far as I was concerned. It was just going to be too hard. It was also going to take too long; my attention span was waning.

I was after something that was going to get me a job, not something that was going to become a job, possibly, at some stage. I still didn't have a proper BBC job that I could live on and that would help improve things for my mother and myself. I liked the excitement and variety of what I was doing, but at the same time we were very poor and my mother was working very hard. The flip side of my taste for variety was a craving for security. In my life up till now there had been a lot of insecurity, so I wanted permanence in things, which at that time meant getting an actual job. Just not in the tobacco factory.

Also, England was even more depressing this time around. When I first went there it hadn't been so noticeable, because I was only 11 years old and didn't have a choice. But when I went back, my mother was still in the same council flat and everyone else I knew was still doing exactly what they had always done.

I decided to move back to New Zealand again — and if you're finding this a little repetitive, I promise this is the last time I will change countries. At least I had made my mind up before I turned 21.

So I moved back to Auckland, determined not to waste any more time dithering about what I was going to do. I wanted to establish security and amass wealth, start businesses, get a decent job in radio. Probably not in that order. At the same time, predictably and in between finishing one thing and starting another, I added a few glittering lines to my CV.

I got a job selling coffee machines and quite quickly became the manager for my region — a deliberate move to divert attention from the fact I wasn't any good at selling the machines.

'I'm going to be found out,' I thought. 'I've got to become branch manager or they'll realise I'm hopeless. They better promote me quick.'

One of the reps was Dutch and everyone else there hated him. I couldn't work out why. I thought it might have been because he had a beard, or because he had an accent or just because he was Dutch.

Eventually I realised it was because he was so spectacularly successful. Also, he didn't like any of them, either. He didn't want to go to meetings or chat about the weekend or drink with them after work. His pockets were full of slips of paper with leads. All he cared about was leads and possibilities. Why would he come in for a meeting when he could be out there selling coffee machines? Somehow he ended up showing me how to sell the machines and he would have been a good teacher if I had been a better student. The only time he wasn't talking about selling coffee machines was when he was running down the other people there. He used to sell these things like they were going out of fashion. He got as many knock-backs as everybody else but he knocked on a lot more doors.

My mother came back about a year after me. We were a good team and it was only sensible for us both to be in the same place. It did take a bit of organising because even though I had been born in New Zealand she had not.

A telephone conversation with my mother

(ring ring)

O: Hello?

P: Hi, it's me.

O: Oh good. What happened to you yesterday?

P: I just got busy in the afternoon but I'll come and see you this weekend.

O: When?

P: I'm not sure but I'll definitely come and see you this weekend. I'll ring you tomorrow. Have you had a good day?

O: Oh well, we won the A and B quiz and we've got bocce this afternoon . . . now . . . (long pause where I roll my eyes and think, oh god, how long is this going to take?)

P: Okay, so I'll ring you tomorrow.

O: . . . Now . . . (long pause where I roll my eyes and think, oh god, how long is this going to take?)

P: Never mind, it doesn't matter. If you can't think of it, it can't be important.

O: No (pause). What was it?

P: I don't care what it was. I have to go but I'll ring you tomorrow.

O: Well I was talking to (pause), oh, you know.

P: No, I don't know and I don't care and I have to go but I'll ring you tomorrow.

O: She's on our floor.

P: Who?

O: Oh, you know, what's her name?

P: I'm going now. I'll ring you tomorrow, I love you very much, have a good night.

O: Oh okay, I love you, I love you so much.

P: All right. God bless.

O: Bye then . . . Paul?

P: What?

O: I love you, you know?

P: And I love you very much. You have a good night and I'll ring you tomorrow and I'll come and see you in the weekend maybe.

O: All right, I love you, you take care . . . Are you all right for money?

P: Yes, I'm very rich, remember? (old lady laughs)

O: Oh, I'm very proud of you . . . drive carefully.

P: I will. You take care, love you.

O: Are you all right?

P: Hang up or I will never talk to you again.
(raucous laughter on both sides)

O: All right, good night love. (it might not be night, doesn't matter)

P: Okay, bye, I love you. God bless. Bye, bye, bye.
(hangs up on old lady)

Because I liked the look of the place, I bought a building in Featherston and opened a cafe and arts and crafts shop called the Inkley Doovery Emporium. Inkley Doovery is a West Country name for something which has a specific purpose but is being used for something else, like a milk bottle that is being used to collect coins. It's a very useful word.

While I was still running it, I joined the Carterton Dramatic Society and went along out of the blue to audition for the part of Macbeth. Of course it was a clique and they had their Macbeth well and truly chosen, which is lucky because it was a much bigger part than I thought. I was Banquo in the end, and I was a damn good Banquo, but I didn't want to be part of a clique. They socialised a lot, and I used to socialise with them a bit because I'd just moved there. I was a local businessman and I knew I had to get to know people. Maybe they'd come and buy a cake or a pie.

Custom at the cafe was sporadic. But sometimes the whole shop would suddenly go dark in the middle of the day because a tour bus had pulled up, blocking the windows. 'Oh fuck,' I thought. 'We're going to need every spoon, cup and plate in the place. We're really going to have to pull finger.' I was there on my own, with my mum working for me part-time. So I had to ring around and get casual staff in if we got busy. We didn't get many coaches, though, because the coach driver always wanted a free cup of tea and I didn't want to give anyone a free cup of tea.

I became a baker and I used to make cakes and they turned out very well. I made tomato soup from real tomatoes. Occasionally, it could get a bit *Fawlty Towers*. Once, as I was walking away from a table, I heard a customer say, 'This is not home-made. This is tinned soup.'

'Oh God, have I given you tinned soup by mistake,' I said. And I took it back to the kitchen and never went back out. They had to leave.

Tipping

I believe you should get what you pay for, which is why I am passionately opposed to tipping. In America tipping is a tax. I never want to see that in New Zealand. Tipping should be a bonus to someone for exceptional service, not for doing what they are paid to do. You shouldn't tip someone because they smile at you. You shouldn't tip them for bringing you a meal. You're keeping them in a job. And you can't opt out. Do you have a choice of going to eat out of the fridge in the restaurant kitchen?

These sorts of annoyances play into my obsessive-compulsive urges, because I do become obsessive about them. In the States, I go out with Americans who accept that they will tip at least 15 per cent. I won't, unless the service has been good. If the service is not good, I won't tip 1 per cent. My friends get worried. I've known them to go back later and tip the staff.

The worst form of tipping in the US is valet parking. You go somewhere in your car and you can see the car park quite clearly, because they're not hidden. But you're not allowed to park your own car, which would be quicker and safer. Instead, you have to join a queue that has formed and hand over your keys to a valet who gives you a chit in return. On leaving you return the chit and he returns your car. Again, you can't opt out. You have to pay $15 for the parking and he expects a tip as well.

I'm appalled at the number of people who apologise when they don't get good service: 'I'm sorry to interrupt. I know you're conducting a private conversation with a girlfriend at work behind the counter and I've been waiting for five minutes but sorry, excuse me, I'm in a bit of a hurry.'

At the same time, I can't stand people who make a profession out of being dissatisfied. You see them come into a restaurant and you know nothing will be good enough. If they get food they don't like, it's probably their fault for ordering the wrong thing. You are entitled to certain expectations and you should only complain when those expectations aren't met.

The cafe was never hugely successful but I lived off the money it made and then I sold it and got a job selling roofs.

Selling roofs was not something I had planned on doing. I had noticed over the years that most people's houses tended already to have some sort of covering that kept out water. But it was just like the encyclopaedia business — you were selling everything but the product you actually talked about. The strategy with selling roofs was to knock on a door, introduce myself and say, 'I happened to be passing and I couldn't help noticing your roof. We need some show roofs in this area, and the position of your house relative to the road would be absolutely perfect for a show roof. It means you'll get a huge discount on the roof if we can just take a couple of photos for our promotional material, that's all we need. Maybe people will drive by to have a look, but you won't know they're there. You'll get quite a discount on the roof, and I have noticed actually that your roof is beginning to deteriorate.'

Ideally, they said, 'What would it cost?' and they didn't know this, but when they asked that question they had as good as bought a new roof.

'I tell you what,' I said. 'I've got my stuff in the car, I'll just quickly measure it up and I can give you a proper quote.' By the time I got back in with the quote all they could think about was their house with a new roof.

'It'll probably double the life of your house,' I said. 'If we can get that weight of the concrete tiles off and a lovely low-maintenance roof popped on there, imagine the relief to the house.'

You have got to knock on a lot of doors to sell a roof, but it's not hard to knock on a door. Many have knockers to get you started.

I think they were good roofs. I hated doing it but I made money. I had to be able to make money because I knew so many people with no talent or ability who were making money doing the simplest things. These people were not particularly bright but they were doing well. I worked out what it was that made them successful. My father had been right: they were doers and not talkers.

Eventually, I got off the sales treadmill and got the announcer's job I had been training for — at 2ZD Radio Wairarapa. The first time I went in to introduce myself they asked me to record a couple of ads on the spot. They were happy with that and keen to use me but said I needed to do an announcer's training course because — and I know this will be hard for many readers to believe — there were a few things I didn't know, such as Maori pronunciation.

I had always — and I still do — prefer radio as a medium. I went on the course, which was as much about qualifications and pay scales as announcing. The A scale was the announcers' scale and the one to be on. The top grade was A9 — Lindsay Yeo and Merv Smith were both A9 so that was obviously what I needed to aim for. The fact I had done some announcing meant I was certain to pass, which I did. I hate to think how many times I reminded them that nearly all my previous announcing had been with the BBC.

Call centres

I'm not good at being put on hold, it may not surprise you to know. That's a shame because putting people on hold is something of a specialty for Telecom with whom I have a bit to do as a customer. They shag you around by giving you a bill which is presumably convenient for them but impossible to understand. You spend half an hour trying to work it out, so that's 30 minutes of your life you will never get back, plus your life is probably another half an hour closer to ending because you've got so emotionally wound up.

Then you pick the phone up to ask them about it and they shag you around for another half an hour waiting for someone to talk to you. That person then puts you on hold, while you listen to music that will definitely shorten your life, and probably forgets you so you have to start all over again. Finally a new person answers and you waste five minutes saying 'Do you know how long I've been waiting on this call?' and it isn't that person's fault. It's not their fault their call centre is in a country where English isn't their first language. They're part of a system which is evil.

It's actually our fault for putting up with it, though a lot of companies are coming under pressure and changing these arrangements.

Horse

CHAPTER 6
ONE IN THE EYE FOR PATSY RIGGER

WHILE I WAS DOING breakfast on 2ZD, the TV show *Top Town* came to Masterton. Whenever they turned up somewhere, they went to the local radio station and got the breakfast host to be the field announcer. He didn't appear on television but turned up at the event and helped liaise with the crowd and get them organised for the games. As 2ZD Radio Wairarapa was the only station in town that meant me.

To be honest, I did a phenomenal job for the two days it took. I know that because it seemed so easy. I had a radio mike and stood in the middle of a field with the people up in the rugby stands. The games were huge and as the contestants watched,

I had to run around the field enthusiastically demonstrating the games for them. That was all there was to it, so it really was easy.

As a result I was asked to audition for a game show called *Every Second Counts*, which went to air in 1987 and ran for two seasons. I got the job and made $500 an episode. It was up against *Coronation Street* on TV1, so was always a dodgy prospect, but the main reason it didn't go longer was that the fee for the rights to produce it locally made it too expensive.

I was amazed by the sheer size of the TVNZ machine. I had my first-ever publicity shots taken. There was a big group working on the show, which was one of the first to make full use of flashing lights and loud music. Everything about it was in your face, especially my suits. I got measured for some extraordinary checked suits that were to be made for me by Bullick & Blackmore in Masterton. I was the trailblazer for that particular style and I think the trail ended with me.

Although the show and the people on it were incredibly professional in all sorts of ways, little things tended to get overlooked. For instance, no one ever told me to look at the camera. At my first rehearsal, I began talking directly to the studio audience, assuming the camera would find me.

The format took three couples who were related in some way — husband and wife, or mother and son. In the first two sections of the game they answered questions and accumulated seconds. The last section of the game was where you won prizes by spending the seconds you had accumulated. The last segment does actually hold up today because it's so quick-fire while they're using their seconds. That makes up for the fact that the questions are banal. It's going so fast you don't really notice that. Also, the prizes were just embarrassing. Looking at it today, I can't believe people were willing to get so excited about the prospect of winning a pop-up toaster.

In the last section you had to pick a subject — say, Maori language or beaches. The contestants all went through a similar thought process: 'Well I know a little bit about the Maori language, but I know a bit about beaches, too. Surely beaches must be easier.' I knew that giving away lots of prizes — say, a trip for two to Club Med Moorea — on any given night would help kick along a show if you thought it wasn't rating. So I learnt the skill of saying, 'Would you like Maori language or *beaches*?' and giving away with my eyes which one they should pick because it would be easier for them.

I continued to multi-task. I've always been of the opinion that if a job is worth doing, another job is probably worth doing as well. At one point, I was setting up my own radio station, which we'll get to later, reading news on Radio New Zealand and filling in for George Balani and Mike Hosking. George Balani was doing the late night talkback and Mike Hosking was doing *New Zealand Tonight*. These were network shows that the community stations used.

I've always loved newsreading, and I have gone back to it several times to fill in. I love the discipline of it. I love the fact that you simply cannot fuck it up — you need to pronounce things correctly, but you also need to make your delivery match the magnitude of what you're talking about. The unspoken message was 'All right, you've had a bit of fun listening to your music. Now sit down, shut up and pay attention.' To do a perfect bulletin is a wonderful thing.

For a while I was in charge of the racing show on Radio New Zealand, which was reticulated to the community stations. I can only imagine that branching out into this area — a sport about which I had no knowledge and in which I had no interest — was part of my subconscious wish to become skilled in every aspect of broadcasting.

I worked with the big names of radio racing: Paddy O'Donnell,

Mary Mountier, Alan Bright. Racing had such a following that the people became stars — the sort of broadcasters who could put out books of jokes or recipes using beer. They were giants in their field, which was fortunate given the depth of my ignorance. However, I was very good at the technical side of things. I could cope easily with three different feeds in one ear — linking, timing things out and putting them into a programme in a seamless way. The relevant authorities had discovered this and decided I could handle the racing show.

Racing was nothing if not chaotic. For a start, as Radio New Zealand's racing controller, I had to organise what races we would cover and when. Some were obvious but not the international ones, like those from Australia, which listeners were also interested in. Saturday was huge. I got in early, went straight to the TAB and got the racing sheets and the latest scratchings. Then I sat in my office at Broadcasting House with these giant, bigger-than-A3 race sheets, printed out from computers on the paper with the holes in the side. I had to time things out — work out from the schedules which races would clash and plan it so we could fit in as many as possible. In some cases we had to record them to play later — and then you had to decide which was more important and should be live.

When the first races started, so did racing control. We had TV feeds of the races and just worked our way through them. The stations would break off their Saturday sports shows to take the feed from racing control, and then resume their other sports coverage. You tried to do the race live, then give the results and preview the next race. You tried to do that live because if you started to record things, suddenly you had a stockpile to get through and quickly fell behind.

Then, all of sudden, something would stuff up — if the first race of the day was at Addington and it began late you were fucked. That meant every race at Addington was going to be on at the same time as the Ellerslie races. All the stations on the community network were doing their scoreboards. In one ear they had me, racing control, but they were trying to do motor racing and rugby, and God knows how many other things at the same time.

Compared to that, TV work was relaxing. As a result of *Every Second Counts* I got to do *Telethon Tonight*, little slots leading up to Telethon. Part of the job was to meet the overseas stars at the airport, show them around a bit and take them out and do some taped pieces with them. Su Pollard from *Hi-De-Hi!* came the year I did it. I was with Patsy Rigger, the country singer, and trying to introduce them. I turned around to point out Su Pollard and turned back and poked Patsy Rigger in the eye with quite a lot of force, because I was enthusiastic in those days. I could feel her eyeball denting against my finger. I was impressed because she was so dignified about it, just emitting a low groan. I carried on: 'Look, Su Pollard's just over there when your eyes come good.'

That was one of the last big Telethons. Outside the Avalon studios in Lower Hutt, we had a row of portaloos for people who were queuing up to come into the studio. They ended up queuing to get to the portaloos instead. The weather was shocking that year — shocking Wellington wind. We had a helicopter bringing in one of the stars and the wind from it was just enough to send these portaloos over like dominos. Doors fell open. People fell out. I can't believe we didn't get it on camera — it was the best thing about the whole Telethon.

My biggest break in television nearly came just after that. Expo 88 was being held in Brisbane and I was asked to go and host a series of programmes from there. That would have been a huge break because it was an opportunity to practise hosting skills but also to be a bit playful and ad lib. You were showing the expo to people who weren't able to afford a ticket to Brisbane. But my wife, Rachael, and I had our second child due about that time.

I had met Rachael when she was a teacher at Featherston Primary School, which was a few blocks from my shop and cafe. She was just out of teacher training and that was her first assignment. Her parents were both educationalists so that was their expectation. She comes from a family of academics. We were very different in many ways — my father would say the doers and the talkers have got together — but sometimes that works out well.

She used to take her kids for walks and they used to slide their hands along my windows, which used to infuriate me. 'That's great,' I thought to myself. 'These teachers, all the holidays in the bloody world, I'm paying their bloody wages with my hard-earned taxes and the best they can do is come around and dirty up my windows.'

So that's how we met. I invited her out when I was in *Macbeth* and in lengthy rehearsals. We got engaged very quickly. We didn't get married quite so quickly. And we didn't start a family for a while because she hadn't been overseas and she wanted to do that first. After we were married she went to Europe for a month or so.

So when the Brisbane offer came up, everything was relatively settled. I thought it would be perfectly reasonable for me not to be around. I thought the birth of our second child would be very much like the birth of our first; I couldn't see it having much to offer in the way of novelty.

'There's no way I would miss the birth,' I told Rachael, when we were discussing the Brisbane offer, hoping like hell she'd say, 'Of course you must go.'

'Of course you wouldn't miss the birth,' she said.

'Of course not,' I agreed, but I was thinking, 'Please God give me a break here, let me go do this great job. Make her insist that I go.' But she didn't. Good for her.

Poshest actresses in the world

1. Dame Judi Dench. She makes Helen Mirren look like a cheap slapper, the kind that would accept an Academy Award with no underwear on.
2. Helen Mirren.

Microphone

CHAPTER 7
SPECULATE TO
ACCUMULATE

> **ALTHOUGH I HAD WORKED IN MANY AREAS OF RADIO I HAD NEVER OWNED MY OWN STATION. ONCE THIS POSSIBILITY OCCURRED TO ME, IT BECAME A MINOR OBSESSION.**

ALTHOUGH I HAD WORKED in many areas of radio I had never owned my own station. Once this possibility occurred to me, it became a minor obsession. This was in 1990, when the radio spectrum was being freed up, and frequencies were being put out to tender.

It was a second-price tendering system, which means the person who tenders the highest only has to pay what the next highest bidder offered. So if I tendered $100,000 and the closest other bid was $50,000, I only had to pay $50,000. That is not the brilliant gift it seems because, when you know that if you get it you're only going to have to pay $50,000, why not tender

$200,000? Everyone else knew that and everyone did the same, so across the board, the bids were pushed much higher.

This was not good for a person in my position — which was that I had no money. Everyone had to pay a deposit, which the government got to keep for as long as it took for the sales to be finalised. Then Maori decided that they owned the frequencies so the whole thing stalled for months and months and months while the government negotiated with Maori over what it was going to do.

In the meantime, schleps like me, who really couldn't afford it in the first place, had our money tied up without knowing whether we had won or whether there was going to be anything left for us to win.

I was sure I could run a successful station. I had acquired a lot of knowledge about radio and I thought I knew what people wanted to listen to. I would be starting in a community that I knew, the Wairarapa, where there was only Radio New Zealand's AM station.

In the end, my tender wasn't successful and my money was refunded and the frequency went to an outfit based in Wellington. It was nice to have my money back, but I would have preferred the frequency. I was just devastated because in the interim, I had, of course, purchased an old hall in Carterton from which I was going to run my radio station. I was certain I would win because I couldn't think of anyone else in the Wairarapa who would bid the kind of money I did. It never occurred to me that people from outside the Wairarapa would be interested.

The only thing I could do was find a new frequency. It seemed impossible that there could be 20 frequencies available in the Wellington area but only one in the Wairarapa.

The government said that if I could prove there was another frequency available on the spectrum then I could have it for six months. At that point it would be put up for tender and I could make a bid — along with anyone else who felt like it — for the frequency I had established. It was better than nothing. Not a lot better, just a little bit. I could make a lot of money. Or I could be left with nothing but a huge financial loss and several disgruntled, soon-to-be-ex employees. Naturally, I jumped at the chance.

I commissioned Broadcast Services Limited (BSL) to find me another frequency. They found an excellent one that didn't interfere with existing frequencies. After securing the frequency, and at the same time as I was plotting to overthrow them, I was still working at Radio New Zealand, reading the news and doing numerous other odd jobs. Naturally they found out what I was doing and I was called into the office of Caroline Lane, who was one in a long line of people employed to eviscerate the organisation.

'Have you considered buying our AM station?' she asked me.

'Is it for sale?' I parried.

'Everything's possible in this environment.'

'All right, I'll buy it,' I said. It had lots of advantages. I could simulcast it on my new FM frequency and if I didn't hold on to that after the six months, I would still have a substantial station making good money. It solved my problem of how to fill up 24 hours a day of airtime; it gave me a staff and the infrastructure I needed. It was brilliant.

After mucking me around magnificently for some time, Radio New Zealand lost the services of Caroline Lane and informed me that there was no way they were going to sell one of their stations, but rather they would be a fearsome competitor.

Meanwhile, back in Carterton, the builders were in and my empire was taking shape. There was a tiny office for me in the reception area, a studio and a small control room, open plan offices and a couple of toilets, and a little area with a photocopier and a big car park next to it.

The costs involved were enormous, especially compared to what can be done with today's technology. I was renting one tape machine from Radio New Zealand for $500 a month. You don't even need tape machines now. I had to have a library with records in it in order to be able to play music. Now you've got a music programme and everything is available to you instantly on the internet. For $20,000 today I can buy a station's worth of music plus the Apple equipment to play it on. Back then I could get a three-CD player with a shuffle function for $800. And it had to be a 24-hour station so people would know that whenever they turned their radio on your station would be there.

I employed Radio New Zealand technicians to sort out the transmission site. I bought a transmitter from Italy; I rented transmission links, UHF uplinks from my building to the BSL tower where I had to put my transmitter. Working out the payments to APRA, the Australasian Performing Rights Association, for the music we played was a nightmare. And although we were in competition, Radio New Zealand sold me their news service.

I had mortgaged my house, putting every cent I had into this activity and I was working as many shifts as I could, reading news and filling in for people to keep the cash flowing. There was also the matter of a wife plus two children under five and one on the way to worry about. Rachael had no idea how much money I was hocking myself up for.

There were so many technical things that I hadn't thought of, like processing. It was all very well to have a state-of-the-art Italian transmitter, but I had to decide what kind of processing I would do to beef up the sound. Actually, first I had to find out what processing was, then decide what kind to have.

One day I got a call from one of the BSL technicians.

'We're up at the transmission site now,' he said, 'and we've just gone to fire up your transmitter and it's slightly interfering with the Concert Programme.'

'Yes?'

'So we're going to need to get a blocker to put on the line — an isolator.'

'Mmmm.'

'Well, we can rent you one for $600 a month or you can buy one for $40,000.'

'Hang on,' I suggested. 'You're renting me the spot for my transmitter. Surely if it's interfering with another transmitter you're renting to someone in an area you're renting, it's your responsibility to isolate the bloody things.' They eventually conceded I had a point but I still had to find the money to fix it. It's not like I had the choice of taking my business elsewhere.

I was bluffing my way through, but at the same time I did not believe it could possibly fail. With my drive and passion and energy it was bound to succeed. My dream was only to start it. I hadn't actually imagined myself running the station day to day.

I had been keeping things reasonably quiet but there came a point where I had to let everyone know that this was happening, if only because I needed to start booking ads. I got my sales team together and held a press conference at the Solway Park Hotel and announced that Today FM was going to be launched. The poor quality of local journalism meant that came as a complete surprise to the other organisations. The Radio New Zealand station had known but hoped it was never going to happen so had been pretending I didn't exist.

But I had to keep the fact that I had only six months of operation guaranteed a secret or nobody would have taken me seriously. I was terrified the local paper, the *Wairarapa Times-Age*, which had taken a slight stand against me, might find out. They didn't.

I worked out how much we would need to bring in to cover operating costs and put together some ad packages that would cover it. They went down well and we soon had enough revenue to keep going.

I made sure we were part of the community. I wanted to get Mitre 10 in Masterton to advertise but knew my competition would say to them, 'Oh they're a Carterton station. They're based in Carterton.' To counter that, I did a noon news broadcast from Mitre 10's shop window. I got Ricky Long, the local butcher, doing a talkback hour every morning. We had great giveaways and competitions, which had never been done locally.

Some people may have resented me. They saw me as someone who had ridden into town to suck all the money out of it. I would have been happy to do that, but the opportunity never arose.

One big advertiser had a car yard in Masterton. When we were up and running successfully, he called me into his office and implied that I was a carpetbagger and told me advertising was being discounted now — by the other station — but my prices had gone up. He just wanted to tell me off. I didn't need this but I didn't want to alienate an advertiser either so I sat there and let him.

'Don't you give five-year warranties on your cars now?' I said as I was leaving.

'Yes.'

'Didn't it used to be a three-year warranty? What if I brought the car in and it was a three-year warranty? Should I come in here and say you're a bit of an arsehole because now you're giving five-year warranties and I've been ripped off?'

He accepted that there was some truth in what I was saying and allowed me to leave his office.

Break-even point was about $13,000 a week, which was a lot for a little operation in the Wairarapa, and every month we had to toil to get there. In my head I was two different people: I was the person who was planning to sell the station or to buy other stations for the future, and I was another person who was trying to work out how I was going to handle absolute oblivion and humiliation in four months' time, then three months' time, then two . . .

But my biggest problem in the early days was what to do at six o'clock in the evening when I was completely wrung out and had no more money to pay staff but still had to keep broadcasting 24 hours a day.

I phoned Doug Gold, who had got several frequencies in the first round in Wellington and created More FM. He was a brilliant radio person and a brilliant salesman. I would go to visit prospective clients only to be told, 'We've spent our entire radio budget with More FM because I got a holiday in Spain.'

'Look, Doug,' I said, 'here's the thing. You've got no frequency in the Wairarapa. Here's what I'll do for you. I will give you the opportunity to tell all of your advertisers in Wellington that if they advertise in the evening their adverts will go on in the Wairarapa. Here's what I want in return. I want to put an FM radio in my control room and I want to switch it onto More FM at six o'clock in the evening and switch it off at six o'clock in the morning.'

'Yeah, good as gold.'

'Do we need to write something? Do we need a letter of understanding or something?'

'This conversation is our understanding. My proviso is that you don't interfere with that transmission once it's on, so all of our ads are played there.'

'Absolutely.'

I had a car radio installed into my rack in the control room and at six o'clock we switched on More FM. There were a couple of problems when one of the neighbours was doing chores and his lawn got mowed in stereo throughout the Wairarapa, but generally it worked like a charm.

My staff was a combination of cheap newbies who just wanted to do anything to get into radio and experienced old-timers who weren't being paid as much as they were worth. When I needed a local newsroom, I phoned up the Broadcasting School in Christchurch.

'Who are your best people?' I asked, because I knew they'd all be cheap.

'I've got two good people who could instantly come out of there and take a sole charge position on a radio station,' I was told. 'The best of the two is Hilary Pankhurst' — who is now Hilary Barry and a network TV news presenter.

'Right, I'll employ her.' She moved to the Wairarapa and all of a sudden she was a one-woman news team, starting her morning with briefings at the police station. She was an object of total contempt to the Radio New Zealand station, who soon decided she was so terrible they needed to poach her from me. I needed to lock her in for six months and decided a company car would be the thing. But I couldn't afford to buy a car. Fortunately, it was the time of the Film Archive's Last Film Search where people were out looking for any old film tucked away around the country. One of their number came into the station to promote the hunt and I took him aside.

'You know what we need to do?' I said. 'We need to get a car, sign write it with "The Old Film Search" or something like that.' I bought an old Vauxhall Viva at a car auction and they helped pay for it. So not only was Hilary struggling with a new job, new town and new place names, working on a WordFirst programme on an old Compaq 64, but she was also having to struggle with a company car which was (1) a total embarrassment, and (2) a Vauxhall Viva, so it hardly ever worked. She had to get the police to push start her after the press conferences.

And always in the back of my mind was the fact that my day of judgement was getting ever closer. I thought the government would advertise that the frequency was being put up for tender. Surely the *Times-Age* would find out about it when it was advertised in their paper. They could hardly overlook that.

I called the staff — who were all on six-month 'trial' contracts — and explained everything to them.

'There's no obligation on me to keep going beyond the six month period,' I said, and in fact I could have legally just walked away. 'But we're going okay, and I'd like to be sitting down with all of you in a couple of months and negotiating your employment from here on in. We can only do that if we win this tender. So I'm just keeping you in touch so that you will know.'

Then I called a small group of these people to my house with a couple of the others. One was a young salesman whose girlfriend worked at the *Times-Age*.

'I need you all to help me disseminate misinformation,' I said. 'I have just stopped paying all my bills. We need the word to be out there that things are financially shaky for us and we can't even afford to pay our bills. If that gets out, then people will think either I'm not going to put in a tender or that if I do it's going to be really low.'

When the tender was advertised I thought there would be quite a juicy front-page story about how the new radio station, which had made such an impact in the area, was on its last legs. But no one rang. The only people who really expressed concern were some of our advertisers because they were getting such good value from advertising with us.

The tendering system had changed so that the highest tender won the contract and paid what they had bid — not the second-highest price. I tendered quite low and Radio New Zealand tendered lower. I can only assume the misinformation plan worked because I got the frequency for what was in reality quite a reasonable price.

Then, for the first time, the prospect of running myself ragged and operating my own radio station that needed to make $13,000 a week to break even started to hit home.

I had succeeded and the Radio New Zealand station was panicked. They were selling $65 spots for something like $8. I wrote to Jim Bolger complaining that my income tax was obviously being used to subsidise what was supposed to be a commercial station. I didn't get a reply. I'm not the first businessman that's had the government undercut him.

Having secured the station, I wanted to get rid of it. I couldn't manage the pace. There was a particular time where dollar for dollar we were earning more money than any other radio station in the country, so I was hopeful of selling quickly and for a good price.

Around this time I was in Wellington when I heard an ad for Bernadino sparkling wine. It was a brilliant ad, just a musical 30 seconds, but I wanted it on our station because I liked the sound of it so much. I rang Bernadino with an offer.

'If you back up a truck to my radio station with a hundred cartons of Bernadino on board,' I said, 'I'll give you a $5000 spend in the month.' They said yes straight away. The weekend it started playing I had Brent Birchfield from Port FM visiting. He was interested in buying my station. I picked him up with Today FM playing in the car and every second ad was this fantastic Bernadino one.

'You've got some big clients,' he said.

I was in full-on sales mode. The books were in good shape. It was a good purchase for him, because it would make a key link in a small network. I didn't downplay how hard I found the work but I thought his structure meant that wouldn't be such a problem. He met the staff, who all behaved beautifully.

We arranged a meeting with my accountant, Darren Quirk, at the Solway Park Hotel.

'Darren, what you've got to know is this guy is going to walk away owning my radio station lock, stock and barrel,' I said on the way in. 'I don't want an interest left in there. I don't want to be part of this radio station any more. So if the figures appear to be not quite good enough to you, we'll settle for not quite good enough. You've got to go in there knowing this.'

Brent was of the view that he got a very, very good deal, and so he did, but I don't think he fully appreciated how much work was involved in making the station money. I also let him have all my debtors, which is not usual with a sale like this. They were worth about $30,000 but I knew they consisted of people who owed small amounts that they were never going to pay. He bought it and walked away thinking, 'I have stolen this radio station from this person', but I think a few months later it became obvious to him that he had paid a fair price.

I took the profit from the station sale and immediately reinvested it, which is what I had been doing since I discovered my natural entrepreneurial instincts as a kid. My father used to say to me 'You have to speculate to accumulate' and obviously he was right. I would buy a business or property, add value and turn it over at a profit, then borrow more and invest in something else, all the while working in broadcasting as my day job. Anyone can do this and it's how you make serious money — not by just making money but by making your money make money for you.

Lodge in the hills

CHAPTER 8
A PEOPLE PERSON

> " I ONCE SPENT AN HOUR TALKING ABOUT SOLAR-POWERED, GLOW-IN-THE-DARK CRUCIFIXES. YOU MIGHT THINK IT'S EASY TO SPEND AN HOUR TALKING ABOUT SOLAR-POWERED GLOW-IN-THE-DARK CRUCIFIXES. IT IS NOT. YOU BOUGHT ONE OF THESE AND CEMENTED IT ONTO YOUR LOVED ONE'S GRAVESTONE. "

ALL OF A SUDDEN I was cashed up and out of work. We continued to live in the old presbytery in Carterton and I went straight to Radio New Zealand as a newsreader. I had done them over in the Wairarapa ratings wars, but they were generous enough to welcome me back. They didn't even complain when I started doing shifts for Radio Pacific as well.

The thought that this was any kind of step back — from owning a successful station to being a fill-in host — never entered my head. If I had been an ambitious person it might have niggled at me, but I am not and never have been ambitious in that way.

I realised having a lot of cash was not a good thing for a person like me. I would just have seen things I wanted and bought them until the money ran out. So I spent most of the funds on a lodge up in the hills.

It wasn't a goer. It had been half-finished by someone who ran out of money, so I got it for an excellent price. There was a big four-bedroom cedar lodge with a giant fireplace and big deck on it which was designed as accommodation. There were about 500 acres of native bush, a kilometre of roading, a dirt track and waterfalls. There were swimming holes and fantastic walks. It was very beautiful but I could see it still needed a lot of money invested in it to bring things up to standard. I knew that and I knew I was not that person.

I had someone living in a campervan up there who sort of ran it, but really Jesus was in charge and it seemed to bring out the worst in him. He was always slipping rocks onto my road or knocking over trees so cars couldn't get through. I had fun there and the kids enjoyed it, but when there was heavy rain the road got bogged and access was a nightmare.

It had been built as a hunting lodge, but I know nothing about hunting and I don't like men with guns. The first thing I did was erect big signs saying 'No Hunting' and put big padlocks on the gate, because people would drive in to hunt the wild deer and pigs. So the most obvious way of making money was never going to be open to me because I didn't want hunters on the property. I did what I usually did: sold it at a profit and put the money into something else.

But that was a sideshow. Radio occupied most of my work hours. A brilliant radio salesman called Errol Wilkinson, who had helped me a lot with Today FM, had started working at Radio Pacific and got me in to fill in on an infomercial hour which played to Wellington. Errol sold me hard to Radio Pacific's manager Derek Lowe, once I had my foot in the door. With its racing coverage, Pacific had now been a network for a while, courtesy of the TAB and Derek's good management.

The infomercial hour was devoted to one person who came in to talk about often very bizarre products. I did so well that they took me up to Auckland to fill in for the guy who did the network infomercials. This was the beginning of what would be a very long relationship with Radio Pacific. I also filled in on the all-nighter, doing talkback from Wellington.

I once spent an hour talking about solar-powered glow-in-the-dark crucifixes. You might think it's easy to spend an hour talking about solar-powered glow-in-the-dark crucifixes. It is not. You bought one of these and cemented it onto your loved one's gravestone. Ideally, everyone would buy one and our cemeteries would look like Hilda Ogden's living room. I don't know exactly how good these things were but I knew they were durable. We threw one around in the studio to prove it. That took care of three minutes. It was tough because it had to be vandal-proof to a degree, though I imagine their appeal to random burglars would be quite low. The crucifix person and in fact, all the people I had in that hour were very sincere. They had to be. Their money was on the line and this was costing them.

Around this time, in furtherance of my dream of sailing around the world on my own boat, I bought an old fishing vessel called the *Clio* which I kept in Wellington. It was the sort of boat that should only be owned by a diesel mechanic who can keep it seaworthy.

One Saturday morning I set out on a fishing trip with Don Rood, who is now head of news at Radio New Zealand. Conditions were not too bad — a little swell, a cold winter's day. I had owned the boat long enough by now to recognise the exceptionally odd noises that would sometimes interfere with the usual odd noises its engine made. We were off the Wairarapa coast when we came upon a huge school of fish I couldn't identify but that looked well worth catching. Don had his rod over the back and I was in the pilot house preparing to circle when there was an enormous explosion under the floor beneath me. It was evident from the fact that all the hatches had blown off and black smoke was coiling out of every fissure in the boat's structure that we were in some trouble.

The boat was laden down with out-of-date and malfunctioning safety equipment and attempts to make a mayday call were futile. For some reason the engine kept going, although the electrics had all shut down. However, the thick black smoke made it impossible to control the boat from within the pilot house.

We tried to put out the fire with buckets and seawater, but we couldn't reach whatever was actually burning because it was under the deck; also, diesel floats, so all we were doing was moving the flames closer to the wood we were standing on. Half an hour had gone by and it seemed inconceivable that we weren't surrounded by rescue craft. It was obvious that our plight had been radioed in because a spotter plane was flying overhead. At the point where the paint on the deck was bubbling and we were considering leaping into the water, a helicopter appeared in the distance. It was not, alas, the Westpac Rescue Helicopter. It was a *3 News* helicopter, there to record the event. It was a comfort to think that our loved ones would have a visual keepsake of our last moments.

Not long after, the Westpac helicopter did appear and we were winched off just seconds before the boat was engulfed in flames. The helicopter circled a couple of times as we watched it sink beneath the surface, and we were taken back to be paraded before the news cameras.

I was supposed to go and hear my daughter Lucy sing with her school choir that night and still had time to get there. I had spoken to Rachael, who had seen the rescue on the TV news, so everyone knew I was all right. I picked up my truck which had needed a tyre change, put the new tyre on and headed back over the Rimutakas. As I neared home, wearing some particularly ludicrous garments that had been found to replace my soaking wet ones, the new tyre came off and I saw it rolling ahead of me. Shit, I thought, this is turning into a really crappy day. But I did get to the concert.

When I went up to Auckland for Radio Pacific, I didn't expect to see Derek Lowe at all. He was a mysterious, legendary figure. His run-ins with Pam Corkery were particularly renowned. But he had a big impact and influence on me. He was a real taskmaster. As far as he was concerned, there was one way to do it and that was his way. Your way might have been better, but it was wrong.

Over the years we eventually grew quite close. He never lost his absolute passion for radio, even when most of his time was focused on the boardroom and operating Radio Pacific as, at the time, the most successful broadcasting entity in the country. He was juggling all sorts of competing requirements. He had a board and shareholders, he was developing an enormous network, buying and selling other interests and making a huge amount of money. His role was more that of businessman than broadcaster, but he still loved radio.

He always had with him a pad of recycled paper — he was stingy, too, though lavish with the people he needed to be lavish with — and even when he was concentrating on a complicated deal, if he got a good idea for a promo, he wrote it down. He wrote all the station promos, which were absolute masterpieces of the genre, on this pad. And once a week he would go into the studio and produce them.

I can't say he ever showed much passion for the infomercial hour, though I know he was passionate about the truckloads of money it brought in.

Derek realised that encumbered with racing, as Radio Pacific was, it was never going to be the number-one rating station, which would have been the goal of many people doing his job. But that didn't mean that it couldn't be the number-one money-making station. If you're never going to get as many listeners as the others, how are you going to create the desire in those listeners you do have to spend, spend and spend? He did it by creating the notion of the Radio Pacific family and producing branded products that you bought to be part of the family.

After a while I got regular overnight shifts on the weekend, so I would commute up to Auckland and stay in a motel. Then I got a daytime show, *Paul's People*, for which I would commute weekly. It was vaguely infomercial but more newsworthy than straight infomercial programmes. Even though they were huge money-spinners, they weren't great for ratings. Derek had brought Brent Impey in to make some changes, which included my new show.

Talkback was something I wasn't very enthusiastic about. I have hovered around talkback a lot, but I always loathed it. I loathe how the insatiable need for a caller makes you say things you don't necessarily believe just to get a reaction.

For Arch Tambakis, an Australian talkback host who was at Pacific for a while, a successful talkback show was a full board of calls, even if every single one of those calls was from a complete moron.

For me, successful talkback is that all-too-rare brilliant caller who says something you haven't thought of or heard before and who makes everyone listening say to themselves 'Where the fuck did he come from?' In those cases, the next thing you think is 'How can someone like that be listening to this shit?' I love talk radio when it is done properly, but I don't think talkback is something you can do properly.

So I tried to fill *Paul's People* with interviews — I could have the luxury of doing a 20-minute interview if the subject was worth it — and I tried to keep the talkback component to a minimum.

The BBC did a survey when they first realised that talkback was a force to be reckoned with and was something they were going to have to do. One of the things the report discovered was that people who call up are not representative of the people who are listening. In other words, talkback consists of a large number of quite intelligent people listening to a comparatively small number of absolute fucking cretins. And those people listen to and enjoy talkback, despite the enormous frustration they get at hearing the morons, because it constantly reinforces their prejudices against humankind. Reading this made me realise why it is so stunning when, on those rare occasions, you do hear someone intelligent or interesting call in.

Arch was the quintessential talkback host. On first encounter, he impressed you hugely with this blunt, brass, crass enthusiasm. 'I could fill a board in a graveyard,' he said to me early on. The full board of calls is every talkback host's goal and safety net because it means there will always be someone to talk to and you won't end up having to fill the empty air with a monologue of your own improvising. I was impressed and wondered how Arch managed always to have a full board.

I soon found out he did it by being truly ignorant and obnoxious. He was entirely bulletproof in that regard with no concern about what anyone thought of him. He was short, overweight and virtually blind. Somehow, despite that, he would intimidate you even when he wasn't trying to. Usually, however, he was trying to. He eyeballed you and, despite his lack of stature, got right up in your face. Part of the motivation may have been that only then was he able to see you. Fortunately his glasses were about six inches thick so he could never get closer than six inches.

Arch did phenomenally good infomercials. He gave the advertisers an extra minute on the phone, which was very valuable to them. And in return they wanted to be nice and offered him their products.

You had to be careful with that sort of thing. For a start, there are only so many glow-in-the-dark crucifixes you can use. Most of us when we were offered great things accepted them politely. We might say that we would do our best for the advertiser the next time they were on, but that was the extent of it. Arch visited them and got to know them personally and took more great things and more great things. That was crossing a line he could never see.

One day, to my horror, it was announced that Arch Tambakis would be doing breakfast with me. It was not uncommon for him to come in, bail me up in that nasty little glass conservatory we used to call an office, shake his fist in my face and discuss the day's programme.

'If you fucking talk over me again, it'll be the last fucking thing you do' was a typical suggestion. He once threw a chair at me in the studio, which was remarkable for several reasons. The chairs in the studio were huge and wired loosely to the ground. Arch got up while we were on air, picked his chair up in his chubby little arms, using every ounce of strength in his incredibly unfit body, and threw it at me. It failed to hit me only because (1) he wasn't very strong, and (2) it was connected to the floor by wires.

I thought briefly that some brilliant radio might have come from the combustion created by putting the two of us together, but I always knew that the chance was extremely small and it was obvious that wasn't going to happen after a few days.

Arch wasn't capable of brilliant radio; he was capable of doing bad radio brilliantly. In the end, he had to go. I think Brent kept him until there were simply too many court cases pending for various offences inside and outside work. His career with Radio Pacific ended in court. Derek Lowe stopped me one day to tell me that Arch was suing.

Left:
My father Brian, 1955.

Below:
My mother Olive, 1956.

Left:
Me, 10 months, conducting
a high-chair broadcast.

Below:
Me, 19 months, and Mum.

Left:
About four years old, with
Gladys, my father's mother,
looking on stoically.

Above:
With the Farmers Santa.

Below:
Nine years old, Cockle Bay Primary School Fancy
Dress evening. Guess what I was.

Left:
Standard New Zealand school
photo, circa 1969.

Below left:
Me with Dad.

Below:
I'm in the back row, but where?

COCKLE BAY SCHOOL
MIDDLE PRIMERS
ROOM 7   1967

Above:
On the panoramic balcony of our council flat.
At 18 years old, I realised the importance of
looking dapper.

'There's an employment hearing,' said Derek. 'Arch has taken us to court, awful man. You'll need to be there.'

I turned up with my written statement and all I had to do was read it and Arch Tambakis would be out of my life forever. I was in the waiting room, ready to do my bit, when Arch came out of the courtroom and walked up to me.

'You fucking turd, you absolute fucking turd,' he began, putting his fists up. 'You fucking say one fucking thing against me you little shit and I'll fucking pound you into the floor. Don't think I can't fucking do it.' That possibility never entered my head.

Arch was so incapable of seeing his own flaws that losing was not an option for him. There was no way people weren't going to see through all these arseholes ganging up against him.

So they got rid of Arch and I went on holiday to Australia. While I was there, Brent rang me to say that I'd been taken off breakfast and the show was being changed. I wasn't too worried. I was going to Bosnia to do some reporting, and when I came back from that Pacific would find work for me. I was focused on the Bosnia trip. After Arch Tambakis, I was looking forward to the more relaxing work environment I would find there.

Gun

CHAPTER 9
HOW I BECAME
BULLETPROOF

> **" I WAS BEYOND EXCITED — I WAS GOING TO WAR WITH THE NEW ZEALAND ARMY AND I WOULD FIND OUT EVERYTHING THAT WAS GOING ON. I DIDN'T REALISE, NEVER HAVING DONE IT BEFORE, THAT MY PERSONALITY WAS REALLY CUT OUT TO DO THIS. I ALSO WAS YET TO LEARN THAT I COULDN'T EXCEL IF I WAS JUST GOING TO BE THE LACKEY WHO WENT WITH THE ARMY. "**

I THOUGHT IT WOULD be a good idea to go to Bosnia and cover the war there for Radio Pacific. It was 1995 and this was to be a one-off. Because Derek Lowe didn't really have anything else for me to do, he agreed. Without either of us knowing it, there was a little seed planted then that would grow into something very big later.

I was left to make my own arrangements. I managed to get the New Zealand Army to agree to let me accompany them on the ground. I flew over and met them in Zagreb where I was getting my United Nations accreditation to go into Bosnia.

I was beyond excited — I was going to war with the New

Zealand Army and I would find out everything that was going on. I didn't realise, never having done it before, that my personality was really cut out to do this. I also was yet to learn that I couldn't excel if I was just going to be the lackey who went with the army.

It became obvious that the benefit of having access to the army's logistics and their knowledge on the ground was outweighed by the fact that any opportunity to find out what was really going on was stymied because I was there with one prejudiced player. My reports were compromised no matter what. If you reported the army was doing great work — which they were — who would believe you weren't just saying that to keep them onside?

I was constantly pushing them to do things that they wouldn't normally do: 'How about you just give me a couple of guys and we go to the front line? You were saying that there's a minefield over there? Can you take me over there?'

'Sorry, Paul. We're not really supposed to go there.'

'Assign me a couple of people, take me to the minefield. I want to see what a minefield is like, I want to see what the trenches are like.'

And they did. The soldiers themselves were excited because they had never seen a minefield either. Soon we were in the thick of it. We were picking over bodies in trenches. I found a Kevlar helmet with bullets and half a head in it, like something that had been mashed up in a mouli.

There were five of us walking along in this place where soldiers wouldn't normally go when all of a sudden the guy in front shouted, 'Stop!'

Although it looked like a pleasant scene, with the silver birch trees standing straight and their leaves covering the ground, he had spotted a hillock where earth had been piled up for a gun. He looked to the other side and saw another one. Then we realised we had wandered into the middle of a minefield.

That is the eeriest thing, because you know that as long as you don't move you'll be perfectly safe, but eventually you will have to or you're going to starve to death. There is nothing wrong with the ground you are standing on but there are several choices to be made about how to get to safety.

Do you retrace your steps? You are taught that, if you possibly can, you should do that and get back to the point where you know you're safe. If you have wandered a long way into the minefield, all you can do is look for the quickest way to safety and follow that. There were so many leaves and we'd walked so far in, we couldn't retrace our steps. You never shimmy. You don't step gingerly because that means you have to take more steps and increases the chance of stepping on a mine.

You have to leap. If you leap onto a mine, of course, you're fucked. But if you step on one gingerly you're fucked too.

I was the third in line. When you can't retrace your steps, you choose the person who is closest to the shortest route to absolute safety. That person leaps out and you follow him. The other advantage of leaping is that you make very clear footprints for the next person to leap into. The person in front of our group was blessed and we followed him safely out.

It's bloody frightening. If the person in front gets blown up, you wait for it to settle and then you keep going on that path because not only has that mine exploded, but you can be pretty sure that if there had been another one within cooee it would have been set off too.

But what is likelier in that case is that your guy is still alive, albeit writhing on the floor in agony, so you'll need to get him out. It's very complicated. Let this be a lesson to us all: do not lay mines. It's only going to cause strife for yourself or others.

I also managed to get the army to take me to Tuzla. I stood there as the refugees from the Srebrenitsa massacre arrived on the back of trucks. These people had just seen their families killed and they told the most harrowing stories. Dutch peacekeepers were still putting tents out and digging trenches as huge numbers of refugees, mainly women and girls, arrived. The men and most of the younger boys made up the majority of the 8000 people killed. The survivors had made this torturous trip from their home and seen the most horrendous things. They all had stories of seeing their families torn from them and killed before their eyes.

I followed one girl through the process. She climbed off the ute when it reached the camp. It drove away and left her standing at the end of a wide corridor of razor wire. She just stood there for ages, then she walked all alone, down the centre of this corridor into the refugee camp. She knew nothing about what was going on or what she should do. She was greeted by someone who looked in her mouth, patted her down and told her to go over to a wall where the surnames of people who had already arrived had been scrawled. This was one of the few ways people had of finding out if they still had any living relatives. In her case, she had been separated from her immediate family before they were killed. Other family members had been killed in front of her over the three days it had taken to get to the refugee camp. After seeing no one's name on the board, she wandered off and was taken to a tent where she would live with people she didn't know for God knows how long. She had no idea about anything.

I had a $30,000 satellite phone. It was so high-tech I didn't fully understand it. The phone was rented and every time I used it, it cost £9 for a connection and £9 a minute. So the first minute was £18. Sending a photo on its analogue system took about 20 minutes and chances were the link would fall out halfway through. I never sent photos but the costs were still phenomenal.

I was on the land phone reporting back whenever I could get access to one. Derek had been supportive but I knew not to spend a cent more than necessary so the satellite phone was used only sparingly. In many situations you can't bring them out because you become a target as soon as anyone sees it. They were inefficient things. They were the size of a suitcase and I remember people dying around me while the phone was saying 'Searching. Searching. Searching.'

After being a foreign correspondent for a few days I realised that the best way to do this was to turn up at the war, uninvited, as it were. There would be logistical problems but I could bullshit my way through anything, or thought I could.

Halfway through the assignment I was starting to worry because arrangements were being made to get me out when my time was up and I didn't want to go. By then I had found a lodging house to stay in on my own, just so I had a bit of distance from the army. I was breaking away. I had also made contact with the British Army and spoken to them. I had got to know other journalists.

'There's a whole interesting bloody landscape here,' I said to the others. 'How do we find out what it is like for the people who are just living here?' The atmosphere in an army town was obviously different from that where the ordinary people were just going about their daily lives as normally as you can in a war.

I decided to hire a car to take me to Split. I had no idea what car-hire facilities were like in the middle of a war but thought I could find someone to give me a lift. I ran the idea past a British Army contact. 'Oh, you'll be killed', I was told. 'You can't just rent cars in a war zone. Between here and Split there's like 25, 30, 40 front lines.' That many front lines sounded extremely exciting.

I found a one-armed local taxi driver with a beaten-up old Mercedes who was prepared to do anything for money. I went to see the liaison woman at the New Zealand Army.

'I've decided to make my own way,' I said.

'Well, we've got a huge armed convoy that's going through in a couple of days. Why don't you wait for that?'

'No, no, no. I've organised a driver.'

'Well, we can't have any responsibility for anything that happens to you.'

That was fine and in fact I learnt more in those few days than I could have in months with the army. In particular, I learnt how close you can get to the heart of a situation, and how much of a feeling you can get for how things really are for people living through something like this.

I felt huge relief when I prised myself away from the New Zealand Army, even as I climbed into this wreck of a Mercedes with my driver and his bad fibreglass arm. Its hand was clenched like it had a bad case of fibreglass arthritis, and it wouldn't move. It was more like an imitation of an arm. He was both embarrassed and proud of it. He had to use his real arm to move his fake one to any position it needed to be in. For instance, if he wanted to drape it casually over the back of a chair he had to heave it into place. The only thing worse than his arm was his English.

The real downside of having a driver with a dodgy false arm was that the car was manual and a lot of the driving was through areas that had been rendered suitable only for four-wheel drives. He had to position his fibreglass arm on the steering wheel to free up his good hand to change gear. If we hit a pot hole there was only his fake hand on the steering wheel to keep the car on the road. And he was very nervous. Anytime we heard any sort of noise he would start to sweat.

I had been told by the army that this was a dangerous trip. Ultimately I planned to go through the heart of Bosnia to Croatia and eventually to Split, but we were first going to the coast towards Dubrovnik. At that time there were shells reaching Dubrovnik, and there were hot pockets everywhere. And because it was guerrilla warfare you never knew where the front line was going to be, hence the British Army's high estimate of death. It was unlikely we would pass many other taxis.

Previously I had souvenired a few items: some bayonets, some poorly exploded hand grenades. They were entirely safe but they were ordinance. I had also secured a small firearm for my own protection. All these things were secreted in the boot of the car.

'I will tell you if we need these items,' I told the driver. 'If we need the gun I will tell you.' So we set off through the war zone, driving through beautiful little villages that had been obliterated.

Travelling this way I experienced the raw emotions that you don't get when you're cosseted by the army. The primary reaction to us was mistrust. Why was this person travelling through this godforsaken zone? We saw kids playing football in minefields, surrounded by the bombed-out shells of houses. Serbs and Muslims were playing together, in the middle of a war between Serbs and Muslims. I stopped in little cafes where half of the cafe was gone and they were still serving that thick coffee you suck through sugar cubes. I wonder if there has ever been another conflict as bizarre.

The funny thing is I wasn't scared at all. I would have numerous similar experiences in the future and I can't remember ever being scared, no matter how dangerous the situation. I can remember times sitting in hotels afterwards, looking back and thinking, 'That was ludicrous. That was such a stupid thing to do.' It's the adrenalin and the excitement that get you through. Also, if there's nothing you can do — which there usually wasn't — there's no point being scared.

One of our destinations was Mostar, site of a famous bridge that had been destroyed, and an important symbol of the whole conflict, representing as it did people coming together. As we approached Mostar there was a lot of heavy fighting going on around us. There were lots of roadblocks. In cases where these were manned by locals, when they saw it was just some fool in an old Mercedes with a one-armed driver, they let us straight through. UN roadblocks had a traffic-light system that told you either you are entering a safe area; there's some dodgy stuff going on; or don't move because it's happening now.

Near Mostar we were in a red area so it was active, which just meant that the UN had been involved in some skirmish within the last few hours.

We were approaching a bridge that spanned a gully, with steep granite mountains on the side. The terrain could not have been harsher. Two angry-looking men had been manning a pillbox and blocking the bridge, but when they saw us coming they came over to block the road. We were told to get out of the car at gunpoint.

'Just do whatever they say, follow my lead,' I told the driver. I got out and looked around. I realised there was nowhere to run, let alone anywhere to hide, which severely limited our options.

I couldn't tell from their uniforms how legitimate these guys were. They were pretty rough. They could have been the real thing or they could have been a couple of opportunists who saw a way to make a bit of money. They clearly weren't the sort of people who would have to fill in forms for their superiors if they killed you. For people like them, the easiest thing was to kill you and throw you over the bank. That's much less trouble than trying to work out what you are saying and help you along in your journey.

But the person I really couldn't figure out was the driver. It's a bad sign when the local is worried, and he was sweating profusely. Suddenly there was gunfire in the background which seemed to spark the guys with guns into action.

'What are you doing?' one asked my driver in broken English, assuming he was a foreigner.

'He's my taxi driver,' I said, for which I got pushed against the car with the bayonet end of the gun.

'What are you doing?' he asked the driver again. The driver answered him in his own language. I had no idea what he was saying but was pretty sure it was along the lines of 'This lunatic has kidnapped me. Please kill him and let me return to my family.'

'Where is your equipment?' the gunman asked me.

'I don't really have any equipment,' I said. And I showed him my pad and camera and the little mini-disc player I used.

'No, where is your equipment?'

I wasn't quick enough to answer before he pushed the taxi driver to the back of the car.

'Open the boot,' he ordered.

And now we were in some degree of trouble. Whoever they were, my cache of weaponry was going to look bad to them. Then my driver managed to take the situation and make it worse.

'Gun?' he asked me.

'You stupid man,' I thought to myself. 'I've never shot a gun in my life. I don't even know if it's loaded. We're going to take these guys on, are we? You've got one arm.'

So we were at odds. I thought we were in serious shit and he thought we could shoot our way out.

'I need a cigarette,' I said to the guy with the gun, in order to buy a little time. 'Would you like a cigarette?'

He wasn't interested. He forced me against the side of the car.

'Open it,' he said to the driver. As clearly as anything I can still hear the little click of the catch in the boot as it was opened. And I knew it was going to be the last sound that I would hear. I estimated we had 10 seconds tops before they saw our weapons. By now the bayonet in my side was hurting. It was a very blunt bayonet so he had to push very hard.

Suddenly there was a long whistling noise not far away. 'That's nice,' I thought, 'Jesus has decided to save me' and there was a phenomenal explosion. I couldn't tell how far away it was but it was close enough to be a concern. We were all hit by shrapnel — not by bits of bomb but by bits of road. There was tarseal going everywhere. The windscreen of the car was smashed. One of the guys with guns was knocked over and then they both started screaming and ran back to their pillbox.

'Get in the car,' I yelled, 'get in the car.'

My driver was distraught and moaning about his windscreen. In fact the car was completely rooted, but we were still able to drive out and made it safely to Mostar where there was more of a UN presence.

That incident had a huge impact on me. For better or worse, it was the start of me believing I was bulletproof. If I can get out of that, I reasoned, I can get out of anything.

I left my driver at the border and made my way to a nearby town where I found a hotel to stay in. It was a people's palace — a communist hotel, built according to communist ideas. It was on the fringes of the conflict, out of range of 99.9 per cent of missiles so you felt relatively safe.

I went to check in. I wasn't expected. I walked through a huge lobby with what seemed like acres of marble flooring. It was completely empty except for two chairs set against one wall. It was probably a 15-minute walk to the next pair of chairs. There was a marble concierge desk about 20 feet long, with no one attending it. I had yet to lay eyes on another human being. Then, about the length of a rugby field away, I noticed a woman standing to attention in a pristine uniform.

I told her I wanted to check in. It soon became clear there was one way of doing everything and that was how we would be doing it. This huge hotel was clearly entirely empty but she made a show of seeing whether they would be able to find a room for me without a reservation. There was no question of a discount because it was off-season.

I was booked in and established there was a restaurant on

the basement floor. I had a view of the Mediterranean from my room, which was small and, like everything else about the hotel, especially the staff, quite stark. After taking a moment to settle in, I went looking for the dining room. I appeared to be the hotel's only guest. Occasionally I encountered someone in a uniform, standing stoically in a marble corner holding a mop or a duster.

I eventually made my way through a labyrinth of grand hallways and reached two enormous doors, with a little sign that said dining room. As I approached, the doors opened before me, not automatically but thanks to two people on the other side who had somehow discerned that I was coming.

I was in yet another aeroplane hangar. I was seated at the table furthest from the door. Immediately in front of me, but more than 50 feet away, in the middle of the room was a rostrum with a Hammond organ. That wasn't a good sign.

I was trying to make conversation and be jovial with the staff but they seemed reluctant to acknowledge I was there. Service was very formal. The menu had just three items and the only thing I recognised was bangers and mash, which is what I ordered. It came with a large bowl of what appeared to be pickled cabbage and a huge plate with one circular spiral sausage and a plop of mash in the middle.

I had just started to cut into my sausage when the doors opened. 'Fantastic,' I thought, 'some more guests.' Instead, a very tall, very large woman wrapped in a black cape came in, carrying a satchel, and sat down at the Hammond organ. She shuffled her papers for some time, while I worked my way around my spiral sausage. Then she started to sing 'The Girl from Ipanema'. She was singing more or less in English, and it was surprisingly loud given that she was so far away, had no amplification and the acoustics were appalling.

I checked out the next day and went to start the long series of hops on planes that would take me home.

Getting through Customs at Zagreb was not easy. This was the location of the UN's major headquarters for their Bosnian activity, where they brought on new staff and briefed people before they went into Sarajevo. The place was effectively in lockdown and security was very tight.

'Do you have anything to declare?' I was asked on leaving the country. What else could I do? I opened my suitcase and showed them the bullets I'd picked up, the hand grenades and the bayonet.

'Souvenirs,' I said. 'Horrible, grotesque and macabre souvenirs.'

The Customs officer looked at me, acknowledged that they were horrible, grotesque and macabre, put them back in my pack and let me on the plane. Those were the days when you could carry bayonets on planes.

Kiwi

CHAPTER 10
IN NATIONAL'S POCKET

> **RUNNING NATIONAL RADIO TURNED OUT TO BE MUCH HARDER THAN I EXPECTED . . . I BUMPED INTO SHARON CROSBIE, WHO I HAD WORKED WITH IN MY VERY EARLY DAYS AND WHO WAS THEN CHIEF EXECUTIVE OF RADIO NEW ZEALAND. I HAD A REASONABLY SIZED CRUSH ON SHARON, DATING BACK TO WHEN I WORKED WITH HER ON *AS IT HAPPENS* DURING MY FIRST PERIOD AT NATIONAL RADIO.**

RUNNING NATIONAL RADIO TURNED out to be much harder than I expected. I had gone back to various bits and pieces at Pacific after the Bosnia trip. At the Radio Awards at the Sheraton Hotel in Auckland I bumped into Sharon Crosbie, who I had worked with in my very early days and who was then chief executive of Radio New Zealand. I had a reasonably sized crush on Sharon, dating back to when I worked with her on *As It Happens* during my first period at National Radio.

She was a huge star and we got on famously. Not everyone got on with Sharon. She could throw spectacularly theatrical tantrums, often involving the flinging of objects, which is generally regarded as un-Kiwi and something many people dislike. However, I was used to them from the BBC, where they were part of the culture. I found them quite stimulating.

'You should really come back,' Sharon said to me after whatever award I was nominated for was won by Paul Holmes. 'You could have the job managing National Radio. Would you be interested?'

'Yes,' I said. It was perfect timing. There was no prospect of anything substantial at Pacific, so it was a good time to move on and an interesting project to move on to.

My agreement, you may have noticed, was given without any thought at all. I had no long-term goal — it would be a challenge to get the job and that was as far ahead as I had thought. The job was part of a changeover process in which National Radio was going from being essentially a government department to a more commercial footing. It was being managed by KPMG in Wellington. They were making the appointments but obviously Sharon had a say and the board had a say. After a few weeks I was approached by KPMG, sent an application form and was interviewed and eventually got the job.

When I announced I was leaving, Derek Lowe took it as a personal slight. As a pioneer of private radio in New Zealand, he reacted to public radio like bulls react to red rags. He was very pissed off that public radio was taking one of his breakfast hosts — even though he had taken me out of that role. In his view I was going to 'a death camp for broadcasters'.

He could have taken some pride in the fact that I was going there to a senior management position thanks to knowledge I had gained from him about how to run a radio business. If he did, he didn't show it.

The new structure was cumbersome. There was a board, Sharon as chief executive and all the senior managers: the head of news and current affairs, the head of finance, the head of commercial activities — essentially the person who sold cassettes, the presentation manager for Concert, the presentation manager for National, and the person in charge of programme acquisitions. My role was officially presentation manager of National Radio, though I always called myself the manager. It was equivalent to being the manager. I didn't have complete control over programme acquisitions and finance and news and current affairs, but I had control over the way news and current affairs was presented and how long a news bulletin was. I didn't have control of the journalists, thank God.

I had not considered when I got the new job that the organisation was being torn apart from every angle, and that the objectives which had to be achieved were not the objectives of 99.9 per cent of the people who worked there.

So I arrived on day one wondering how to furnish my office.

On my first day, I went to see one of the senior management team. He was the manager of transition, employed and paid for by KPMG. His job was to get this ramshackle group of broadcasters, who thought they were managers, to move Radio New Zealand out of the past and at least into the present. Possibly into the future. For the 99.9 per cent, he was the enemy.

'We've been waiting for you,' he said. He didn't yet know that I was more likely to side with him than anyone else, but he may have had an inkling because of my commercial background and some things I'd said to KPMG in the process of getting the job.

He almost cried during that first meeting.

'My hair is matted with blood from banging my head against the wall,' he said.

'That's entertaining,' I thought.

For the rest of the day I had no idea what I was going to do apart from furnish my office. Working in the room outside my office were all the people who had wanted my job and felt they should have got it. I could read their minds. 'Who the fuck is this little shit coming from Radio Pacific? What does he know that we don't already know?' The answer was nothing. I didn't know anything that they didn't already know about what they were doing, but I knew all the things that I needed to know about what they were going to do or what I thought they should do.

I went into my office and sat down. I had no radio. I couldn't even listen to my own network. I had a chair and a desk and some empty filing drawers and cupboards. I positioned my jotter pad and checked that the stationery was all in order in the top drawer, which it wasn't, so I went out and bought some stationery.

I went to see Sharon, who described the situation in slightly different terms than those used by the manager of transition.

The reality was that the staff hated the management team, hated what they were doing, did not believe they could do it but did believe they were destroying public radio. The worst part was that deep down most of the management team agreed with them.

To sum up: the staff hated the management team for what they were supposed to do; and the management team hated what they were supposed to do so much that they were trying not to do it — delaying making decisions and then making bad ones.

There were absurdities wherever you looked. Elizabeth Alley was a wonderful person and a talented broadcaster. She was in charge of purchasing programmes, and she knew a lot about programmes, but she didn't have the budgets to actually purchase them. She had endless meetings about what programmes would be bought if and when the money became available.

We had a lot of meetings. Sharon sat at the end of the table and I was gradually moved to sit next to her, not because of my place in the hierarchy but so that she could kick me under the table or hit me over the head with a glitter wand she used to have. This would occur, I felt, whenever I said something that sounded like it was getting close to the truth.

At these meetings we pored over documents that were tabled and discussed the ramifications of the restructuring and how the huge number of redundancies that were necessary could be kept from the staff because they would mutiny if they found out. It was obvious to me that they had to find out if anything was ever going to happen. Plan A seemed to be talked about for so long, I wondered if the others were hoping the government would change its mind before anything final had been done. That would also require someone to come up with an extra $50 million so wasn't very likely.

Another constant irritation was that I was the only person at the table who understood that we had entirely enough money to do what we needed to do to meet our obligations under the broadcasting charter. Everyone else seemed determined to prove to the government that we didn't have enough money.

I was turning into one of the things I loathe most — a bureaucrat. There was hardly any time to focus on presentation and the way the programmes sounded. I wanted to update the sound of National Radio. It has a fantastic role and it's a brilliant opportunity. It's commercial-free, which meant we had an opportunity to push the boundaries with news and drama. They had very talented journalists. I wanted to make more of the news. It was ridiculous that there were extraordinarily dull access programmes on, when they could have had extended news bulletins. There are times of the day when you simply don't want to listen to fusion music. Not for a whole hour.

Then someone on the management team decided the bird call had had its day. There was a battle we didn't need to have. It wasn't like we were getting a lot of mail complaining about the bird. Fortunately, if I achieved nothing else in my time I managed to save the bird.

There was no reason why almost all of the suggested restructuring shouldn't have happened. There were too many people. There were staff there wandering around with their heads up their arses. There was a belief that nobody else in the country could produce radio like they were producing it. Well, there were lots of people who could. I used to plead with the others to bite the bullet on the redundancies and then see whether that would leave us enough money to do what we were obliged to under the charter. But I was told we couldn't make people redundant before Christmas. After Christmas I was told we couldn't make people redundant while they were on holiday.

There were regular meetings with staff that management were rostered to attend. The only staff who went were the agitators, who had no shortage of fuel. There were weeks when management representatives were eaten alive. There were managers who avoided walking through the newsroom because of the hostility in the air.

Most of the staff who were agitators and who were anti-change didn't realise that the reason it was being done so badly was because those on senior management charged with doing it were siding with them. But they couldn't tell the staff they were doing that because that would've been embarrassing. They would've looked silly so instead they looked incompetent. There were faults on both sides but the greater fault was with the management for allowing it to happen.

When Dick Weir was made redundant, it was done incredibly clumsily, partly because there was a huge reluctance to do it, and so to do it properly was inconceivable. Everyone knew it was going to happen before it did, including Dick.

Someone decided we should display floor plans to show the staff how lovely the new building would look, in order to boost morale. I mentioned that the staff were not stupid and one of them was almost certain to count the desks and realise there were fewer of them in the new building than in the old. However, the pictures were put up and the number of redundancies, which we had known for some time, became general knowledge and another storm blew up. That was really irrelevant by now because, given we had decided not to make people redundant before or after Christmas, we had got to the point where we couldn't make people redundant at any time because we had used up all the redundancy money by continuing to pay the salaries.

While all this was going on, we were also supposed to be going digital. Staff had been assigned to make it happen and flew around the world looking at systems. Because not only were we going to go digital, which was obviously a good idea, but we were going to lead the world, which was a bad idea. We couldn't afford the airfares we were paying for.

I tried to explain that we didn't need to lead the world. 'Digital world leaders' wasn't core business and certainly not relevant to the charter. 'We don't need to be new,' I said. 'Let's find a system we can afford that'll do the job easily. Let's lead New Zealand now and make sure we can upgrade later.'

In the end, the troops were brought home, the process came to a halt and all this money was wasted. It would have cost less to buy a whole package that didn't work and then ditch it than the money we spent getting halfway there.

But the ultimate example of things that were sacred and didn't work was the 'commercial arm'. This was essentially two things. Replay Radio, which sold recordings of programmes by mail order and the sale of news services. Apparently this would be our financial salvation by making up for the money we weren't getting from the government. I thought a commercial arm was unnecessary because there was no requirement on us anywhere to make money and we could afford to do our job with the money we had. It was obvious, too, that the internet meant we were just a few years away from a world where no one would be buying recordings of radio programmes.

I believed that it cost more to run this department than we made and I believed it was the job of the person in charge of the department and in charge of finance to prove that it was contributing to our bottom line. If it was a good idea, then at the end of every year we should have had money to spend on public radio, thanks to our commercial arm.

In the time I was there, no one was ever able to prove that.

At one meeting the commercial arm arrived with a report that had been *typed* on a *typewriter*. It contained a list of numbers where the bottom line was presented to everyone and to put to rest my concerns. This is the money we would not have without the commercial arm.

Unfortunately, I am no financial genius and needed things explained to me. 'Is this number the turnover of the department, or does this represent a true net gain for Radio New Zealand?' I asked. No one could tell me.

I decided I had to leave. I had never dreamt of doing the job. As usual, I just wanted to get it. I kept pulling out the charter and reading it and thinking, 'It's all so easy. Why is it being made so hard?'

Many commercial radio stations are operating professional broadcasting units by any criteria you choose, including National Radio's own. But they don't have National's sense of self-importance. Grandeur doesn't increase the quality of your news.

In some ways my standards were even more conservative than theirs. I don't believe that music should just fade out and the news should start. I think the music should stop and then the news should start. On the hour, if you're going to have time signals they should be heard clearly, not over a piece of music that has run over because it wasn't started at the right time. I think all those disciplines are important.

But I don't think it's important to have wall-to-wall pomposity. An interview isn't good just because it's long. And it isn't good just because there are a lot of pauses when people are thinking hard before they answer questions.

'We're giving them time to breathe,' I was told.

'Tell them to breathe faster,' I said. Actually, they had nothing to say and all we had done was bore people rigid.

Nearly every time I have resigned from a job I have been asked to stay, but I've never done that. I would never try to persuade anyone to stay. If they've decided to go and they've worked through the process, they're going to go no matter what. The only thing a manager can do is offer the departing worker something they really want. But if you're doing that, you're a bad manager, because you should have seen this coming and done that earlier.

Sharon was genuinely surprised and very disappointed when I quit. She tried to persuade me to stay and when I wouldn't stay she tried to persuade me to stay a bit longer, which I also wouldn't do. That never works. I was offered considerably more money to stay but I knew we couldn't afford to pay me that much.

Many people doubtless thought and think that I wasn't the 'right fit' for National Radio and they are absolutely right. But I was what was needed because I was prepared for change. Someone who was the right fit would've been the wrong person for National Radio at the time.

The only right thing to do was leave.

There was definitely an element of copping out on my part. It had become too hard. Perhaps I should have stayed, pegged back my immediate expectations and gnawed away at it — but I'm not a gnawer. I hate the thought of going to work every day and just chipping away. There were people making decisions who were actually hurting public radio by wasting huge amounts of time and money. At the same time, there were great broadcasters and people doing great work who could have done twice as much great work if they'd been allowed.

I started talking to Brent Impey at Radio Pacific to tee up the next job, as was my practice. In the back of my mind there was this idea forming about working as a foreign correspondent.

Best advice

The best single piece of advice I've ever received
was from Annabelle White, on barbecuing steak: no
poking, no pricking and only one turn. Apparently
the last point is now the subject of some debate,
but I wouldn't want to get involved in any sort of
controversy over such an insignificant matter.

Yacht

CHAPTER 11
'PAUL IS IN THE WATER NOW'

> **" I WAS VERY HAPPY TO BE PART OF THE PROTEST. I HAD ALWAYS DESPISED THE FRENCH TESTING. I HAD NEVER MET PETER, THOUGH I WAS AWARE OF HIS REPUTATION AS A LAWYER AND PENAL REFORMER. HE WOULD BECOME A FIRM FRIEND, ALTHOUGH, LIKE MOST OF MY FRIENDS, I HARDLY EVER SEE HIM. "**

MY NEXT BIG OVERSEAS assignment was covering the French testing at Mururoa in 1995. I think it was Derek Lowe's idea. If not, I'm happy to give him the credit as he's not getting any money from this book, even though he was responsible for so many of the things in it.

A lot of journalists were making the voyage to Mururoa to cover what would turn out to be the last French nuclear tests in the Pacific. Many were going with the New Zealand Navy on the *Kiwi*, others had hitched rides on miscellaneous craft. There would be the inevitable protest flotilla and Greenpeace representation. As well as the French Navy, French media vessels would also be in the area, so it looked like it could get quite crowded.

It was decided that I would go with the flotilla on Peter Williams QC's 53-foot yacht, the *Aquila d'Oro*. I was very happy to be part of the protest. I had always despised the French testing. I had never met Peter, though I was aware of his reputation as a lawyer and penal reformer. He would become a firm friend, although, like most of my friends, I hardly ever see him. I found him to be a strange mixture of socialist, capitalist, friend to all and enemy to all. It was also obvious he had an absolute belief in fairness, except when he was arguing with you.

He and I flew to Rarotonga while a small crew sailed the boat up. We were then going to take it to Tahiti before sailing to Mururoa and back again. That is a sea voyage and a half. Peter put a lot of money into this protest. A good sailor himself, he also employed a full crew.

As we were farewelled from Rarotonga, there was a huge hurrah and our hearts were full of pride. Within half an hour we were in a major swell. I was feeling queasy and the photographer was seriously seasick. We retired to our bunks but I ascertained very soon that your bunk was no place to get better. Instead, I went back on deck where I vomited the last of the sickness out. I think I had got competitive, too, and it helped that the photographer was nearly dead.

Peter and I passed the time with some intense philosophical debates. He is extraordinarily opinionated, which I admire very much. Better still, he can be opinionated because he's very clever and extraordinarily well read. We had some phenomenal discussions which were very exciting but entirely unwinnable for me, because if things weren't going his way Peter would turn into the courtroom performer, against whom a mere broadcaster had no chance at all. Mainly we argued about Jesus creating the world. One evening, we were becalmed, the skies were clear and you could see the galaxies and the rim of the earth in every direction. There was just water, sky and the most amazing starscape.

'This is how you know that God created the universe,' said Peter.

'What?' I said. 'How?'

'Look at it. Look at how vast it is. Do you know how many things had to come together perfectly at exactly the right time for this boat to be on this water, under this sky, surrounded by this air, with these people skippering it?'

'Actually, Peter, I believe what we're looking at now proves just how *likely* it is that all of those things would come together in one place at one time to create this environment.' I based this on the fact that the universe is so big and contains so many possibilities that it's impossible to imagine that somewhere this wasn't going to happen.

'But happening here, what are the odds that it would happen here so that we could be alive?'

'Anyone could say that on any one of those stars, but for the fact that it didn't happen there so they're not alive to say it. Don't you see?'

He couldn't understand. In the end I was persecuted and made to feel like an idiot for holding the beliefs that I held. It was extremely enjoyable.

I love boats, but not yachts and I came to despise the *Aquila d'Oro* because the trip was so unpleasant physically. Peter's description of yachting is 'prison with an increased risk of dying'. When we finally got to Tahiti, the photographer was indeed on the point of death, and if we hadn't arrived when we did we were going to have to tip him up and push things into his bottom to keep him alive. I was opposed to that. Obviously on some boats people are tipped up and have things pushed into their bottoms all the time. It's a time-honoured way for crew and passengers to get to know each other. So we were talking about it, but on balance I thought it was preferable to let him die.

There was a small group of locals gathered to meet us at Tahiti. These were the people most affected by the testing, and they were appalled that the French would again thumb their noses at the rest of the world and be doing this.

Peter became incensed that no one from Greenpeace was there to give us an official welcome, given we were there to support a cause they claimed to own. Malodorous as we were, he decided it was a priority to track down Greenpeace immediately to give them the opportunity to apologise for not fronting up. The photographer was improving before our eyes. Peter grabbed him and we headed off to the Greenpeace office, which was not far away.

'You know, Peter,' I said on the way there, 'it is bad that they weren't here to meet us, but maybe we should just hear their side first.'

The door was opened by a young German man, sipping, we couldn't fail to notice, an imported beer.

'Yes?' he said, and at that point I had absolutely no interest in hearing his side. I stood back so as not to get in the way of the tirade I knew would be coming from Peter, who uttered words to the effect of: 'I'm Peter Williams, this is my dying photographer, and this is Paul Henry, a journalist of extraordinary renown in New Zealand. We have just piloted a 53-foot boat in rugged seas from our country to be part of the anti-nuclear protest and we were greeted by a small bunch of local people. Why were you not down there to greet us?'

I'm paraphrasing.

By now he had forced his way with his words and his body into the centre of this room, which became his stage. It also contained a group of attractive, youngish women and, you'd have to say, attractive, youngish men. He proceeded to tear them to shreds. He destroyed their work. He didn't bother to find out anyone's name.

'You're German, aren't you?' he snapped at one young man, who reluctantly admitted he was.

'Typical,' said Peter, but he never backed that up. He simply added that they might like to share some of their imported beer with us. He went on to tell them that we intended to go to Mururoa.

'You better go quickly or you'll be too late,' said the first young man.

'Too late for what?'

'Oh, I can't really tell you.'

'What do you mean you can't tell us?' I said.

'What do you fucking mean you can't fucking tell us?' said Peter. 'I've just told you we're sailors. We've been out there in the rugged ocean risking our fucking lives and you've got something planned?'

In the end the Greenpeace functionary, fearful, I think, for his life, told us that something was going to happen that he couldn't tell us about but that would have international impact, so we should go very quickly. So our time on land was regrettably short as we made our way back out into the ocean straight away, leaving the photographer behind in Tahiti, for everyone's sake.

Mururoa isn't a destination, because you can't get within 12 nautical miles of it. For us, it was a GPS point and the voyage to that point seemed to take a lifetime. The tropical heat and humidity meant we had condensation constantly dripping from the ceiling, so essentially you were permanently showering in other people's distilled sweat. You've got spots all around your genitals because you haven't been able to wash for days, and when you have it's been with salt water and you've put damp clothes on over the top.

Some nights we went backwards. Several times after finishing a shift, having been lashed to the wheel to prevent the boat from rolling because the weather was so bad, I looked at the GPS and saw we were a nautical mile further from our destination than when I started. We knew when we had arrived because the GPS eventually told us we had. A few other boats were there. The French had a couple of massive, heavily armed war frigates bobbing about.

We found the *Kiwi* and got some fresh water from them. They were observers, sanctioned by the government, so they weren't allowed to have anything to do with anyone who might be going to break any international rules. We had to be very careful what we said to them because clearly we were there to cause trouble for the French. But we also wanted to stand on their boat because it was so much bigger than ours it felt almost like being on land.

All the boats were bigger than ours except that belonging to David McTaggart, the founder of Greenpeace, who was there. He was a very impressive man, a real adventurer with a lot of mana.

We got offside with the other protesters because our love of fine wine led Peter and me to gravitate towards the people from 2 France, the French television network covering the protests. Greenpeace instructed everybody not to talk to the French, but seriously they had an amazing cellar in their fish hold. They also let me use their satellite phone to file reports, which was a godsend as all the other equipment I had access to seemed to be cursed. Greenpeace were convinced the French TV people were spies and told everyone so. They may well have been. They seemed very interested in my reports and we spent a lot of time talking to them. They were curious about what the activists were planning, but they would have been whether they were spies or simply doing their jobs as journalists.

I did notice that their cameraman, who was using a Betacam to shoot interviews with us, had to interrupt the interview frequently to swap the camera from shoulder to shoulder

I HAVE LITTLE TIME FOR GREENPEACE!

because his arm was getting tired. That was a hint that perhaps he wasn't a full-time cameraman.

One thing Greenpeace did like about us was Peter's legal knowledge, which came in very handy. The French boarded our boat to serve papers, and then Peter served his own papers on them, but they claimed they couldn't understand English. Peter was in an awkward position, because he hadn't been able to get any insurance for the boat. First of all, he wasn't prepared to pay the outrageous premium but, moreover, if your boat was seized, even if you had insurance, you wouldn't get a payout because technically you were involved in an illegal activity. It was obvious that if you made any attempt to cross the 12 nautical miles of the exclusion zone to Mururoa itself, it would be impossible to land and the likeliest option was death.

Keen to find something to do as a protest, we eventually decided to make ourselves a distraction for the French. The plan was for Greenpeace to try to get into the atoll and for us to create a diversion to enable that.

Another of the crew, Rusty, and I volunteered for this job. We had been doing quite a bit of running around between boats at night in the *Aquila d'Oro*'s nine-foot inflatable with its nine-horsepower Johnson motor. Before we set off, I did a report back to Radio Pacific, which was magnificently stupid in retrospect. 'Here's what we're going to do,' I was screaming across the airwaves. 'Hello, world — this is our secret plan.'

We set off in the pitch-dark into a huge swell. We had no GPS. From the inflatable the only point of reference we had was the light on the top of the mast. You didn't have to get far from the yacht before you could no longer see that.

When we got into the boat we knew which direction Mururoa was — but after a few moments the direction changed. So we headed off roughly where we thought it would be. The next moment, from the horizon, the whole planet seemed to light up. The French, on one of their frigates, had us in their massive spotlights and were hurtling towards us. I had no idea they were Pacific listeners.

'Shit, Rusty, shit,' I yelled, and he just about did. We couldn't see our own boat. The only thing we could see was the frigate, which could only see us occasionally because we were so small and the swell kept concealing us from them and them from us.

Every time you went down you wondered where the frigate would be when you got back to the top of the swell again.

One of the most frightening moments was when the frigate stopped. We were at the top of the swell and we saw huge arms swing out from the side and drop Zodiacs into the water. We're puttering away with our nine-horsepower while NATO-quality might, including dozens of sailors, was bearing down upon us. But once they were down at our level they had trouble finding us. Before they did, we caught sight of the little light on the *Aquila d'Oro*'s mast and were able to get back on board before they could take us into custody.

While all this was going on, Radio Pacific had got in touch with the boat. They wanted to talk to me because it was so long since I had told them about our plan. Fortunately, Peter was there to fill in for me and did the live cross.

He told me later what he had said. 'Well, your man's in the boat. He's very brave, he's gone out with a crew member, Rusty. I can see them now, I can hear them now, I'll be handing you back to Paul soon.'

Not that soon. Just as I got back, trying to synchronise with the swell, I put my hand up to the railing, but the yacht went up and the inflatable went down and I ended up in the water.

'He's in the water, Paul is in the water now. This is a very dangerous situation, listeners.'

That was great radio — reporting on the reporter dying. It doesn't happen nearly often enough. For the handful of people who were up at whatever time it was in New Zealand, it was broadcasting gold. Not to mention as expensive as hell. So, good for Derek.

The crew threw ropes down and hauled us up on deck. From there we watched the frigate retrieving its Zodiacs and felt very cocky about having eluded them.

In the next couple of days, we learnt, largely from Greenpeace intelligence, that the French were very close to the first test. Peter and I had gone over to the 2 France boat for yet another interview and wine tasting with the rather attractive pair of reporters. I had just done a report from their ship and went out on the deck. They had a hydrophone, too, and I noticed a slight blip. We walked to the stern and looked in the direction of Mururoa. We were very close to the edge of the exclusion zone.

Without actually knowing that a bomb had gone off, we knew that it had gone off. You couldn't see anything and you couldn't hear anything. If anything, it was as though you were hearing less than you had heard before. Then a mist rose from the surface, like a frothing of water, and a sort of rain cloud developed and gradually dispersed.

Everyone just stood there in silence. The swell stopped. It was almost the opposite of what you think would happen. It was a moving experience because you realised how big this thing must be to be able to see it from so far away. We had been doing a lot of mucking around and joking, then suddenly the mood turned intensely sombre and you thought: 'This is why we're here. This is what it's all about. How fucking dare they?'

At the same time, in the back of my mind, I was thinking: 'I wonder if this is wise. I wonder if we're going to rue being here in this atmosphere on this day in a few years' time.'

We lost a lot of our enthusiasm after the event. It was hard to justify staying, certainly from a journalistic point of view. No one knew how many tests there were going to be.

No one thought they could stop it, but I thought we could delay it, and the more spectacularly we delayed it, the more it would cost the French and the more it would agitate the world. There were a lot of people in France who were against it. I'm sure it was more the agitation at home than the sanctions abroad that made the French pull their heads in to the degree that they did.

We sailed directly back to Rarotonga with the sense that we had done something, but also with the sort of anti-climactic feeling you get when you've achieved a goal and have to make the long trip home to ordinary life again.

'Be careful of the boat,' Peter told the crew. 'Be careful of the equipment, but go like the fucking clappers. Let's just get back.'

We were exhausted, barely existing. Conversation, which had played such a big part in the journey up, was too much of an effort. We did dress for dinner, however, which entailed putting a shirt on. Sometimes we didn't bother with pants but we always had a shirt.

On one of these days in the emotional doldrums we caught a marlin on our line. This huge fish leapt out of the water. It was the sort of magnificent thing that would normally make a fisherman scream with joy. There was no way we were going to be able to pull it in on a hand line. I looked back at Peter and he looked at me, and without saying a word or even looking at the fish, he reached over, grabbed this huge knife and cut the line.

At one point a big storm blew up. That's when you really have to concentrate because if the boat yaws in the water and a wave catches you beam on, then that's it — possibly you're all dead, definitely the trip's going to take a lot longer. Later that night the weather had calmed down, but only slightly, and the spinnaker was up. When a boat's got the spinnaker up it's under a huge strain. We were inside, playing checkers, when Peter suddenly said, 'Is the spinnaker up?'

'Yeah, we're making really good time,' came the reply.

'The spinnaker shouldn't be up,' he said. 'The wind's too strong.'

At that exact moment, there was an unbelievable explosion, as though an incendiary device had gone off next to us. The boat stopped. We had been going fast and then we weren't moving. I looked out of the porthole, and it was like a blizzard of confetti coming down. The spinnaker had blown into a million pieces.

Peter had been lying on the top bunk. I watched from the bottom bunk as two wizened little old man legs swung around and came down onto my stomach. He climbed over me with all his force and shuffled down next to me.

'Six thousand fucking dollars,' he said. 'That's what that's cost me.' A huge tirade of abuse followed. Then he slothed back into his bunk, his point made, and we continued on at a much slower speed.

The other highlight of the trip back involved the bearded, almost feral cabin boy. His bunk was right up in the bow with the sails — the worst place to be on a boat. We seldom saw him. It was as though he wasn't on the boat. At this point, the boat having been very poorly provisioned, we had pretty much run out of everything to eat except Hubbard's carob breakfast cereal. We could have kept the French navy and Greenpeace supplied with Hubbard's carob breakfast cereal. Naturally, men alone at sea for a long period start to fantasise to themselves. I used to dream of Georgie Pie. I pictured myself walking into Georgie Pie and buying a pie and sitting down at one of their squalid little tables and eating it. It was partly because I loved Georgie Pie pies, but I think mostly because I could not imagine a harder floor, a more stable building. I could not imagine a more rock-solid item of food, come to that.

One day the feral cabin boy came on deck and announced that he was going to make scones. Peter and I watched him disappear into the bowels of the ship. We heard the occasional clatter of pots and pans, but without speaking it was obvious we both knew we would never see a scone. The cabin boy had presumably yielded to insanity due to the rigours of the voyage, which was very sad.

But after what seemed like a very long time, the aroma of baking scones wafted up from below. We hadn't had anything that remotely resembled food for a long time and I'm sure we were both intrigued, but not sufficiently to inspire conversation.

Then another inordinate amount of time went by and through the gloom of the dark cabin, this bearded little troll of a man appeared, bearing a tray of scones, with a little bottle of jam and a little dish of butter. He walked gingerly up the stairs and stood before us. And before we could say anything, the boat went up a swell and we just had time to notice the sorrow in his eyes before he fell backwards and all the scones and jam and butter went flying into the bow. We barely had time to realise how magnificent it would be to eat a scone, before it was taken away from us. That's the ocean. It gives and it takes away.

Peter looked at me and I looked at Peter.

'Jesus fucking Christ,' he said.

We got off the boat at Rarotonga, at which point we started to buck up. As I walked down the wharf, I could not bring myself to turn around to look at the *Aquila d'Oro*. 'I've done it,' I told myself. 'I didn't need to do it and I certainly don't need to do it again. I will never get on a boat like that again.' All I wanted to see was land. To be honest, even though I've always loved boating, I've never got sailing.

Many years later I finally had the boat of my dreams — roughly 60 feet, 40 tonnes and $2 million worth of it. I prided myself on my ability to berth this boat singlehandedly. When I was a child, my father used to take me to watch people making a hash of backing boats down ramps. That was his idea of entertainment. In my case, boat and man were one. There were times when people at the marina applauded when they saw me bring this

I HAVE NEVER LIKED YACHTS

boat in unaided. I was piloting and also doing the ropes and fenders on this huge thing.

Once I was bringing it in with my eldest daughter Lucy on board. We were outside the breakwater and doing seven knots.

'Hold it on this course,' I said to Lucy, 'while I go down and put the fenders on.'

I left her in charge, thinking nothing could go wrong at that speed. Little did I know while I was on the lower deck that Lucy was fighting with the wheel, trying to get the boat to remain on course.

Then, vaguely, in one ear I heard a not terribly alarming scream — definitely not the sort you would expect to hear from someone facing death. I looked up and could see that we were moments away from driving straight into the breakwater.

I leapt up. Lucy had completely removed herself from the wheel and was standing metres away with a look of inevitability about her. I managed to avoid complete disaster by the narrowest slither of margins. I was seconds away from not only making a substantial insurance claim but also from that thing boaties hate more than any other — embarrassment.

I AM SORRY LUCY — WHAT WAS I THINKING!

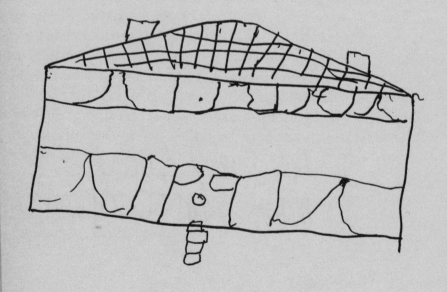

Homebush

CHAPTER 12
I SEE DEAD PEOPLE

" IT FED INTO THE IDEA OF THE RADIO PACIFIC FAMILY — NOT ONLY WOULD PEOPLE TAKE OUR PILLS, RUB IN OUR POTIONS AND SLEEP ON OUR MAGNETS, BUT THEY COULD SIT AT HOME AND VISIT OUR DANGER SPOTS WITH ME AS THEIR GUIDE. OTHER PEOPLE WENT TO NEWS-GATHERING CENTRES; I WANTED TO BE IN NEWS-HAPPENING CENTRES — IN THE TRENCH NEXT TO THE PERSON WITH THE GUN. "

BOSNIA AND MURUROA CONVINCED me that working as an international correspondent was the way to go. Both experiences were incredibly stimulating and satisfying. Also, no one else in New Zealand — and no one radio station — was doing exactly this. Other networks used local people. My plan was to base myself in New Zealand and travel to where the story was. Derek loved the idea that he would have someone in an area that National Radio or ZB didn't. And very often we did have that: I was where major news organisations didn't have people.

It fed into the idea of the Radio Pacific family — not only would people take our pills, rub in our potions and sleep on our magnets, but they could sit at home and visit our danger spots with me as their guide.

Other people went to news-gathering centres; I wanted to be in news-happening centres — in the trench next to the person with the gun. It was more than just reporting the news, it was getting inside it. Bosnia had shown me that the key was to travel with no infrastructure to slow me down. With no resources, I had to push harder and take more risks. I didn't have an advance team setting up interviews and booking my accommodation. I couldn't possibly get accreditation in many areas, let alone actually achieve anything that wouldn't be achieved better by the battalions of journalists already in the most obvious places.

Admittedly, it was challenging organising this from home on the outskirts of Masterton using the services of the local AA travel agency.

I spent a lot of time in Singapore, which was an efficient place to use as a hub. I could rent hotel rooms there for half a day. The beauty of them was that they were in the airport so you didn't have to go through Customs. You could collect your baggage and go straight to your room, do stuff and get on another plane without actually going to Singapore. Sometimes I arrived without an onward flight to New Zealand booked so I could ricochet off somewhere else if another story came up.

Singapore is good for getting to Asia, obviously, but also Europe and even Africa. If I was going to Africa, I tried to get on an Egypt Air flight from Singapore, because if you timed it right, they weren't able to take you on from Cairo straight away and they put you up at a much nicer hotel than I could afford myself. Sometimes they had to put you up for two nights and provide transfers and accommodation. It was fantastic.

As much as I loved the travel, I loved coming back to Homebush, where we had moved from Carterton. It was a wonderful place, especially for the girls. We had an idyllic five acres at the end of a no-exit street and a small mansion — the original homestead, which is why home and area share the same name. I just loved it, even when I sat basking in the sun and the quiet was interrupted only by the creaking sound of another piece of spouting falling off.

Much of my money had gone on cars, like my Rolls-Royce. With a Rolls, by far the cheapest aspect of ownership is the initial purchase. They are so hokey they almost don't qualify as showy. What I like about them, and a lot of other showy cars, is that they are for dreamers. Dreamers design them, dreamers manufacture them and dreamers buy them. Only recently, since BMW have started making them, have Rolls-Royces become viable as vehicles. Before that, when you went out in one you practically had to have someone following behind with a decent Japanese car so you could be confident of completing your journey. I breathed a sigh of relief every time I got mine back in the garage.

There were lots of little differences between Rolls-Royces and Bentleys. The Bentley was for people who liked to drive. If you were going to drive yourself you had a Bentley, if you were going to have a chauffeur you had a Rolls-Royce. I liked the fact that someone had decided it should have a full picnic table in the back, and a place for champagne. How wonderful to be able to hear nothing but the electric clock — you bought the advertising line, even though it was never true. All you could really hear was the wind howling by because the doors had been so badly assembled.

I got my first Rolls when we were running Homebush as a homestay and had a Japanese person staying. It was a beautiful Silver Shadow 2. My guest wanted to play golf and I organised to take him to the course in the Rolls, which spent most of its time under a tarp in the shed alongside the Massey Ferguson tractor, the ute and the fire engine.

When I got it started I always let it run for half an hour to make

These are a few of my favourite cars

1. Aston Martin Rapide
2. Bentley Mulsanne
3. Hummer H1
4. Mustang 1969
5. Mini Clubman (BMW)
6. Ferguson 35 tractor
7. Land Rover Country (9 seater)
8. Maserati Gran Turismo
9. Toyota Hilux ute
10. Bristol Fighter, 2008

sure it was going to be okay. At this time it was playing up very badly. I dropped my visitor off at the golf course in Masterton and when I pulled up in the car park to get the golf clubs out, not intending to turn the car off, the engine stopped.

He didn't notice anything.

'What a wonderful car,' he said as he walked away.

It wouldn't start. By the time he had finished and come back to the car park, the mechanics I found to come and fix it had only just left. I had been there the whole time dealing with my very expensive problem.

'You're already here,' said the Japanese man. 'I finished a bit early.'

'Yes, I came early, just in case,' I said. 'I've heard it's quite a fast course.'

Homebush sucked the financial lifeblood from me for several years — all my own fault. I built a little airport out the back, with a helipad. I had a real fire engine and a windsock. I put a lake in and roamed around the place on a Massey Ferguson lawnmower.

The contrast with where I had been for work was usually very stark. I was conscious that I was now safe, yet breathing the same oxygen as people I had just seen getting killed next to me. In the laundry basket were clothes with other people's blood on them, waiting to go in the wash.

One Sunday in 1997, when I hadn't been home very long, I was chopping some wood. While I was away Rachael had taken the opportunity to have some trees cut down that she knew I would not have wanted cut down. It was a pleasant day, and I was enjoying being back with my family, gritting my teeth bitterly and chopping these giants of the forest up into fireplace-sized logs.

The radio was on and I heard the first report of a car crash in Paris that might have involved Princess Diana. I went inside and turned on CNN, which was a major source of stories for me. I used to watch what was happening, try to work out where the story would be in the three days it would take me to get anywhere and make that my destination.

'I'm going to have to go to France,' I said to Rachael after realising what was going on. I rang my AA travel person, Margaret. At home. On a Sunday.

'You've got to get me on a flight, preferably straight to Charles de Gaulle, Paris. If not, then to London and I'll find my own way after that.' But by the time I had finished the call I had already calculated that I would be wasting my time going to Paris and I should go straight to London.

On the way, with my cell phone and a camera, I realised I could not possibly cover the accident and her death. There was no way I could get near any of that. I had to find another story. And it had to be a story I could sell, because the arrangement was that Radio Pacific covered my expenses but to actually make any money out of this work I had to sell stories to other broadcasters or newspapers.

So in London I slept with the people who were camping outside Westminster Abbey and carrying their flowers to Kensington Palace and talked to them all through the night, which, of course, was daytime back in New Zealand, about why they were there.

There was no point trying to cover the funeral. Other people had much better vantage points and were doing a much better job of that angle than I could possibly hope to. I would have been swamped in the global wall-to-wall coverage. Miraculously I got a brilliant photograph of the wreaths on the casket which I sold in London and got good money for.

But I still had to come up with something, and by now the 'Let's talk to these people who are standing here in the rain/ brilliant sunshine/fog' angle had been pretty much beaten to death. I decided it would be interesting to see how many people

were around who weren't part of the event, who had opted out of participating in this piece of history.

I went down to the shopping area of Kensington, where all the shop and house windows were papered with pictures of Diana. The streets were deserted. I stood in the middle of the road and everything was still. If you were going to make an apocalyptic movie in London, this was the time to make it. The only humans in sight were snipers dressed in black stationed along the roofs of the buildings, obviously prepared for people to break in.

I found, in the end, six people who were walking the streets going about their normal business. In the background of these interviews, at one point, you could even hear Elton John singing his song at the service.

'When you could just walk for five minutes and be part of this huge event, why are you here instead?' was the question I put to them all. What was in the psyche of someone who was there and not part of it? One of them had opened his shop in case there was a rush. He didn't even have his TV on. He just stood in the doorway as the extraordinary sound from the service echoed around the empty streets.

'Aren't you tempted,' I said, 'to walk for five minutes and see her casket pass by or see the crowds or see the big screen?'

'No.'

Another person was a vagrant.

'Are you aware of what's happening today?' I asked and she was appalled that I might think she wouldn't be. She was extraordinarily well informed about the event, but it wasn't part of her world.

I never made a lot of money from these stories. There are agencies in London that you can use, who will take 20 per cent to send your work around the world. But it's very difficult to organise, especially for a story with any currency. You needed an office to do that for you if you were out in the trenches. Usually I was in a place where it was very hard to get the information out except for my phone calls to Radio Pacific. I couldn't transmit photographs. I could write the occasional feature as long as it wasn't time dependent. However, by the time I had enough hours to do that I was usually too exhausted.

One of the most extraordinary things surrounding the death of Diana was that only a few days later Mother Teresa died. After the Princess of Wales' funeral a lot of people were mourned out, but I was sure there would be something worth doing in India. I phoned Derek from London because he approved all the trips.

'We should do this Mother Teresa thing because I think there's a lovely thing there between these two people.'

'It sounds expensive, Paul.'

'Almost certainly, but I think we should do it. I think it's good for our audience'.

Derek was tight-fisted but his love for radio used to override his reluctance to spend money. And to his credit, he never once said: 'Wasn't there a cheaper way to get there?'

I went to a travel agency in Regent Street in London.

'I've got to get to India,' I said. 'Any airline other than Air India.' I didn't want to arrive with intestinal complications. There'd be plenty of time for that later.

'I can't.'

'All right, Air India.'

The travel agent got me a flight to Mumbai and a transfer to Calcutta, but I had to wait for a couple of days, and that was frustrating because I knew how far behind I would be when I got there. I read all the background I could and managed to worry about everything. What if I couldn't get near the casket? No one knew what it was going to be like there — whether the whole thing would be run by her order or if the government would take charge. It might be impossible. To take my mind off things I went down to Bristol to visit my gran, who I hadn't seen for years. She was still in the squalid little terraced house that I used to go to when I was a little boy in my Jesus boots. My schoolboy photo still hung on the living room wall. I had to interrupt her conversation every time my cell phone rang because I was negotiating global travel to cover a major event. I was reminded again of how different everything could have been if I hadn't had the idea of something better lodged in my mind from an early age.

As I was leaving Heathrow the whole project fell into place. I saw a newspaper poster that read: 'Two Saints Die in One Week'.

What bollocks.

No matter how much you idolised and idealised Diana, and no matter how much you can reasonably criticise Mother Teresa, because she was saintly but she was far from perfect, you have to admit they were living totally different lives. One of them had dirty hands and the other one didn't. There was a nice feature — the contrast between these two holy celebrities. I had the guts of the yarn written in my head by the time we reached India.

Mumbai was a nightmare. Between the stench and people pissing in the streets and sifting through dust looking for food, it's a nightmare at the best of times. When the whole world is landing on its doorstep, it's even worse. There were journalists arriving and being swept away in the cars they had booked, by the drivers who would be with them the whole time. No one was interested in helping me. I thought I was going to have to wake up a beggar to get any assistance.

Eventually I got on board my flight to Calcutta. I was squashed in next to an obese Russian journalist. It was my practice to try to befriend other journalists for various reasons. Some were great to get information from, others were good to cadge off, though I always made sure there was something in it for them. Usually you could exchange information that was of use to each other. When the journalist was from a big organisation, the New Zealander with the backpack and a cell phone was a novelty.

The Russian journalist was moaning from the moment he sat down. He was sweating torrents and appeared to have every illness under the sun, including some that were new even to India. He thought the assignment was ridiculous and he was going to do it as quickly as possible and get back home to collect his mafia bribes or however he earned most of his living.

When the hostess came around with our meals I went to take mine but was stopped by a hairy Russian paw.

'Wait one moment,' said my new friend. 'We are both very hungry but very scared. This food will kill us, won't it? What is it?'

'Lamb korma,' said the hostess.

'As I suspected. It will kill us. No, no, no, we won't be having any of that. Bring me something that is entirely shrink-wrapped and my colleague will have that too.'

When we arrived at Calcutta he asked where I was staying. I didn't have anything organised but it certainly wouldn't be a luxury hotel like the one he had booked. There's a paradoxical law of travel: the worse the country is, the more expensive the expensive hotels are, but the less chance you have of surviving in a cheap hotel. In the end he put me up in his hotel and we agreed to split the bill.

Obviously, I was more enthusiastic about this story than he was.

'We've got to go to the slums,' I said. 'We've got to cover the work she's done, we've got to talk to the people who are in there, the sisters who are doing the dirty work and everything like that.'

He waddled along reluctantly. We went into some of the missions Mother Teresa had in the slums. I have never seen anything like it before or since. The concrete floors were on an angle so that the people who were brought in covered with maggot-filled wounds could be put on the floor and hosed down and the maggots would be washed away. The stench was what you would expect under those conditions. There was not a surface that you could touch that wasn't blazing hot. Your shoes became impregnated with the filth that was on the floor. It was truly squalid.

It's not hard to get into the slums where the missions are based, but it is dangerous. These people have good reasons to kill you and not much to lose. When you go into the missions themselves, you ask yourself why anyone goes there if they don't have to — like the Australian girl we met who had committed to six months helping the nuns.

Some people had criticised Mother Teresa for not doing more to publicise the plight of people she helped. By exploiting images and other PR tactics, they argued, she might have done more for them. Her answer was that that was someone else's job. She was too busy helping the people in front of her. I've even heard her criticised for living the high life — by which the critic meant eating the odd banana when those around her couldn't afford even that. Well, it wasn't very high.

All in all, the contrasts with the earlier funeral in Kensington could not have been more marked.

In London, no expense had been spared. Everywhere you looked, there were lovely sepia or black and white photos of Diana looking thoughtful and sometimes carrying black children. Most read: 'Diana Princess of Wales, 1961–1997'. In Calcutta, there were hand-painted pictures and the words: 'Mother Teresa, 1910–Forever'.

We got to the hall where Mother Teresa was lying and saw the seemingly endless stream of people waiting to file past her casket. They had as many fans and air conditioners going as possible but it was hot and she was decomposing. They put a cover on her to keep flies off but there was no denying the smell.

When it came to the funeral, again, the big guns were doing all the blazing. Huge rigs had been built for the lighting and there were podiums erected for the cameras so the anchors from CBS, NBC, CNN and the rest could all do their thing.

My Russian friend got out as soon as the funeral was over, absconding under the shadow of darkness without telling me, though he did pay his share up to then. I was left again with the quandary of how to do something nobody else was doing. I decided to take a shortcut and go straight to Mother Teresa's headquarters, Mother House, which was where she lived and where she would end up.

The next day I was the first European journalist who was allowed through the door, and one of only a handful who were there as the casket was taken in. After a while I was ushered into the room where her casket had been placed with the first candles lit by its side.

'You are number one,' a nun told me. And I thought, if I never did another story, if I never made a penny out of this one, that moment in time was worth all the effort.

I made quite a bit actually, and got a good story out of it. I used a picture I had taken in London of a girl in a public school uniform who had paid £3.75 for a small bouquet of flowers, which were being sold outside Green Park. She had stood in line for some hours, drinking a Coke and waiting for her turn to place them at the palace gates as a tribute to Diana.

Alongside this, I had followed a girl who had never been out of the Calcutta slums and who had stolen a flower and waited for three days in 98 per cent humidity, with no food, to walk past Mother Teresa's body and leave her flower. As she walked away, certainly heading back to horrendous squalor, one of the nuns blessed a petal from a flower that had been taken from Mother Teresa's body and handed it to her. I took a photograph of her clutching that petal. And in the contrast between those two girls you had the difference between Mother Teresa and Diana. That was my story, which ran in the UK and generated a lot of complaints for the way it allegedly denigrated Diana.

Black forest cake

CHAPTER 13
HOW TO MAKE
JOURNALISTS
LAUGH

> ❝ I THOUGHT IT WOULD BE EASY. DESERT STORM HAD BEEN NOTHING IF NOT A MAJOR MEDIA EVENT, SO I WAS SURE THERE WOULD BE ROADS WHERE THEY WERE NEEDED AND LOTS OF POINTS WHERE YOU COULD GET LINKS AND TRANSMIT YOUR MATERIAL WITHOUT TOO MUCH DIFFICULTY. ❞

IN 1998 THERE WAS pressure being applied to Iraq over allowing UN military inspectors into the country. Weapons of mass destruction and all that. Tensions had flared and looked like they were going to ignite. There was a stand-off between the US and Saddam Hussein. The military build-up in the area had begun. The frigates were in the Gulf and stealth aircraft were in Jordan. Well, if the inspectors couldn't get in, I would have to, on behalf of Radio Pacific.

I thought it would be easy. Desert Storm had been nothing if not a major media event, so I was sure there would be roads where they were needed and lots of points where you could get links and transmit your material without too much difficulty.

As I was deciding when to go it suddenly looked like the country might be closing its borders entirely. So I left in a hurry, which meant I got off to a bad start. I had no idea what I was going to do. Would the war have started by the time I got there? Would it be over? Was it even going to happen?

I had just $1000 in cash and a credit card to pay for hotels. I couldn't afford a satellite phone, and hoped I wouldn't need one but was sure that, if I did, I could rent one in Jordan, which is the most westernised of the Arab countries. I was going to get into Iraq through the Jordanian border.

It took myriad flights to get to Jordan. On the last leg, I met a young English man, Simon, who explained he was going to tidy up his affairs in Jordan where he had been working for a member of the royal family as a tutor for their children.

'I haven't got anywhere to live,' I told him. 'Do you know of anywhere?'

'My hotel is nice and modestly priced for what it is,' he said. 'I'm going to be staying there for a couple more days and you could have it after me.'

When we got to Jordan, I had my first run-in with Jordanian authorities while paying for my visa. I hate all bureaucrats anyway, but after the long journey I was tired and in a foul mood. East–West tensions were high at the time and the officers were hostile from the start, waving their guns around and threatening to deport me before I had even got into their country.

'Why am I paying $50 to be abused like this?' I said. 'I could commit a crime and get treated like this for free.'

Eventually I met up with Simon and we went to the hotel, where everyone seemed to know him, which I thought was a good sign. We went to his suite, which was full of his possessions, and he generously gave me one of the two bedrooms to stay in. 'I'll be out all day tomorrow,' he said. 'And then I'll be gone for good.' I went to bed early and got up early again the next morning to look into what I needed to do to get into Iraq. Its embassy in Jordan was one of its last operating anywhere. I thought it might take a few days to get through, so I also wanted to sniff out some stories in Jordan while I was waiting.

I got back to the hotel in the middle of the afternoon. Clearly there had been something of a kerfuffle in the room during my absence. A slightly dishevelled Simon arrived not long after me and began throwing a few belongings into a bag.

'I'm not going to take all my things,' he said. 'I've managed to get a flight this afternoon.'

'Where are you going?' I asked.

'I can't remember where, just out of here,' he said, which struck me as a little odd. 'I've got to go. I'll leave some money at the desk.'

'Don't worry about it too much,' I told him. I was grateful because he had helped me. I was now in a good hotel and all in all it had worked out quite well. Plus he seemed to be under some stress.

'If anyone comes looking for me, just say I've packed my bags and gone to England permanently.'

'Who might come looking for you?'

He stopped throwing clothes around for a moment.

'It's very easy to make enemies in this place,' he said. 'Just take care. Here, this might help you.'

With that, he handed me a very elaborate edition of the Koran. The Koran is elaborate to start with, but this was a spectacular volume.

'Oh God,' I said, 'you can't leave that with me.'

'It's too heavy for me to take.'

I had talked to him in our time together about how much I would like to visit Algeria, then listed as one of the 10 most dangerous places to travel. Customs formalities there were reputed to consist of someone looking at you to see if you were mujahedin and, if not, shooting you. 'It will be great for Algeria,' said Simon. 'If they're planning to kill you and you're kneeling on the ground with your hands on the Koran then they're not allowed to.' So I took it and he went, or, rather, fled, panicked and dishevelled, leaving behind all sorts of things.

That night there was a knock on the door — one of those knocks whose purport is 'Open the door now or we will break it down'. I had gone to bed early, so I could get up in time to talk to Ewing Stevens at Pacific. I wrapped a towel around myself and opened the door to see several very official, very aggressive men. They were in uniform, but were not police.

'You're not Simon,' they said.

'No, no, no,' I confirmed.

'Where is he?'

'Well, here's the thing . . .' I began. And I was thinking: where the fuck did I put that Koran? I was choosing my words carefully, trying to think of the best way to frame things. It wasn't happening quickly enough for the men in uniform. By now they were in the room.

'Where is he?' the leader demanded. 'Is he in here?' It was soon obvious he wasn't. 'What's your relationship to him? How do you know him?'

'Look, I actually don't know him.'

'You flew here together from England.'

'Well, technically yes . . .'

It didn't sound good, when he put it like that. I started to tell the yarn and after a few sentences realised it wasn't going well. So then I started to hesitate, which looked even worse. Every word that came out of my mouth went straight up my arse and screwed me.

'I didn't board the plane with him. I just happened to be sitting next to him and we started to talk and he said this would be a good place to stay.'

Then they found the Koran. I had no way of knowing whether that was good for me or bad for me.

'So this is yours now, is it?'

'Did he leave the Koran? Did he leave that here? It's not mine. I wish it was, it's a beautiful book, isn't it? But it's not mine, no.' Then I had a brainwave. 'Actually, he's left a number of things. Do you want me to get them together for you? I tell you what I'll do, I'll pack together all of his things very quickly.'

When I got the things together, of course, it turned out that there weren't very many and nothing of any interest to them.

'We will take this,' said my persecutor, holding up the Koran. 'And when the man you don't really know contacts you, you tell him never ever come to Jordan again.'

I said I would be certain to pass on their message in the unlikely event that I ever laid eyes on Simon in the future. Avoiding Simon had quite recently become one of my main aims in life.

When they left, I'm sure they didn't fully believe my story but clearly their gripe was personal and with him, not me. I still don't know what he had done, but it obviously had pissed off some reasonably important people. I was annoyed that I had lost the Koran, because it was so heavy it would have been almost impossible to get into trouble while carrying it.

Next morning, I needed to get my visa, so I headed to the Iraqi embassy. This was really the ambassador's home, with an annex and lots of security. Apparently, you went in, slid a few dollars across a big counter with your passport and you got a visa.

Before I went to the embassy I researched the best way to get into Iraq, so that once I had my documentation I would waste as little time as possible. I had to go to the land border, where oil trucks were constantly going back and forth down a huge highway through the desert. Empty tankers going into Iraq, and full ones coming out again. It would take the best part of a day. That was if there wasn't a traffic jam, which apparently there often was, with lines of trucks stalled for kilometres. This went on 24 hours a day.

I was told by other journalists that you could go by bus but that it was a bit rickety. You could also get a ride on one of the trucks — they weren't supposed to take you but would for a few dollars. You could hire a vehicle and take a self-drive package. Or you could bludge a ride with the BBC or CNN. But you couldn't do any of that until you had your visa.

I was also told that the only person who could issue a journalist a visa for Iraq was a Mr Sadoon, and for reasons that will soon become clear, his is a name I will never forget. I was further told he started work at ten so I should present myself at ten.

I turned up for my appointment and entered a room with a large number of people in it — many Arabs, and many also, clearly, western journalists. Among the latter I could feel an obvious competitive edge. All eyes were on me as I walked up to the counter.

'Ah, Paul Henry here from New Zealand,' I said to the man behind the desk. 'I have an appointment with Mr Sadoon.'

A wave of laughter surged, broke and washed over me. All the journalists roared.

'Mr Sadoon is not here, you'll have to take a seat.'

'You don't seem to understand, I was told to be here at ten o'clock because Mr Sadoon would be here and I need to get into Iraq.'

Howls of laughter. I think someone even slapped his thigh. Clearly I was the butt of a popular joke and everyone had been through this at some point

'You don't have to take a seat if you don't want to,' said the man at the counter. 'You can just leave if you prefer.' So I took a seat in this comparatively squalid, albeit convivial environment.

'How do you think that went?' I said to the room in general, generating a round of guffaws.

One journalist shuffled over and sat next to me.

'How long do you reckon I've been waiting for my ten o'clock appointment with Mr Sadoon?' he said.

'Please tell me a day,' I begged.

'I've been here three weeks, and do you know what really pisses me off? It just comes down to money. You go up to that counter now and you slip that guy a thousand US dollars and you'll be talking to Mr Sadoon within half an hour. That money won't get you into Iraq but it'll get you a meeting with Mr Sadoon and the opportunity to slip him the same amount or more. I don't know how much. In the weeks that I've been coming here for my appointment with Mr Sadoon, I've seen the big boys come and get straight into Iraq. The BBC just flying in, CNN flying in. They're playing a game.'

I learnt the authorities would want another $1000 for the right to take a satellite phone into the country. Not to rent one — merely to carry it with you. I had $1000 for everything.

'What are you going to do?' I asked my informant.

'I don't know. My time is almost up. The war hasn't started and I just don't see how I'm going to get in.'

I wondered if logic would trump money for the first time anywhere in the world. I went back to the desk.

'There are a few pretty annoyed people here from the world's media,' I said. 'We want to go in and tell your story, not someone else's. The only way we can tell your story is to get in there.' He appeared to have heard that before.

I wondered if anyone had tried winking.

'I'm not going to sit and wait with these other people, I want to see Mr Sadoon,' I said, and winked. I winked like a man who had more than a thousand New Zealand dollars on him. 'I want to see Mr Sadoon, just tell me when he's going to be here. I can be here at any time night or day to see him.'

Weeks went by and I spent most of my time in this room. I gathered a few little stories. I observed some riots that were happening and I got some great war yarns and kept up with what was going on. But always I had to keep coming back to that room where we all waited for Mr Sadoon.

I did glimpse him once or twice as he arrived in his Lexus and moved through the compound. The cry would go up: 'Is that him? Is that Mr Sadoon?' Our spirits soared. We all stood up and watched through the bars as Mr Sadoon drove in. Every time it happened I was sure that I was going to meet Mr Sadoon and would soon be on my way to Baghdad. That day never arrived. He came into the room once or twice to give people an opportunity to slip him money. He obviously had a spare moment when he hadn't been given $1000 for a few hours, so he displayed himself to the gathered masses.

Occasionally we were told to wait in another room and that made me very excited. I was sure that meant I was one room closer to Mr Sadoon, but the other room, which had lots of small pictures of Saddam Hussein and a huge number of doilies, merely sheltered more journalists who I hadn't seen before.

A newly arrived BBC producer approached me one day: 'We're here to get our visas. Do you know where we go?'

'I don't think there's anything you can learn from me,' I said. 'Do you need anyone else on your team? Are you short of anyone? I'll work for nothing if you can get me into Iraq.'

'Oh, it's like that is it? We were told that we had to see Mr Sadoon.'

'Yeah, I think he's the guy.'

The BBC producer called a colleague over. They went into another room and I heard him say, 'We're here to see Mr Sadoon. BBC.' Sure enough, that was the last time I saw them. And the Iraqis weren't making an exception for them. They paid, but the sums being asked meant nothing to them. They were there to get in and cost was no object. A thousand here and there, as a percentage of the total cost of their trip, was nothing. Fuckers.

Back home, Derek Lowe never quite got it when I tried to explain the problem. 'Why didn't you report him?' he always said. Or, 'Why didn't you call the police?' I could have tried that: 'Hello, police? I'd like to report the Iraqi embassy.'

I knew I was getting nowhere. I could have gone home. I had some reasonable stories. But having got that far I couldn't leave without one last effort to get across the border. I went to see a Finnish journalist I had got friendly with.

'You are not going to get a visa to go into Iraq,' I said. 'And neither am I. It's not going to happen.'

'Oh, I'm going to give it a few more days,' he said.

'There's no reason to imagine that a few more days will make any difference.'

It wasn't like they were gradually whittling through people. We were just seeing new faces added to the group every day. I had been there about two weeks. He had been there longer.

'I don't want to spend the next few days waiting for this bunch of arseholes to sell me a visa that I haven't got the money to pay for. Why don't we rent a four-wheel drive and go for it? There's a war on — almost. How efficient is the immigration department in Iraq going to be?' To my eventual regret, although he was wearing a suit and seemed quite stuffy, he immediately embraced this very stupid idea.

'Where will we get a four-wheel drive?' he said.

'Have you been outside? They're everywhere.'

Within half an hour I had contracted a driver with a substantial four-wheel drive. His English was bad but his price was good. I didn't tell him whether or not we had documentation, so he probably assumed we did. As we made our way to the border I reported home and told the listeners about having no documents, so that became part of the story.

Night fell quickly as it does in that part of the world, taking the temperature right down with it.

'Iraq,' said the driver suddenly, and pointed. Apparently we were there.

'Can you just pull over and stop for a moment?' I said. We stopped where we could see Iraq in the distance.

I still wasn't sure what our chances were so I decided to confess all to the driver.

'We have no documentation,' I told him. 'We have been told we can fill in our documentation at the Iraqi border.' I had convinced myself that might be possible, especially because Mr Sadoon would not be there.

'I do not think that is possible,' said the driver.

'Well, that's what I was told at the Iraqi embassy,' I lied.

Our driver had been to Iraq many, many times and taken many loads, but he had never taken foreigners without visas. He was not keen.

'I think this is the end of the line,' said my colleague.

'It can't be the end of the line,' I insisted. 'One way or another we've got to get into Iraq, even if it is only into the bloody Customs booth.'

And then I came up with a way to make my original plan even worse.

'Let's just drive in. There's no fences as such. It's night time. We've got a four-wheel drive. We don't have to be on the road.'

We decided to edge our way a little closer on the road and then turn the lights off, go off road and cross the border that way. We considered the possibilities of being stopped without documents after that and talked ourselves into believing that the closer you got to Baghdad, the more lawless it would be.

So we got virtually to the border, then did a cunning duck around and, despite it being pitch black and the middle of the desert, quickly drove into an Iraqi military base.

'We're going to have to rely on you to translate,' I told the driver. 'Just plead ignorance, say we're fools from another country.

We both look stupid enough to make that convincing.'

But before there was any time to put that into practice we were all dragged out of the car and had the shit beaten out of us by men with guns.

'Sorry, sorry, it's been a terrible mistake,' I kept saying. I was about to fall back on 'It was all his idea. I never wanted to do it', when the beating stopped.

My Finnish friend panicked and started talking about the Geneva fucking Convention. Even though I was hurting badly I was still able to register that he was being an absolute twat. He and I were taken and held at the Iraqi checkpoint. God knows what happened to that poor driver. He was beaten up as well, but he wasn't taken to the checkpoint.

We were hauled into a room with the compulsory giant portraits of Saddam Hussein staring down on us. The guard running the checkpoint was bemused more than anything.

'Documents,' he snapped and we handed over what we had. 'No visa?'

'We'd like a visa. Yes, please,' I said. Well, it was worth a try.

'You don't come here through the desert to get a visa,' he said, and I was relieved to hear that he spoke English very well. 'You must get a visa in Jordan.'

'They told us . . .' I began, and as I heard the words come out I knew it wasn't going to wash. I changed tack and told the truth. 'I'm sorry, we just thought we'd give it a go. Do you know Mr Sadoon?'

'Sadoon?'

'Yeah. People are bribing him at your embassy in Jordan. He's making a fortune selling visas and I can't afford to buy one. I'm from New Zealand. I want to tell your story. This guy is from Finland, he wants to tell your story. We just can't afford to pay the bribes to Mr Sadoon. Where's your family?'

'In Baghdad.'

'When did you last see them?'

'It's been some time.'

'How much do you get paid?'

'I haven't been paid for six months.'

'Have any of your colleagues been paid in the last six months?'

'Some have not been paid for much longer than me.'

'So you haven't seen your family, a war could start at any time, you haven't been paid for six months, Mr Sadoon wants a thousand US dollars a week for me to bring a satellite phone into this country and he wants at least the same amount for him and his cronies to give me a visa. And you want to send me back to get a visa.'

And with that we were locked up. The room I was put in was like a toilet without the bowl. There was a locked door, a light bulb hanging on a wire and a panorama of shit. Previous occupants had pissed and shat almost everywhere. There was shit all over the wall with the door in it and two of the other walls. Left untouched was a wall covered by an oil painting of Saddam Hussein.

I had been allowed to keep my satellite phone. I crouched down in the middle of this underground shithole and tried to get a signal but failed. After a while I was taken back to see the guard who had questioned me. By now it was late at night and absolutely freezing.

The room was decorated with opulent and appalling taste. There were drapes like theatre curtains, made from shimmery satin fabric with golden tie-backs and faux gold fittings, and, once again, doilies on every piece of furniture. It was not what I expected at an Iraqi border post in the middle of the desert.

'What do we do with you?' said my interrogator.

'Is my colleague around at all?' I replied. 'We have been here for some time. Have you been determining whether or not we will get a visa?' I reasoned he probably wanted to get rid of us and had been making arrangements to do so. I considered what life would be like as a human shield and concluded it probably would not be that bad. I knew there would be good stories in it, and I already had quite a good yarn to tell.

'We will keep you here for longer, I think,' he said.

'Really? It's very unpleasant down there and it's very cold. Feel my hands.'

For some reason I liked this guard. I felt sorry for him. Everything in his life was crap. That apart, we had a lot of common ground. I showed him photos of my daughters.

'This is my life,' I said. 'I travel around countries like this, and they live in Homebush, a lot further away from Baghdad.' Then I saw photos of his family. It was humanity in a war, and I was eavesdropping on it.

Then it was back down to the cell and an hour later back up again to the room with the bad drapes and my new friend. The television was on.

'Mr Henry, come and sit with me,' he said, without turning his gaze from the screen. I did as I was told.

'I want you to watch something,' he said.

It was Iraqi television and, I learnt later, what I was watching was being played every hour on the hour. It was CNN film of Madeleine Albright and other US officials talking to US college students, who were asking them very tough questions about policy in the Middle East.

But Iraqi television had edited this — very badly. They cut out the answers, so all you saw were the aggressive questions and looks of alarm on Albright's face in response, so that she actually appeared evil.

After it had played for the third time I had had enough.

'I know what happens in this,' I said. 'I've seen it before. You've seen this before. Why are you wasting your time watching it?'

'This is not a waste of time,' he said. 'This is war talk. Even the young people in your country think you are persecuting us.'

He said 'your country' because we were all Americans if we were white.

'Can we speak frankly?' I said. 'Do you recognise that this is heavily edited? She can actually speak, that woman on the screen.'

'Look at the way they're talking to her.'

'Don't you see?' I said. 'That's what this fight is all about. It's called democracy. What would happen to those students if they tried that on with Saddam Hussein in Baghdad? What would happen to them? Would it be put on TV for everyone to watch?'

This was followed by a long silence.

'It changes nothing,' he said eventually.

'It changes everything because that's what we want to bring to this country. Do you think those students would put up with not being paid for six months and having their families imperilled in another city, or do you think they'd ask even harder questions to executives which would then be broadcast on television around the world? This is the difference between our two countries. I can go back to my country and I can say "Iraq is great and you're a pile of arseholes" and they won't shoot me.'

Our relationship changed at that point.

'I'll get you a cup of tea,' he said.

'Thanks. Do you smoke?' I said.

'We have no cigarettes.'

'Neither do I and I am a fearsome smoker. Is there anywhere I can access cigarettes?'

He left the room and came back with some guards. They put me in the back of a jeep and we drove to a duty-free store. It was a huge Palladian building with not much inside except for three fridges and several glass counters containing a few watches and cigarette cases. But in one corner there was a mountain of cigarettes.

It was US 50c for a carton of 200 Iraqi cigarettes. I splurged on two cartons.

Back in the jeep I asked if there was anywhere we could get something to eat. They took me to an Iraqi burger bar that was somewhere between a really bad McDonald's and the worst truck stop you can think of. It actually had truckies in it.

I took one look and knew that anything I ate here would give me a savage dose of the shits before finally killing me, but I didn't care. I ordered and ate a brilliant burger, dripping with fat. I bought the guys who were escorting me food, too, and they devoured it like they hadn't eaten proper food in a long time.

I was allowed to make a satellite phone call back to Radio Pacific. I'm sure they thought I was ringing my family, as most people would have. It was so cold I could hardly talk, but I managed to get through and tell Geoff Sinclair what was going on.

As a result, Rachael opened our front door at Homebush the next morning to see one of our neighbours standing there.

'We hear your husband is imprisoned in Iraq and we've baked you a cake.'

So that's how the family found out I was a prisoner. I became a national and international news item, though only a small one because I wasn't the only person who had been captured in Iraq.

Back at the bunker it was obvious both that my captors weren't going to kill me and also that they didn't know what to do with me. I had laid eyes on the Finnish journalist a couple of times, so knew he was all right, too.

I began talking to the guy in charge again, chatting about things like the price of cigarettes and how much a loaf of bread cost in Baghdad and Masterton. I gave him a cigarette and we sat there smoking from my cartons.

'I'm going to leave these cigarettes when I go,' I said. I offered everyone else cigarettes. 'I'm going to leave these cigarettes here but I'm reluctant to give them to anyone but you. Why don't you distribute them as you see fit. But I do need to leave here now. I think I'm becoming a problem to you. It's really uncomfortable,

I'm very cold. So we should get me some transport.'

There was a significant, but not awkward silence.

'That can be arranged,' he said finally.

'I'll need to take my colleague with me. He's hopeless, isn't he?'

He agreed wholeheartedly and a couple of hours later we were in a vehicle taking us to the Jordanian border. Relief soon turned to concern when it became apparent that we were in the unusual position of entering a country that there was no record of us leaving. This provided much puzzlement. It was obvious where we had come from.

'How long have you been in Iraq?'

'Two days.'

'How did you get there?'

In the end there was only the truth to tell. And it became a matter of pure bureaucracy: You haven't left, so you can't come back. You can't enter Jordan if you haven't left Jordan. After a couple of hours, common sense prevailed and we were allowed, if not to enter, at least to be in Jordan. And a couple of bus rides later, I was back at the hotel from which I had never checked out.

ON ASSIGNMENT

PAUL HENRY
FOREIGN CORRESPONDENT
RADIO PACIFIC NETWORK

Fish

CHAPTER 14

'WHY WOULD YOU COME HERE TO THIS TRAGEDY?'

> **"** I KNEW AFRICA QUITE WELL BY THEN. THE BRITISH INTRODUCED RUBBER STAMPS AND CARBON PAPER, SO THE BUREAUCRACY IS EXTRAORDINARY. ADD THE CORRUPTION AND THE CHIEFS TO THAT AND YOU HAVE A VERY COMPLICATED MIXTURE. I UNDERSTOOD WHAT THE PEOPLE THERE LIKED AND DIDN'T LIKE WHEN IT CAME TO FOREIGNERS COMING IN. **"**

DOUGLAS KEAR WAS A Hamilton man who had been one of a group of tourists kidnapped while on a gorilla safari in Africa. This was international news in 1998. Efforts had been made by his family and at diplomatic levels to find out what was happening, with no success. I knew Africa quite well by then. The British introduced rubber stamps and carbon paper, so the bureaucracy is extraordinary. Add the corruption and the chiefs to that and you have a very complicated mixture. I understood what the people there liked and didn't like when it came to foreigners coming in.

It was obvious that the people trying to locate Douglas Kear were getting nowhere. No one could even prove whether he was dead or alive. All they knew was that he had been alive when the kidnappers released a couple of the hostages. They were believed to be in the Democratic Republic of the Congo, somewhere close to the border with Uganda and Rwanda. That is a very specific, quite small area, largely consisting of impenetrable forest, in a very large country.

The idea of finding him, or simply trying to find him in that sort of environment was very exciting. Derek was excited because this was not just an international story but one with a strong New Zealand angle, unlike most of the things I was doing.

I went to see Kear's family before I left. I didn't want to give anyone false hope and didn't shy away from the fact he was quite possibly already dead. That said, I thought I might at least find out what had happened to him or get close to the people who took him, which no one had managed to do.

One of the Radio Pacific copywriters stopped me and made enquiries about my sanity in light of my plans. A lot of the things I did were obviously dangerous once I was doing them, but not so obviously dangerous during the planning. This was a case where what I was doing was unquestionably dangerous — attempting to track down people who were at best hardened killers.

I first flew into Uganda, landing at Entebbe airport, but my ultimate destination was a town called Kisoro, which was the starting point for most of the gorilla tours.

While in Kampala, I went to the offices of the local newspaper, *New Vision*, to see if I could drum up some publicity for my search. I thought that might speed things up by smoking out someone close to the kidnappers. They gave me a great front-page story about the search for Douglas Kear which threw up some good leads. I also told the journalist I spoke to I needed someone in Kisoro who knew his way around and could cut some corners and liaise with the various parties to find out information for me. He recommended a cousin who I took on as an assistant.

I flew out of Entebbe airport in a small plane. As we took off I could see some of Idi Amin's planes off to one side, slowly rusting away. And, within moments, I was flying over Lake Victoria and looking at the hippos in the water.

Kisoro was smaller than I had imagined. There was some communications infrastructure but I would have been lost without my satellite phone. There were places to stay that could almost be called hotels. Mine was a collection of huts in a compound with a kitchen and a bar area. The shower was a big piece of plastic on top of a mud roof that would fill up with rain water and heat during the day, and the plumbing was very sparse. My bed was made of thatched sticks but it had a mattress because I was in the best room. I loved it all. I got a discounted rate on the best room because I was staying for so long, and possibly because I was the only guest they had.

I met the cousin, Didas, who didn't know much about the story but did know a lot about the various factions there and people I needed to speak to. I reasoned that the more people knew about me, the likelier I would be to get in touch with the kidnappers.

'I want everyone in this village to know exactly who I am when they see me,' I told Didas. 'I want them to know exactly why I am here, exactly where I am staying. I need them to know I'm not in support of any faction or another. I'm not with the police. I'm not with the tour company. I'm not here to make a judgement or bring someone to justice. I just want to find out what happened to this man.'

Because I behaved so differently from everyone else who had come looking for Douglas Kear, there was no distrust surrounding me. Progress was slow, however. Near the town was a knoll where I used to go sometimes when I felt like a bit of peace and quiet. It was in Uganda but you could touch the Congo from there and you could almost touch Rwanda. You could look down on the mist in the forest and know that was where the gorillas were. It was the strangest feeling, the same as I had when I stood in Mother House in Calcutta and thought: 'Even if nothing comes of this expedition, being able to experience this has made the trip worthwhile.'

I soon felt at home in Kisoro. With time on my hands I got to know the people at the hotel well. I organised a working bee. We planted flowers and whitewashed the walls. I showed them how to prune and train their roses. I also got sick to death of eating goat, which was what you were fed on if you were prosperous. There were about ten ways of cooking a goat and they were all exactly the same.

'We need fish,' I said. 'I fancy a bit of fish. I go to the markets all the time and they've got fish at the markets.'

'Oh no, we can't get you fish,' the hotel cook said. So I went to the market myself and bought a huge fish, took it back, slapped it down in the filthy area where the chef used to cook and said, 'This is my dinner.'

They laughed. I ignored them.

'Cook it up for dinner. We'll all have it, it's a huge fish.'

By dinner time I was sitting in the dining hall and the room was full of people, with more looking through the windows, all there to watch crazy Paul eat a fish. It looked fantastic when it came out. I made the manager sit down with me and we both had a plate. I took the first bite. There is no way I can adequately convey to you how awful it tasted. It was like eating shit that had been cooked in vomit. I'm sure that fish had subsisted on nothing but excrement its entire life. And I have a sneaking suspicion the locals all knew that.

One day I noticed a change in the town's mood. Normally the air was heavy with menace, but this day there was an almost festive feeling in the town, with no festival planned that I was aware of.

'Something's different,' I said to the manager.

'The locusts are coming,' he said.

'When?'

'Probably tomorrow, maybe the next day.'

'Is there anything I need to be aware of?'

'Just make sure your door is closed. It will be much excitement. They are a delicacy, nothing tastes like fresh locusts. Then, after the locusts go — fried locusts.'

I thought locusts meant plants being devoured and the clothes being stripped from people's backs. The next day there were no locusts but there was increased excitement. People were collecting up every container they could find, every plastic bag and plastic bottle.

That night they rewired their huts and put all their light bulbs outside. They stood and waited, and when the first locusts arrived, they grabbed them out of the air as they flew past and stuck them in their mouths. A few hours later, there was a wall of locusts and people were frantically grabbing them and stuffing them in their containers. By the next morning the whole place was just swarming with locusts. By that afternoon, there were dead locusts everywhere. That night, there was a huge feast of barbecued locusts. And within two days it was all over. They came, they were conquered and they left.

Behind all this, violence was always in the background. This was a time when there was a lot of distrust in the air and a lot of killing going on. Some people called it intertribal conflict. Other people called it a war. I concluded that the difference was merely the size of your tribe.

Every night there were murders. The impenetrable forest was populated by pygmies who came into the village during the day and were very hostile to everyone. One used to play his guitar for you and then expect to be paid. If you didn't hand over any money, he hit you with his guitar. I thought of hitting him back but he was probably much stronger than me.

One day I went to see the impenetrable forest. I did not expect to be able to get in, it being impenetrable, but I got in a little way. I didn't want to go very far because as well as the pygmies it was inhabited by a lot of anacondas. But it was as extraordinary as any natural phenomenon I have ever encountered; it was so fertile that when I crouched down I could see things growing. Climbers moved before my eyes.

One especially bad night some 50 people were murdered in the village. I could hear the screams from my hotel. Next day, I walked to a market across the border in the Congo. One of the murder victims had been slit from his throat to his genitals and pegged open on the path as a warning to others not to support his group: 'Don't help these people or this will happen to you.' Women and children going to market to sell or trade their six potatoes had to walk past this grotesque sight.

There were not many other foreigners around. The violence had slowed the tourist trade right down, with few people keen enough to risk kidnapping to look at some gorillas. One aim of the kidnappers was to destabilise the Ugandan economy by disrupting the tourist industry and in that they succeeded spectacularly. The whole time I was there only one group of tourists appeared. They stayed only two days.

In a short period of time I gained a lot of intelligence and I was pretty sure that the Interahamwe, the Hutu paramilitary organisation, had taken Douglas Kear. Because of my contacts, other people came through wanting to cash in on my intelligence. A pair of Africans from Kampala attempted to befriend me. They wanted messages taken to the Interahamwe. This was all to do with Ugandan, Congolese and, to a degree, Rwandan politics, and I wanted no part of it.

'If you help us, we can help you,' they said, but I couldn't really be sure who they were. I didn't understand their motivations and had no way of finding out.

One day I got a message telling me to call the British high commissioner in Kampala.

'Mr Henry, this is the best possible intelligence we have,' said the high commissioner when I finally got through. 'You are being hunted down and you will be killed. You need to know that the only responsible, reasonable thing you can do is get out of there now. And I mean right now. You should not be there tonight. There is one other thing you need to know: if you choose to stay, no one is going to come in to get you out if you go missing. You are entirely on your own.'

'Well, I feel I'm getting quite close to finding out what's going on,' I said.

'You must be getting quite close for people to want to kill you,' he said.

So in a way the trip had been a success, because I had got closer than anyone else. But I hung up wondering how I could explain to people that was a success and that this was the time to leave. Was I leaving because I was scared or because I was not stupid? Why was I leaving instead of staying when I was so close and could presumably go all the way?

So I decided to stay.

After that phone call I started sleeping on the floor in case anyone tried to shoot me in my bed. Every night I would wake up at the slightest sound, which was often gunfire. It was an uncomfortable and unpleasant time.

When I needed to arrange meetings I communicated with people I didn't know and couldn't see via messages I put in newspapers with my contact details and where I could be found. There would have been no point making my location secret. One of the people who worked for me passed on the newspapers to people in the impenetrable forest or wherever they would be likely to see them. Then he was killed, and I had reason to think it was because he was a local and helping me. That changed things for me. It was my adventure but it wasn't just my life at risk. And for what? I was sure Douglas Kear was dead. Staying didn't really make sense.

Not long after, one of the Africans from Kampala who had contacted me before came to see me.

'We need to go and meet some people,' he said. 'I've arranged it.'

It was a four-hour walk to get to the meeting place, and I had a very bad feeling about it. I thought about calling it off, even as we were on our way. Then I realised that, as dangerous as it was, this could be as close as I would get to finding out what happened to Douglas Kear. So I carried on, knowing it was quite dangerous. We came to a clearing where the meeting was to take place, and while we were waiting my companion told me he had a gun. I was furious.

'You shouldn't have brought a gun,' I said. 'There is no chance that you can kill all of the people that are coming to this meeting before they kill us, so why would you kill any? You kill one and there's no chance we're going to stay alive.'

The next minute about 20 men carrying machetes and guns came out of the bush. There were a lot more we couldn't see and only a couple, obviously the leaders, did any talking. My companion was translating, but not everything that was being said, and things seemed to be getting tense.

'Tell me what you're saying,' I asked. 'Tell me what they're saying. Have they seen Douglas Kear? Can they bring me his hat? I know he was wearing a hat. I need to see something because I'm not doing anything else until I have some evidence that these people know he's there.' If they had wanted to take me then, they had the perfect opportunity.

I used to make a point of touching people in tense situations because I knew it helped calm things down. I went up to one of the leaders and put my hand on the arm that was holding the machete.

'Do you understand what I'm saying?' I said. 'This is the only reason I'm here. If you want publicity in return for Douglas Kear or information, I will give you publicity. I will put you in touch with radio audiences around the world. I will come back here, and talk to anyone who wants to talk to me, but before I file another report I need to have some evidence that you have seen the man I am looking for.'

There was a lot of aggro going on and I ascertained that there was more being discussed than I knew about, and this had almost nothing to do with Douglas Kear. The men offered to take me into the bush to meet more people, but not to see him.

I was a tool to get a message out and it became obvious that I was potentially another international story, another white person killed in this terribly unsafe part of the world where you should not go if you wanted to stay alive. I think that was one of the times when I came very close to death.

They definitely did not know where Kear was, so in the end, having made my offer, I simply said I was going and turned and left. I was sure I was going to be killed as I was walking back. All I knew about finding my way out of the jungle was to keep walking down. It was like following a river — keep going and you will come to the sea in the end. I kept going and for the hours it took I was thinking, 'Are they behind me? Am I being hunted down now?'

I didn't see my contact again. God knows whether he was one of them, or if he was trying to get me killed. After I got to Kisoro, there was no way I was going back to meet those people again. Within a few days I decided it was time to get back on the plane and go.

The most widely accepted theory about the fate of Douglas

Kear is that he was not killed by his captors but died when, being an old man, he succumbed to the rigours of being dragged through the jungle and treated roughly.

One of the big lessons from the experience was something a *Time* photographer said to me: 'The funny thing about this game is that the further down the road you go, the better the story you get, but the less the chance you have of getting the story out.'

Often when I was in the middle of a dangerous situation, I found myself thinking, 'I must bring the kids back here.' Five years later I was back in Kisoro on holiday with Lucy, sleeping in my old room. The roses were looking fantastic and the whitewash had held up well. There was even a photo of me on the dining room wall.

I wanted to take her across the border from Uganda into the Democratic Republic of the Congo, just so she could say she'd been there. I had hired a RAV4 and employed my old contact from the *New Vision* newspaper to be our driver, and one day we set off for the border. I took Lucy in to see the police chief there, who was another old friend. There was another conflict going on at the time — French peacekeepers arrived at the same time as us.

'How are things today?' I said. 'Do you think it's safe for us to go across?'

'I think you'll be all right,' he said. So we headed for the border along with a couple of people who were going to the market. The border was a 30-metre strip of no man's land between a pair of trees on each side.

We went to the hut on the Ugandan side, where they checked our passports, and then we walked quietly across. And you could have heard a pin drop as we were walking. It seemed a lot longer than 30 metres. There were people sitting around with semi-automatic weapons, their gaze following you every step of the way. This is a place where so many people are killed that

Top:
Bosnian refugee camp.

Above:
My one-armed taxi driver (hiding fibreglass arm).

Above:
On board the Greenpeace ship Manatee. Dave McTaggart, one of Greenpeace's founders, and Peter Williams QC.

Right:
Filing a report.

Below:
With the Malaysian Prime Minister.

Bottom:
A camel underneath me.

Above:
Posing in Israel.

Left:
Making a satellite
phone call in the
Jordanian desert.

Above:
Checking out the accommodation in Cambodia.

Below:
My driver and interpreter (front) in Cambodia.

Right:
Uganda.

Below:
Boarding an old Hercules to deliver aid in Sudan.

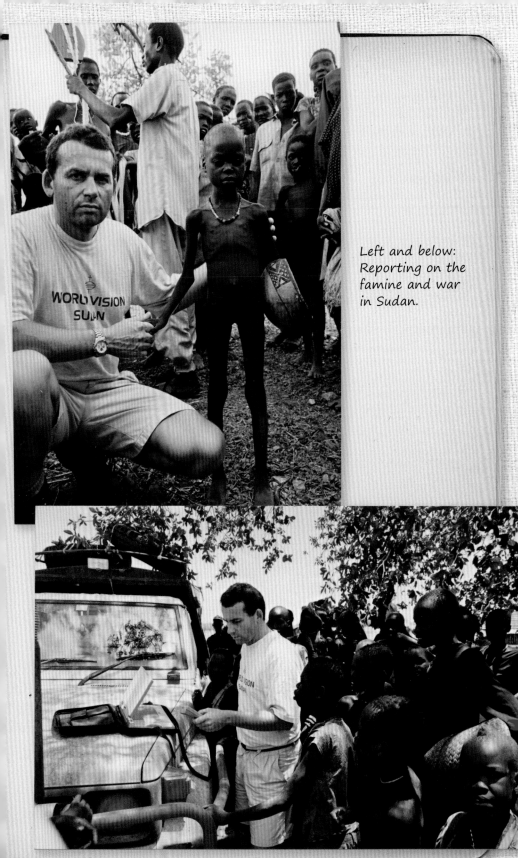

Left and below: Reporting on the famine and war in Sudan.

Above:
Below Everest.

Right:
In the Tibetan
capital Lhasa.

everyone is suspicious of everyone else. Lucy, who had never even seen a gun before, reacted with a mixture of fright and excitement, which is just the right response in an environment like this.

People say it was irresponsible to have taken a child to a place like that, and it sounds irresponsible when I recount it, but there is something about being there and knowing you're okay. It's living on the edge, but it is living — it's really living. The closer to the edge you are, the more living it is.

We went into the little kiosk on the Congo side with our passports. A large sombre Congolese woman was in charge.

'Why would you come here to this tragedy?' she said.

'I was here five years ago working,' I told her, 'and I wanted to show my daughter, because it's a sad but beautiful part of the world, and people should know about this part of the world.'

'It is a sad part of the world. How long will you be here?'

'We just want to literally walk through the village and then we're going to go back.'

'I'll keep your passports so that you will go back,' she said, and waved us through.

We walked along the track, and the trees on either side were all shot up. There had been a lot of killing here. There was a lot of movement inside the little shacks on one side. People were starting to run and get their guns. They seemed strangely at one with their guns.

'We've got to go,' said Lucy. 'We've got to go, we've got to get out of here, let's go now.'

'We'll just get a Coke,' I said.

We walked into the little border village and it was effectively closed too. However, there was no shortage of people sitting around waiting for something to happen.

I went up to someone sitting outside his shop. 'We'd like a Coke,' I said. 'Can you get us a Coke?'

So he opened his little shop and got us a Coke. I opened my hand, in which I had a collection of different kinds of money — Ugandan and American — and he took some and gave me old Congolese money, back from when it was Zaire, which was very cool. I gave Lucy and my driver their Coke.

'Okay,' said my driver. 'We are out of here right now.'

'We don't run,' I said, as we turned around and headed back with our Cokes. 'No one runs in a place like this, we just stroll back.'

When we got back to the Congolese woman and our passports, I said: 'I didn't buy you a Coke.'

'It would have been nice if you had,' she said.

She handed us back our passports.

'No stamp?' I asked.

'You never came here.'

'That's a real shame,' I said, 'because this 15-year-old girl is going to want to talk about this amazing experience when she gets home.'

With that, the woman got a scrap of paper out, stamped and signed it, and handed it to Lucy. We walked out.

'I so wish we were still over there,' said Lucy, when we were safely back in Kisoro.

My experiences in Africa and parts of Asia made me start thinking about what could be done to help people whose lives were a few short years of hungry, miserable poverty. I set up something called everyhorizon as a foundation to channel some of my own and other people's money to where it could be useful.

I saw so much need and I saw how easy it would be to deliver solutions. I thought, naively, I could dramatically change these people's lives by spending a small amount of money in the right place at the right time. I could do that because I could so easily set up chains to these areas through people I knew, and for $100 you could do so much in these little villages. Before long I discovered the great flaw in that idea. If you ask people for

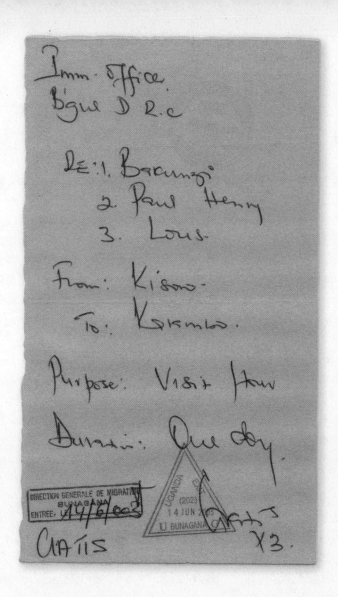

money, those people have a reasonable expectation that you should tell them, indeed prove to them, what you've done with it. And that costs a fortune. So I let the foundation dwindle away and decided just to do things with my own money.

One of my many pet hates is people who promote the good work they do and I have no intention of doing that. But I would like to tell the story of one aid project which demonstrates how effective aid can be if it's done without a bureaucratic mindset.

In Phnom Penh all of the city's rubbish goes to one dump.

Trucks arrive all day, ferrying rubbish. Because the city is so poor, by the time the rubbish goes to the dump it has been picked over by umpteen people who have extracted anything of value. It is pure rubbish.

Children live and work in this dump. Their families live around it on stilt houses in lakes of ooze, which seeps out of the dump. Some of the children burrow into the rubbish where they live. In a day, they may find enough rags to get a dollar. Around the dump, work the adults who buy the rags. You can hardly call this system exploitation because no one gets any profit worth speaking of.

One aid organisation took the kids off the dump and put them into schools. Those kids lost their place in the only social structure they knew and their entire way of life. They weren't quite equipped for anything else, but they couldn't get back into the dump. Meanwhile, the charity had moved on to its next media-friendly crisis because all the kids were off the dump. Like so many charities, they had not appreciated the realities of life. If your choices are thief, beggar, prostitute or the dump, the dump is the best one. The kids are not unhappy, despite having no education, being poorly nourished and being prone to infections from standing in shit and on sharp things.

Another charity went there and offered the children a dollar a week if they would go to school for one day a week. They also gave them shoes to reduce the risk of infections. On the day they took them to school they gave them a great nutritious meal, which was the only food they gave them.

This didn't disrupt the families who the children were supporting. It didn't disrupt what they actually did. But it did improve their lives dramatically for next to nothing.

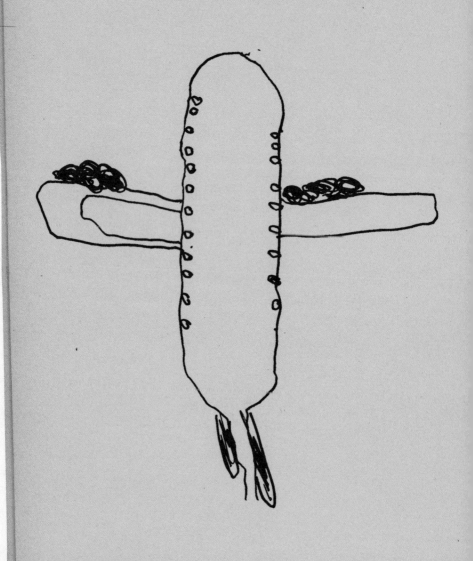

Aeroplane

CHAPTER 15
AWARD-LOSING RADIO JOURNALIST

> " BECAUSE MY RESOURCES WERE ALWAYS SO SLENDER, ESPECIALLY COMPARED TO THOSE OF MY RIVALS, I HAD DEVELOPED A LOT OF STRATEGIES TO COMPENSATE. IN THIS CASE, I WENT TO THE PRIME MINISTERIAL RESIDENCE, BUT MY COMMONWEALTH GAMES ACCREDITATION DIDN'T COUNT FOR ANYTHING. SO I STARTED TALKING AND CONNED MY WAY THROUGH THE FIRST, SECOND, THIRD, FOURTH LEVEL AND I GOT RIGHT TO THE PRIME MINISTER'S PRESS SECRETARY. "

I HAVE NEVER BEEN much interested in sport — certainly less interested than someone doing my job should be. I once bumped into Graham Henry, the All Blacks coach, at the airport. He was surrounded by a group of burly young men.

'Hello, Graham, where are you off to?' I asked. On reflection I should have known that the All Blacks were playing an important test the next day.

So when the Commonwealth Games were being held in Malaysia in 1998 and Derek Lowe thought it would be a good idea for me to go, I wasn't keen. The logistics would be impossible because there would be thousands of journalists already there with full accreditation and facilities.

But on my way a real news story emerged. The Prime Minister, Mahathir Mohamad, had his deputy, Anwar Ibrahim, imprisoned for sodomy. That and the synchronised swimming were the highlights of the trip.

Because my resources were always so slender, especially compared to those of my rivals, I had developed a lot of strategies to compensate. In this case, I went to the prime ministerial residence, but my Commonwealth Games accreditation didn't count for anything. So I started talking and conned my way through the first, second, third, fourth level and I got right to the Prime Minister's press secretary.

The angle I was interested in was that Mahathir had chosen to take this extraordinary step at a time when the world's media were watching. If he was truly appalled by sodomy, surely he wouldn't want his country to be known for it.

The Prime Minister was refusing all interviews. But I told everyone I encountered that I wanted to tell his story his way. I would give him an opportunity to answer questions he would be keen to answer. Because there was so much media attention, he agreed to a few press conferences and I was invited to one. I sought out his press secretary, who by now I had got to know.

'The thing is,' I whined, 'I've got a little tape recorder and a cell phone and that's me, this is my whole network here. What I'd really like is a one on one with the Prime Minister.'

At the end of the press conference there was a barrage of questions but Mahathir ignored them all and left. An assistant took his place at the podium and pointed at a *New York Times* journalist and at me and said, 'Could both of you come with me, please?'

We were taken to another room as the other journalists filed out and from there I was ushered, alone, into another room. There were guards everywhere and suddenly Mahathir came in. And the thing that will never leave my memory is that, despite being the leader of a country with a population of 20 million, he had a badge pinned to his chest — one of those black plastic ones with white writing reversed out — and it said simply 'Mahathir'.

We had 20 minutes together and it was extraordinarily frank. I asked him why he had chosen this worst of all possible times to do something that brought so much negative publicity to Malaysia?

'Look at me,' said Mahathir. 'I'm an old man. I don't know if I'll be around tomorrow and if I weren't, and I hadn't addressed this, a sodomist would be running my country. I can't let that happen. I can't run that risk.'

That was a very disarming answer because it appeared so truthful. After the interview I walked out, clutching my mini-disc recorder and passed the other journalists who were still milling around. As far as I knew, I was the only person in the world to whom Mahathir had explained the reason for his extraordinary actions. The other people there could have put it out over their global networks instantly. I was going to cue it up and play it over the phone to Ewing Stevens in the middle of the night.

Malaysia was bizarre but not that gruelling. Cambodia on the other hand was one of the worst places I visited as an international correspondent. I went to cover the Hun Sen uprising. The background was very complex but it was essentially the dying days of the Khmer Rouge and the ultimate end of Pol Pot's grip on power. Hun Sen was a former member of the Khmer Rouge who worked to overthrow Pol Pot and ended up running the country.

At the time I went, Hun Sen had tried to take over and was exerting pressure. The king was standing by, waiting to see what would happen and which way the police and army would go and which way the militants would go. No one had seen Pol Pot for a long time and I was interested in seeing how close I could get to finding him. He was known to be still alive and living in a stronghold in the countryside.

When I arrived I did what I always did, which was to make a story of whatever I found there. I discovered you could buy landmines near the airport. You went to a little building and a man took you out the back where for a couple of dollars you could choose from a selection. I briefly thought of getting a couple for my front garden to keep strangers out.

I went to Siem Reap in search of Pol Pot, made some enquiries and got nowhere, so decided to return to Phnom Penh. I did, however, have my usual departure tax meltdown when I was told I had to hand over $25 to an airport official. Given the huge number of holes in the ground and the generally dilapidated state of the airport, I found it hard to see how such monies were being used.

'There's no airport tax here,' I said. 'You're just going to take the $25 and keep it, aren't you?'

'Airport tax, $25,' repeated the local extortionist.

'I'm the only person standing here, there's no toilet, no gift shop, you can't buy a knick-knack or anything. The whole place is bombed. It's cold. Where is my $25 going?'

'There's your plane out there. If you want to be on it, $25 airport tax.'

So I slammed $25 down on the counter as hard as I could, and the official picked up my bags and threw them out of the building onto the runway where they burst open, scattering my belongings everywhere. He and his colleagues stood by laughing while I gathered everything up.

That was $25 well spent.

Back in Phnom Penh journalists at the Foreign Correspondents' Club told me there was a big story at Pailin, which was run by Pol Pot's former number two, Engsari. He had his own army of about 6000 armed militia working for him, operating mainly around the border with Thailand.

It sounded like the wild west.

I thought that if I went there I might find the trail that led to Pol Pot himself. Why wouldn't he want to speak to me?

At a town called Batdambang I found a young man who spoke English and offered to pay for someone to fill in for him while he came along with me to help out and be my translator.

We hired a Toyota ute with a driver. This was a part of Cambodia that still showed all the effects of Pol Pot's destructive regime. There were mortar holes in the road as big as spa pools. There were also lots of mines still in the ground, so you followed tracks where people had walked as the safest option.

We were headed for a village where I had been told fighting was going on. As we approached I could see people laying mines, which was against every law you could think of. The UN had sent people into Cambodia to clear the mines for years and here were people effectively coming along behind them laying new ones.

The road narrowed to one lane. On either side was low dense bush which I had been told would almost certainly be mined. Suddenly we came to a clearing where there were tanks firing on the town.

Against his instincts, I persuaded my interpreter to attempt to talk to the soldiers who were engaged in this conflict. I sat down on a box of ammunition and waited while he tried and failed dismally to convince someone to come out of his tank and be interviewed.

We explored a little more and found a group of about 12 people who had fled from the village and they told us terrible stories of the rapes and killing that had been going on. There was a *Time* magazine journalist there and when I told him we planned to keep going in the general direction of the village, he knelt down and he held my legs and said: 'I'm going to be the last person to ever touch your legs. You are not seriously going down there are you?'

'I'm just going to see what it's like just a bit further down.'

'You are either brave or very fucking stupid. There is no way you'd get me any further down there. We are pulling out.'

'Are you going to take these people with you?' I asked.

'All of these people will be dead within half an hour,' he said. 'We're going, we're out of here now.' And with that he was off. My driver was worried that if we went any further and the road got any narrower, we wouldn't be able to turn around, which was something we might need to do in a hurry if people started firing at us. Driving off the road wasn't an option.

'If you drive off the road, you go over a mine, you're all dead,' he said.

I didn't believe that. I thought you would just be wounded and die later.

'Tell him we'll go just a little bit further down the road,' I told my interpreter.

So we drove painfully slowly and carefully along. There was a lot of gunfire and a lot of movement in the trees. Then even I saw sense.

'Okay, we can turn around here,' I said, and as we were about to do so an old man ran out of the bush carrying a sack with blood pouring out of it. It turned out to contain bits of his grandson that he had gathered up after the boy had been killed by a mine.

We got the old man on the back of the ute and kept going. As we drove away we could sense people coming behind us ready to kill us, but they were moving slowly. It was war in slow motion because no one wanted to stand on a mine or set off a booby trap. We got back to the clearing where the villagers were.

'Every one of these people I want on the back of this ute, get these people on the back of this ute now,' I said. The interpreter was terrified. He was gingerly helping an old woman up.

'Just fucking throw her on and get out of here,' I yelled. Against all common sense I also tried to get through to Radio

Pacific to describe what was happening, which would have been brilliant radio, but I couldn't get a signal and really there were other claims on my attention. Just as we had got everyone on the vehicle and started to turn around, bullets began buzzing around us, fired by people we couldn't see from inside the bush. We got everyone back to the main highway, where we just dropped them off. I know they would all have been killed if we hadn't been there to get them out of danger.

Our next destination was Pailin, which was just as dangerous. This was the last hurrah for the Khmer Rouge, whose numbers had been whittled away to a tiny fraction of what they had been. Engsari controlled this part of the world with his private army during the day, but the Khmer Rouge would come out at night.

The driver left us when we got there and I was left with my satellite phone, a briefcase full of cigarettes and money to bribe my way out of problems, and my interpreter, who was no less scared than he had been. We fetched up at a bombed-out hospital which a girl of about 14 was running as a hotel. She rented us a ward.

My interpreter was more scared of getting malaria than anything else. It would have been fatal for him, not because he would have died from it but because it would have prevented him from working. So when we went to bed we were wrapped up in mosquito nets like two mummies. I was using my briefcase full of money as a pillow and the ambient temperature was approximately a million degrees.

'Are you frightened, Mr Henry?' said my interpreter in the dark.

'No,' I said. 'I'm wary. How about you, are you frightened?'

'I'm very, very frightened.'

'Fear will achieve nothing,' I said. 'There's no point in being frightened but tell me if you were frightened, what would you be frightened of?'

'Where do I begin?' he said. 'I can hear the gunfire, I can hear the screaming. Can you not hear those things?'

'Yes, I'm aware of those but you must never think that screaming is necessarily just down to people being shot.'

'I'm frightened of mosquitoes.'

'Now that's reasonable, let's worry about mosquitoes.'

There was another long silence before he spoke again.

'What are you thinking, Mr Henry?'

'I'm thinking there could be a radio award in this for me,' I said. Which was true. I spent a lot of time in foreign parts worrying about having a great award-winning story that no one would ever hear because it was so hard to get them out and on air. At other times, I started to tell people stories and ended up not telling them the truth of what happened simply because it was so incredible I couldn't expect them to believe it.

An example of something in that category occurred this night in the hospital. As we lay there, we heard horrible screaming. It was clearly a young person's voice and it was very close.

'We need to go and find out what's happening here,' I said.

I guess the interpreter was more scared of being on his own than of whatever we would find so he followed along behind. I took my cigarettes with me, just in case. This was a system I had developed for defusing tensions. No matter what, someone will always let you take out a cigarette if you say you want one. It's a good way of buying time. And if you can offer someone a cigarette you form a small but useful bond.

All of a sudden, as we walked along outside in the near dark, we were confronted at gunpoint by the Khmer Rouge. There was a gun at my chest. My interpreter was knocked to the ground and a bayonet held at his throat.

The only edge you can have in a situation like that is novelty value. You play on the fact that these people would not have been expecting to bump into a white man. Just as when someone has a heart attack and there is a golden hour in which they can be saved if they get medical attention, in a case like this there is a golden minute. If you're still alive after a minute, you have a good chance of surviving.

'Just don't say anything,' I yelled at my interpreter, who was whimpering quietly on the ground. I figured that shouting at him almost made me one of them. I also noticed the screaming had stopped, so these were presumably the people who had been responsible for it.

'I'm lost,' I said to the Khmer Rouge. 'Do you speak English?'

There was no reply.

'Do you smoke?' I said. Every second was like an hour. I told them I was staying quite close but had got lost in the dark. While I was saying this I reached into my pocket. I felt these men bristle as I did so, but they relaxed when they saw I was only getting my cigarettes. I slowly opened the cigarette packet and pulled a few out. I put one in my mouth and offered the leader of the group one.

After an awfully long time — at least two seconds — he put his gun down, put his hand in his pocket and took out a coin, which he gave me as he took the cigarette. At that moment I knew everything was going to be all right.

'Just get up and start to walk back down the path,' I said to my interpreter. As he did so I took out my matches and lit our cigarettes. 'Have a good night,' I said to the gunmen. I turned and walked a few steps before stopping and handing him the packet, which was half full. Then we walked back to the hospital, wrapped ourselves up again and eventually got to sleep.

When I got back to Masterton I went to a jeweller and had that coin put on a chain. I wore it for a while but stopped because the last thing an obsessive-compulsive person needs is a fucking lucky coin.

Not long after, I gave up on the search for Pol Pot, even though I had been able to find out where his base was. The main reason

I gave up was that two people whose judgement I trusted told me with absolute certainty that if I persisted I would be hunted down and killed before I got there. If I had thought I would be killed on the way back from seeing him, I probably would have continued but there really didn't seem any point if I wasn't even going to lay eyes on him.

The enigma of Pol Pot drew me to Cambodia. When I went to southern Sudan I didn't have a story in mind but I was fascinated that this was the site of the longest-running civil war in Africa — a conflict that would endure for more than two decades. There were Muslim/Arab Africans in the north, largely supported by the government, persecuting the Christian Africans based in the south.

I also wanted to cover the relief effort there and was travelling with a couple of people from World Vision. I went on an aid flight in an ancient Hercules that even the New Zealand Air Force would have spurned. To save money they don't land and they don't use parachutes when making drops of Unimix, which is a food that has been developed for people with malnutrition. They double bag the food and fly as low as they can before letting it fall. That's quite safe because it's desert so there's nothing to hit. Pilots in such areas tend to be flyers who can't get work for regular airlines — ageing alcoholics, in other words.

From the plane I looked down on the parched landscape where hundreds of thousands of people faced imminent death by starvation. You're so low you can see their faces as they look up and often they don't know whether the plane will drop food or bombs — save their lives or end them.

Inside Sudan, I stayed in a compound with aid workers. I couldn't work out how to convey to an audience what it means when you say 300,000 people are facing death. The figure is so large it's incomprehensible. I decided to make it a story about one person. I found an eight-year-old girl, called Acolgern. Her whole family was dead, and the extent of her possessions was a string of beads her mother had given her. I just followed her for a day as she waited patiently in queues to be given a handful of Unimix.

People walked for days to get to this camp when they heard there might be food. I watched stick figures hobbling out of the horizon, with barely any will to live left by the time they arrived. Sometimes it was simply too late and they sat down under trees to die. There wasn't enough food for the people and there weren't enough aid workers to help everyone who needed it. In many cases the people had faced starvation before. They were brought back to health to go through the whole cycle again while their country was being fought over.

They were very powerful stories. They were about people living their lives simultaneous with ours. They look up through their dying eyes and they see us fly over in business class. Our lives are all totally intermeshed even though we may never meet.

A New Zealand journalist, of course, had less life-threatening but equally pre-occupying concerns. The huts where we slept were home to termites that fell on you and bit you unless the large lizards who also shared the huts got to them first and ate them. When they got a bit much I moved outside to sleep, on a pile of sticks because you needed to be above the ground away from the snakes. The only trouble with sleeping outside was the hyenas, so you had to weigh up a lot of things when you were deciding where to sleep.

The rain came while I was there waiting to get out. Everything turned green, everyone was able to drink and the guinea-worm eggs hatched in the water. So as they consumed the life-saving water, people also swallowed guinea worms which grew in their bodies, feasting off such nourishment as they could provide and then exploding out of them, usually through their faces or arms. People with guinea-worm wounds were everywhere.

The sanitary conditions were appalling. The toilet was a pit that you tried desperately to avoid using. The first time I went to try and crouch on it, the smell was too much and I suddenly found I didn't need to go. The second time, I got a bit closer, but the same thing happened again. Likewise the third time. The fourth time, I simply had to use it. I was crouching almost ready to go when bats flew out around my arse.

When it came time to leave, we were to meet a plane at Bahra-Ghazal. There was a severe fuel shortage and this would be the last one to fly for several months. I did not want to miss it. We waited and waited and there was no sign of the plane, which first had to pick up some people about four hours' drive away.

'Get on the UHF,' I said to one of the aid workers waiting with us. 'Where is this plane? I don't hear it.'

You can hear planes from a long way away in the desert. Finally we got through and found the plane had crashed. We learnt the pilots thought they could take off again, but they wouldn't be able to land because of damage to the front of the plane.

I said something that you don't often hear: 'I would rather get on a plane that I know can't land than stay in this fucking country a minute longer. Tell them not to take off. We're coming.' They said they would wait three hours but after that they had to leave whether we were there or not. So began a panicked drive across the desert to get to our plane.

At one point we were passing through a small village of a few huts and there was a beautiful, beautiful woman, 19 or 20, glistening in the sun and the heat, completely naked and washing herself down with a gourd using water from a fresh puddle. In the middle of the war and famine and ghastliness it was the most beautiful thing I had ever seen. As we drove past she lifted this gourd up and the water tumbled down over her breasts, down between her legs to the sand.

We carried on driving and I kept begging the driver to go faster.

I know I say FUCK A LOT ∴ Soary

We were driving through the ruins of people's lives — every village seemed to have been bombed or burnt. Finally there was a speck on the horizon that eventually turned into a plane.

When we saw the damage it looked like the plane had no chance of taking off. Its tail was up in the air and its nose was buried in the desert. There was a large number of people standing around looking at what would probably be their new home because there was no way this thing was ever going to move.

'Get all of the baggage out and ready to load,' I said. 'If nothing else, for a moment in time, let us at least imagine we are leaving on this plane.'

I walked over to the pilots.

'How bad is it?' I said. 'It doesn't look too bad to me.'

'I reckon if we weight down the back and pivot it we might be able to lift the nose and take off,' one said.

'Well, that's all that matters, isn't it?' I said encouragingly.

I got on the plane and one of the pilots stood at the back and pointed at the heaviest of the people standing around.

'You, you and you,' he said. 'You're all coming to Kenya.' They obligingly got on. There were no seats in the plane, just half-arsed benches and webbing to hang on to. The pilot climbed in last.

'It could be iffy,' he said. 'Wind your limbs through these ropes.'

And miraculously we took off. The noise inside this thing was fantastic, the vibration was extraordinary but it lumbered into the air. The people who were being relocated went pale.

It was a perfect flight and not long before we could see our destination. Then an alarm started to sound and a mechanical voice began to repeat 'landing gear, landing gear'. The co-pilot got out of his seat, got a broom, opened a hatch in the floor and poked the landing gear, which had got jammed, to force it down. Then he turned to us.

'This is going to be a very rough landing,' he said redundantly. 'It's not going to be a crash landing, it's going to be a rough landing. What I want you to do is get out of the plane with urgency when we stop.' I was happy to go along with that.

The plan was to have the plane going as slowly as possible before its front hit the ground. Recovering alcoholics or not, the pilots pulled off a perfect landing, but we still seemed to be going very fast when the nose crunched into the ground and started shaking everyone around wildly. It was uncomfortable but nothing could overwhelm the joy of knowing that we were in Lokichoggio, Kenya, and there was even the possibility of a poor-quality shower before the end of the day.

Finally we ploughed to a halt. The deafening noise ceased and all you could hear was the whimpering of the injured. Two men carrying buckets ran across the runway to the plane. They were the airport's fire service.

The next day we were on a flight to Nairobi. I was starting to feel some uncertainty in the belly area because I had had a big feed the night before. We took off in our small plane for the two and a half hour flight to Wilson airport, 5 kilometres south of Nairobi. After about an hour the person in the seat in front of me, whose belly was in no doubt, exploded. Within milliseconds an unbearable stench filled the plane.

My first thought was: 'Thank God it's not me.' My second thought was: 'I think I'm going to explode, too. Just let me make it to the airport, just let me get into a toilet in the airport.'

I was almost gagging and had another hour and a half of this to look forward to. Shit continued to seep out of this man. His seat was touching my knees and my feet were under it. It was certain that no one was going to leave that plane without at least having some of his shit on them. When we finally landed and the door opened, people crawled over each other's heads to get out and away from him and the horror. I didn't explode until much later that night, back in my room after dinner.

That trip embodied all that was both good and bad about

being an international correspondent. You'd go to something, you would face death, you would see the worst of the world, you would see the worst deprivation, you would see the most wondrous beautiful things. And take Imodium to be sure you won't explode.

I decided I wanted to stop the travelling after nearly dying — ironically, not far from home.

When I went on a trip I left my car in Auckland and drove home to Homebush when I got back. The longer I spent being an international correspondent, the worse my driving got. I was going faster, taking corners more quickly and one night on a back road I took a corner too fast and shot off the road and over a bank.

'That was my fault,' was the pointless thought that went through my head. I didn't consider for a moment that I would be hurt. Look at all the incredibly dangerous experiences I had survived. And sure enough, within moments I was on my feet and able to stop a passing farmer who helped me get the car back on the road, and I drove it home with bits hanging off it. But I knew I couldn't keep doing that.

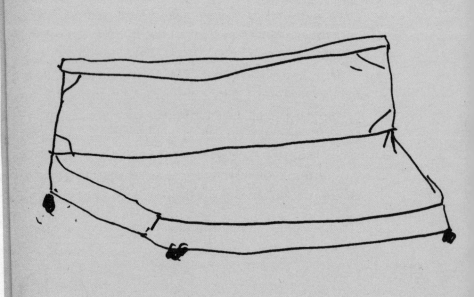

The couch of death

CHAPTER 16 STANDING JOKE

" I HAD ALWAYS BEEN FASCINATED BY POLITICS, AND THOUGH I HAD NEVER SERIOUSLY CONSIDERED RUNNING, I CERTAINLY HADN'T RULED IT OUT. 'GOD, I COULD BE A GOOD POLITICIAN', IS A PHRASE THAT RAN THROUGH MY HEAD REASONABLY FREQUENTLY. IT SEEMED TO ME ILLOGICAL THAT YOU COULDN'T ACTUALLY GO INTO PARLIAMENT AND ACHIEVE SOMETHING. WHY WERE SO MANY OF THEM A WASTE OF BLOODY SPACE? "

I HAD ALWAYS BEEN fascinated by politics, and though I had never seriously considered running, I certainly hadn't ruled it out. 'God, I could be a good politician', is a phrase that ran through my head reasonably frequently. It seemed to me illogical that you couldn't actually go into Parliament and achieve something. Why were so many of them a waste of bloody space? And this was in the days when they weren't nearly as big a waste of space as they are now.

I had been living in the electorate for some time when a couple of Wairarapa National Party people approached me to stand.

'I'm not even a member of the party,' I said coyly.

'But you're a National supporter,' they pointed out, and indeed I was. At least, my political beliefs were more closely aligned with the philosophy of the National Party than any other party. National was going to have to work its way around the fact my non-membership meant that I technically didn't qualify to stand for them, but they were confident that they could do that.

Part of the appeal was that my peripatetic lifestyle had meant much less family time than I was happy with. Everywhere I travelled I met journalists whose families had been left in tatters by their careers and, as much of a domestic strain as politics would be, it was more stable and less life-threatening than being a foreign correspondent.

The people who wanted me to stand were confident that I'd win selection, even though they didn't know who was going to be up against me, if anyone, at that point.

I went to see Derek Lowe, with whom I had discussed the possibility of politics over the years. With Derek in his office was someone I at first took to be the Angel of Death but who turned out to be Stephen Joyce, who now owned the company.

We sat on the Couch of Death, enjoying Derek's panoramic view of Auckland Harbour, and it soon became apparent that politics or not, the role of international correspondent was not one that Stephen saw having long-term relevance to Radio Pacific. In short, everyone thought it a good idea for the role to be terminated. In short, I was fired. That made it much easier for me given how I always feel I am letting people down when I resign. I would much rather be sacked.

I instantly forgot I was ever a foreign correspondent and set my sights on winning the safe seat of Masterton, then held with a majority of more than 8000 by the Deputy Prime Minister, Wyatt Creech, who had decided to become a list MP. Masterton had been in National hands for a good number of years.

The other person vying for selection as the National candidate could not have been more different. For a start, he belonged to the National Party — in fact, had been a conscientious hard worker and party stalwart of many years. He was generally regarded by many as in line to succeed Wyatt. I was the outsider to start with, who people had heard of because I had a media profile and had run a business and created jobs in the area. For reasons still known only to themselves the committee selected me as the National Party candidate for Wairarapa in the 1999 general election. To be honest, I was clearly the better man. Once selected, I took a year off any work commitments and put what money I had into the campaign.

I had a few things I believed in that I should have told voters and the party straight off, but the nature of political campaigning in New Zealand is that you moderate things. I should have let the electorate know very clearly that I believe New Zealand used to be a country populated by people who were engrossed in building it, and who knew that if they didn't build it, it wouldn't exist. They were building a future for themselves and their children. I believed we should all still think like that.

But in just a few generations, we have become a country full of people who expect to be handed things on a plate; of people who wonder why their grandparents didn't build roads and other infrastructure that would last forever, and expect someone else to do it for them now. Thankfully some people still do those things, but individual initiative is thin on the ground, which is extraordinary because arguably we're all still pioneers. People think they have a right to a good life that will be created for them, and with that has come distrust of people who seem to be better off.

I didn't want to be a list MP. I was standing for an electorate and I should have been cut loose to win it over. If I had said more of what I believed, it might have been different. I think I said just enough to burn off some people. After that, I was reduced to a large extent to being an apologist for the stupid things National had done over the last nine years.

I support what National stands for, not what they do. Anyone who reads the party constitution — which an alarming number of people in the organisation haven't — would be likely to think it sounded like the way to go. Ultimately I don't care who people vote for. I care about how New Zealand is run. I was one of the biggest supporters of some of the things that Labour did because they were the right things to do. Also it helps that I've got a strong social conscience and there's nothing in the party constitution that would indicate you shouldn't have a strong social conscience.

The campaign launch didn't bode well. The highlight was John Falloon's honky-tonk rendition of 'God Defend New Zealand' on the piano, a guaranteed crowd pleaser. The guest speaker was the Minister of Finance, Bill English, and when he spoke you could see people looking around, hoping desperately that John Falloon was going to come back and give us another tune. Even I almost fell asleep during Bill English.

A candidate meeting in Dannevirke was typical of what went on in the campaign. The sort of people who go to political meetings in the Wairarapa are exactly those people with a pioneering spirit I was after. They were hard workers in the rural heartland, but they're older people. They are also the last people you would expect to vote for a candidate like my extremely high-profile transsexual Labour opponent — and former Today FM employee — Georgina Beyer. But it turned out that if you were a voter in the Wairarapa in 1999 who wanted to send a National Government a clear 'fuck you' message, a transsexual Labour candidate was *exactly* who you would vote for.

At the meeting were Georgina, myself, Cathy Casey for the Alliance, some fool for the Greens and a greater fool for Act.

The audience were there to listen to people who could safely say anything they wanted, knowing they would never have to deliver on their promises, and to wait for the National guy to stand up so that they could boo me because I represented all the evils of an incumbent government and the tide was going out on that.

The Alliance speaker essentially promised a public hospital at the end of every street, and she was applauded. The Labour candidate agreed that would be a great idea and said the Alliance couldn't do it but Labour could. The Act candidate fumbled his way through the most extraordinary load of bollocks you could possibly imagine. So no surprises there. And I glazed over for the Green candidate. Everyone was met with rapturous applause, except for the Act candidate.

I walked on stage to the sound of booing. I looked out at the audience and knew we were on the same side. They were people who worked like navvies on their farms every day.

'I'm appalled with you,' I told them. 'You just applauded a woman who has said that you can look forward to a public hospital at the end of every street. You're not stupid, are you? You must know that that will never happen and yet you applaud her.'

I pointed out that when people are asked what qualities they want their politicians to have, honesty is always near the top of the list. 'Evidenced today is the fact that you don't want honesty at all. You want to be sold a lie. We cannot afford the sort of health system the Labour and Alliance candidates are promising. In fact, New Zealand can probably only really afford one public hospital for the whole country, plus a lot of very fast ambulances. So let's talk real. You people have worked bloody hard for everything other people are taking advantage of, and you're now applauding when those people who haven't worked very hard want to take more of the wealth that you've built up.'

My electorate people were appalled, but I knew there wasn't

a vote in that room for me to win. They worked hard and were great, but they were used to Wyatt and I still don't think they had come to terms with MMP. The whole political landscape was changing very quickly — I was one of the first candidates in New Zealand to use the internet to campaign. That was never going to be a huge hit for me, though, because no one had the internet. It was another option but it was really not much more than a website address that was twice as long as my car.

Wyatt Creech came to several meetings to support me, and so he could be seen to be passing on the mantle, but he was also Deputy Prime Minister and his time was limited. He was busy overseeing National's whole campaign and helping a lot of other new candidates.

He took me to the local fast food chicken outlet once to try to convince me I would win. 'Look, like all candidates just starting out, I know you're worried,' he said. 'I know you think you're going to lose but it won't happen. You don't overturn an 8000 seat majority.'

'Yes,' I said, 'but Wyatt just have a look at where they voted last time. Look at where that 8000 majority came from last time and you'll see that it doesn't exist anymore.' All sorts of things were happening to that vote. People were dying off for one.

'Look, you're going to lose a few thousand, but you're in an electorate where you can afford to lose a few thousand. You will be the next Member of Parliament in the Wairarapa.'

For a split second I was completely at ease. Then I reverted to reality.

'Is it possible that I know more about this than all these people?' I said to Rachael. There were analysts and a huge party organisation. They couldn't all be idiots. But they failed to look back prior to the last election, when Wyatt had lost. He only got in after a lot of legal to-ing and fro-ing and with a slim majority. Wairarapa was all over the shop.

Healthcare, education and welfare

Medicine and the social policy around it interest me greatly. There are three things we know for sure about healthcare: (1) We have very good state healthcare in this country; (2) It isn't as good as it should be; (3) It is never going to be as good as people want it to be.

It would be good if healthcare and education and the justice system, which are all core things, could be taken away from political parties. We should acknowledge the minimum we will accept and work towards an ideal we all agree on. But first, we have to realise how lucky we are and then, in our own reasonable, non-victimising way, fight both to retain what we have and to improve it.

Generally, I love user pays, and I hate non-user pays. But I am happy as a non-user to pay tax for some things. You have to pay for people who, for one reason or another, have been dealt a bad hand through no fault of their own and need help. Obviously you want a good health system, you want good stopgaps to look after people, you want good social policy.

Apart from those things, all I want to pay for is what I use. I'm prepared to pay a proper price for that and I would be able to afford to if I wasn't sucked dry paying for all the things I don't use.

But the killer was the combination of anti-government resentment and Georgina Beyer's huge profile. She was the first candidate with any appeal who Labour had put up for some time. People saw her as the courageous underdog and me as the rich arsehole. And they failed to see that, thanks to MMP, they could have had both the underdog via the party vote and the arsehole via the electorate vote.

The Alliance candidate, Cathy Casey, was also funnelling people to Labour. She was a great friend of Georgina Beyer and the author of her book, which was released during the campaign. It was the first time she had represented the Alliance in the electorate as their candidate, replacing Dave McPherson, an extremely popular politician whose massive support from the previous election was clearly not going to stay with Cathy.

The Minister of Senior Citizens came to help me by addressing a meeting. It was almost like he was working for the opposition, though it's not hard to make old people stampede. It seemed to me like he didn't even understand his own portfolio let alone anyone else's. Often when I was in the company of sitting MPs I found myself thinking something was very wrong. I knew more about politics than anyone else in the room.

I would also admit it when I didn't understand policy fully. I read all the policy documents, but they sometimes made no sense. I expressed doubts. At that point my colleagues said, 'The policy's not that important.' Then I realised that I had a better grasp of policy than any of them because I at least understood the impact of the policy. I could understand what people were worried about. I didn't know dates and document numbers but I could answer questions by telling people what I believed and what I wanted to do for them.

Prime Minister Jenny Shipley came to help. That may have been my idea, but it was not a vote-winning manoeuvre at this stage. I took her around some schools and a couple of businesses. We made the most of photo opportunities, and the media followed along obligingly.

I got to sit in her car and it infuriated me that she didn't have the New Zealand flag flying. I thought then and there, one day I'll be the Prime Minster and I'll have the New Zealand flag flying on my car all the time, even when I'm not in it. Why bother being Prime Minister if you're not going to have your country's flag flying on the official car?

I had a New Zealand flag flying on my old $6000 Volvo, which was painted with my election advertising. I still have the New Zealand and US flags flying at my home. I got a lot of flak just for driving a Volvo, even though it was the cheapest car I ever owned. People used to boo as I drove around the district. Whether they were booing me, the car or the flag I'm still not sure.

However, Jenny Shipley was very generous with her time, and we ended the day back at Homebush with a do for about 80 key supporters. It was very pleasant but I remember it most because the girls climbed up onto the landing on our big staircase in the vestibule when she finished making her speech, and Sophie thanked her and handed her a New Zealand flag that she had bought in the two-dollar shop the day before.

The family were brilliant throughout. The girls turned up to dreary functions in their party frocks and Rachael worked hard to keep the day-to-day domestic worries in the background. I was so proud of them. We had campaign headquarters at the house, which wasn't easy. I didn't focus enough on the family that year because I was very worried about the election slipping away from me. I was in to win. Campaigning wasn't a part-time job. I used to look at my rivals and see them doing their day jobs while electorate organisations were doing the work for them.

My father came to visit me once during the campaign. He was based between Singapore and Australia at the time. It was typical of him to just turn up every couple of years or so. 'I'm in New Zealand. I'm in a rental car, I'm on my way down' or 'I'm in Wellington, I've just arrived. Can you come and pick me up?'

He didn't have much time for politicians, and I was increasingly coming to share his views, but I think he may have been a little bit proud because he gave me a cheque for $10,000.

'This is just to help out,' he said. That meant a lot, and it did help because I was making no money and my overdraft just kept going up.

I lost the election. Once again, the exciting part of the project would have been getting in. I saw myself possibly as a one-term politician but there were things I wanted to achieve in that one term. I wanted to shake the country up and also have the chance to be an honest politician. I suspect I could be Prime Minister by now if I had succeeded. If you have a look at the way things went when Labour got in and the way National completely disintegrated, it was that National intake who are in very strong positions now. I was the orator. I had the dream. I could see the light. But it wasn't to be. No matter.

There's a wonderful photograph which the *Wairarapa Times-Age* took on election night. It shows Wyatt and me in the Frank Cody Lounge of the Masterton Town Hall. There is no mistaking that we have lost.

The night itself was torture because I knew what the result was going to be, but our figures were among the last to come in. I was in the odd position of waiting for the inevitable to occur. But there were people around me who had still not accepted that I would not win. They spent the evening saying things like 'Shit, it's not looking good. Obviously, we're going to win but it's going to be close', before moving on to 'Just a couple of booths could change everything', and 'It's not over till it's over'; so when the final result came they were genuinely shocked and that shock and disappointment is somehow contagious.

And, of course, I had to make my dignified, conciliatory, morale-boosting, gracious speech of concession at the end of the evening, when all I wanted to say was, 'I told you so. Maybe if we'd done it another way it would have been different.' As well as myself and my family I felt I had disappointed my wonderful campaign team. The National Party had disappointed me.

Soon afterwards, true to form, the *Wairarapa Times-Age* ran a story about how bitter I must have been because I hadn't taken the election stickers off my car. It was the only car I had, and they had seen me driving around the day after the election with my campaign paint job still on it. Apparently candidates who are not bitter stay up all night peeling election stickers off their cars when they lose. Like most newspapers, they have their fair share of arseholes.

A few years later I was asked to comment on that time, and I said I didn't win because of the pig ignorance in the electorate. That has been quoted several times subsequently by the *Wairarapa Times-Age* — quite recently, in fact.

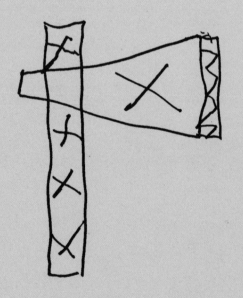

Axe

CHAPTER 17
THE ONE
THING I KNOW

> **" I WASN'T BRILLIANT WITH BABIES. I COULDN'T DO THE NAPPY THING. ACTUALLY, I COULD. I HAD TO DEAL WITH FAR WORSE, FAR MORE FULLY DEVELOPED NAPPY SITUATIONS AS AN INTERNATIONAL CORRESPONDENT. BUT IN THE CASE OF THE CHILDREN I REASONED THERE WAS NO POINT US BOTH GETTING OUR HANDS DIRTY . . . "**

WHEN RACHAEL AND I got married my vision for a family extended exactly as far as one daughter. In the end I got three. I don't know why I wasn't keen on having a boy. Perhaps because boys are lovely for a while but then they turn into people like me. A daughter, on the other hand, seemed like a fine thing.

I had just moved a step beyond my father. 'You don't want too many children,' he advised me. That was rich, coming from someone who hadn't wanted any. At least I was up for one. Actually, I was up for two, because when Rachael got pregnant I said to myself, 'If this is a boy we will definitely be having another one.'

Lucy was born in 1988 in the old maternity annex of Masterton Hospital in the middle of a horrendous storm that rattled its old foundations. Trucks were blown over on the road that night. Because I was the breakfast host on Radio Wairarapa, which passed for a celebrity in those parts, there was a photo of us in the *Wairarapa Times-Age* the next morning. Next to it was a picture of a truck lying on its side. I couldn't imagine why anyone would be even slightly interested in what had happened to the truck and its driver when they could be looking at my daughter.

I wasn't brilliant with babies. I couldn't do the nappy thing. Actually, I could. I had to deal with far worse, far more fully developed nappy situations as an international correspondent. But in the case of the children I reasoned there was no point us both getting our hands dirty, and since Rachael was going to be there all the time, it made sense for her to be the one.

Our parenting was very structured. Rachael stopped teaching to be a stay-at-home mum. What's more, she enjoyed it. She is one of those natural mothers who love every bit of it and excel at every aspect of parenting. She was even good with other mothers and had get togethers in the house. I occasionally came home to find a circle of topless women in my lounge with their breasts out and wondered why I didn't find it even remotely attractive.

It soon become clear that left to her own devices Rachael would have kept conceiving well into double figures. I was more than happy when she wanted a second child. Sophie was born two years later and Bella two years after that.

Every time the subject comes up people say, 'Did you want a boy?' as though we kept trying in order to rectify a mistake of nature. Obviously, not having a son meant I missed out on things like rugby practice. Equally obviously, given my lack of interest in sport, that has not been a sacrifice. Fortunately, none of the girls was particularly interested in ball sports.

Lucy was spectacularly uncoordinated but would give anything a go. Having a go and not persisting has always been my philosophy and I've always made that clear to them.

Lucy could never be accused of not giving things a go — she was in the choir, lead performer in the musical at the school, did ballet and tried ball sports. She got so excited if she touched the ball. Usually if it came near her she threw her hands in the air and you could see her thinking, 'Am I supposed to touch that?'

Rachael is an academic and believes academic qualifications are vital. I, on the other hand, believe personality will carry you through anything. I worry that being hell-bent on academic achievement can suck the life blood out of a human being. If you can manage both, that's great.

I wanted them to have a similar childhood to mine — but without the emotionally distant father. I wanted them to enjoy freedom, be close to nature and have the opportunity to try lots of experiences.

In Carterton, and later in Homebush, they could come home, dump their bags on the floor and head straight out into the garden. They made up songs and games. They loved trees. Some of our trees had huge supple branches they could play on like rocking horses. They gave some of them names, like Jockey Rocky Lines. We had a deep hedgerow in front of the house, made up of trees that were deciduous so you could just see through it in the winter, but in summer it was completely impenetrable. They were convinced, partly because I had convinced them, that fairies lived in the hedgerow. Sophie saw the fairies from her room. We created a magical world. I had a full stage built into the hedgerow, wired with twinkly lights as well as spotlights and a sound system for when we put on shows. At Christmas I hired a performer to host the evening and we invited the whole street. They came with blankets and sat on the lawn while all the kids did a turn. It was the professional's job to encourage everyone and most of the neighbours got up and did something.

But to some extent, both the international correspondent work and then my attempt to win Wairarapa brought the magic to an end. Magic is time-consuming and takes a lot of energy. I didn't value it quite as much then as I do now. Those were the best years of my life and I had no idea. If there is one thing that I would change, if I could go back, I would try to appreciate more the value of that time.

One of the things that's organised very badly in life is that most of us have small children at an age when we are also focused on things that we hope will establish our — and their — security and prosperity. You know these lovely things are happening here and now but you're also focused on the future. And you kid yourself you are doing things that take you away from your children for your children. I was looking forward to being able to take the kids wherever we wanted and being able to do whatever we wanted. But what was happening at the time was better than anything we could have done.

It's nice to be able to give them all university educations but they will probably be able to do that themselves if you've set them up properly. The important thing is to just live in the moment at that time and just exploit it for all its worth. It's basically the only thing I've learnt in my entire life that's worth learning. Not only is it the carefree time when children should be having fun, it's also the time when money matters least. Kids don't know if you have lots of money and they certainly don't want it themselves. They have no idea. I used to think the people having a cup of tea and a lamington at Farmers were rich.

How and why to say no to your child

How: Say 'no'.
Why: I was walking along the street with Bella, my youngest daughter, and as we passed a pet shop she said, 'I'd like a dog'. I didn't say no, I said, 'Great, let's go in and have a look for one!'

Introducing Louis, the least productive, most problematic of my family members. Show name Professor Spanky. Though for obvious reasons he's never been shown.

One point on which Rachael and I differed considerably was our attitude to safety. I wasn't really that interested in it, to be honest. Thanks to her, we were probably the first family in the southern hemisphere to embrace fully the concept of the car seat.

Obviously the evidence suggests it's ludicrous to have a loose object, such as a child, rattling about in a car, but when I was a boy we used to beg the school bus driver to drive back and forth, from one side of the road to the other so we were thrown about, and he always obliged. When we were staying up north a lot and travelling back and forth, my father used to take us out in our lethal, steel Vauxhall Velox and drive fast along loose metal roads through the night, which was equally exhilarating. All inadvisable, of course, but suddenly finding myself expected to strap all my children in like astronauts just to go to the dairy came as a shock.

We compromised. For instance, if we had been out in the truck, as soon as we got to Homebush Road the girls were allowed to sit on the tray for the last leg of the journey. The free and easy approach to safety, while invigorating, didn't always end up on the right side of the ledger. You can't watch the little scallywags all the time.

Once, the day before Lucy's birthday party, I was hammering at a waratah with an axe, going ferociously, swinging the axe back and bashing it in again. All of a sudden she found something she wanted to show me.

'Daddy,' she shouted with glee, and came running towards me, just as the sharp end of the wood splitter went back. She ran straight into it. Funny what you think of in those situations. My first thought was: 'I've split my daughter's head open with an axe.'

She was screaming uncontrollably, which you don't enjoy but logically you know it's a good sign because it indicates life. Children scream all the time on a farm, so as I carried her inside Rachael had no idea how serious it was. Then she saw the blood, which was everywhere.

'What did you do?' said Rachael.

'I smashed her in the head with the axe,' I said, handing Lucy over. 'Make her better.'

As it happened, the axe must have been at the point where it was just about to swing back, so the accident had been more of a case of her running into it than it hitting her. And now she has a conversation point whenever people look at photos of her birthday party from that year.

'Oh, what's wrong with your nose?'

'Daddy hit me with the axe the day before my birthday.' She didn't even need stitches, but it's amazing how much blood there is in a nose.

Bella was involved in a similar incident. I had a big paddock at the back that I used to mow using the tractor whenever I needed to destroy some nature. I was also a great buyer of junk at farm auctions and had implement sheds full of things that probably didn't work but it didn't matter because I was never going to try to use them or even learn what they were for.

I had bought a flat-based tractor trailer for $20 at one of these auctions and used to tow things around Masterton, often at night, because if the police had seen it there would have been trouble. Sometimes the kids came too.

One night as we were coming home, Bella and one of her friends were sitting on the back of this trailer, with their legs over the end where it was hooked up to the tractor. As we drove through the paddock I went over a particularly big bump. The girls bounced up in the air, fell between the tractor and the trailer, and the trailer rolled over them. Fortunately they didn't stick their heads up, or there could have been an accident. Both of them were hysterical but apparently not hurt because they ran into the house, holding hands, with me following behind saying, 'You're fine, you're fine. Hop back on the trailer, everything's great, I'll buy you an ice-cream later.'

'Daddy's run over us with the tractor,' alleged Bella, between sobs, as she ran into the kitchen where Rachael was standing at the sink. She turned and looked at the girls and then over their heads at me.

'Rachael,' I said, 'do not believe a word they're telling you.'

'Bella, turn around,' said Rachael. And she turned around, allowing me to see the trailer tread marks that ran down her face and across her chest. Rachael then tried to introduce a ban on children riding on trailers but it didn't last because she could see the fun they were having.

That wasn't nearly as dangerous as a game we had called Fire in a Box, which is one of the most accurately named games ever invented. Certainly more so than tennis. It entailed me playing the part of a delivery man. I had a great big cardboard box with screwed-up paper in it and stood outside the house while the girls waited inside. I lit the paper, put the lid on the box and knocked on the door.

'Delivery,' I said.

'Oh, we weren't expecting anything,' the girls said. 'What is it?'

'Fire in a box for Bella.'

'Oh, we weren't expecting fire in a box.'

By now smoke was coiling out of the box.

'Do we have to sign for it?' they said from behind the door.

'Yes, I need you to sign for it.'

The challenge was to see how long you could delay opening the door or getting rid of the box.

Who was going to give in first? Was it going to be the delivery guy or one of the three recipients. Sometimes, by the time they opened the door, their father was standing there with a box that was completely ablaze.

'Oh, that's past its best, we don't want that,' they said in that case. No matter what, the game always ended with me frantically trying to get the box on the lawn before it burnt a hole in the carpet. It was so much fun, why wouldn't you do it? In the worst-case scenario, someone gets badly burnt and the house is razed to the ground. But that happens to people all the time, without the enjoyment of playing Fire in a Box.

Once we drove past a house on fire and Sophie said: 'They must have been playing Fire in a Box. They're better at it than us. No one gave in.'

Oddly, despite their affinity for fire, the girls were much less comfortable around water. Although it is one of my passions, Bella, Sophie and Rachael have no interest in boating whatsoever. Lucy pretends to be interested, for me, but they really can't see the point in investing that kind of money.

So naturally, I decided to take them on a boating holiday to show them what fantastic fun it is.

We had a 24-foot fibreglass launch that I kept at a marina in Wellington because it was too big to be regularly towed over the Rimutaka Hill.

'We're going to go across Cook Strait on holiday,' I declared.

By the time we set off, thanks to Rachael, we were practically sinking under the weight of the safety gear we had to take. On the day we were leaving the weather forecast was good. I had a very early model GPS chart plotter which took so long to find a signal that you were usually at your destination before it had fired up. That didn't bother me. How hard could it be to find the South Island?

We went out into Cook Strait and something was obviously wrong with the weather forecast because a storm had come up and this was a watery hell. We turned around and went home.

The next time we tried to leave the weather forecast failed to match the weather reality again. There were a lot of people in boats bigger than ours who were packing up and going home but I was sure the forecast would be proved right, the weather would change and we should give it a go. My crew, in their ignorance, supported me.

I knew the sea would soon be calm. It quickly grew much worse. We battened down all the hatches, so the waves crashed over the boat, and kept on going. Bella had crawled up into the bow and was trying to sleep. Sophie and Rachael were sick and clinging to anything that didn't move. Lucy had the emergency radio beacon and was also holding on to a rag she was using both to clean up her own vomit and to wipe the window so I could see how high the waves were.

In hindsight, had I known it was going to be that bad, I wouldn't have kept going, but you get to a point where it's more dangerous to turn around. I was grasping the wheel to make sure the waves didn't tip the boat over. At the same time I was telling Lucy what she should do when the boat sank.

The feedback I got was that, if they decided to have anything at all to do with me after this, which was moot, the family would not be going near a boat again if I was in it. And should we survive, they wanted to be taken straight to a hotel in Picton, where they would book flights home.

Then the water calmed down somewhat — we went from life-threatening to unpleasant. When we got to Tory Channel the water was like boiling soup, but we managed to skip over it and on the other side it was like a lagoon. It was perfect.

Within seconds the mood on the boat changed. The children wanted to stop and have a swim in the channel so of course I said yes.

'I'm going to make you all certificates, because you survived this amazing journey,' I told them. And when I got home, I did. When it was time to turn around and head back, I made the journey while they were asleep, and they woke up as we were going into Wellington Heads.

Today, Lucy is a nurse. That was something she found for herself and she is spectacular at it. Sophie is having her gap years and deciding what she wants to do. And Bella is spending an exchange year in America.

Ultimately, of course, the marriage didn't last. Rachael changed a little bit and I changed a lot. Her changes were consistent with the family staying together, mine were not.

I regret a lot of what happened then, but you can't go back and change it. People say you can't live with regret. Actually, you do, every day. But there's nothing to be gained from immersing yourself in it.

At the time it's going bad, you don't imagine there are alternatives to ending a relationship, when, of course, there are. You also don't imagine that it's damaging, when, of course, it is. You kid yourself into believing that leaving is going to be okay and the family will be different but not worse. That's bullshit. History will tell you, if you look at people you know who have done it, that it's always a disaster, but you still think you can manage it.

When it became obvious that it was broken down completely and I wasn't living there and was probably not going to live there, there was a time when the children distanced themselves from me, and that was really, really hard. I sometimes wonder, even though I consider I have brilliant relationships with them all now, if they've entirely come back. Is my relationship with them now as good as it would have been if things were different?

I like to think I handled the separation, as far as the girls were concerned, better than my parents did with me. Rachael and I both wanted the best for the children, but it's easy to say that when you are the person who has wronged someone else. For the person who has been wronged, it's a lot harder to put on a brave face for the sake of the children. Rachael was extraordinarily mature about it.

When it came time to make a settlement, we didn't surround

ourselves with lawyers and make them rich. We were both very clear that essentially what we were doing was juggling the children's money. We didn't throw their money away.

The split up was almost entirely my fault. I could have done a million things differently but whether or not that would have kept the family together I don't know.

When it happened, it was hard knowing that I had taken something away from all of us — that dream that so many people have of the perfect family unit, which had been our reality for a while. You console yourself with the idea that it's better to split up than stay in a bad marriage, but I wasn't in a bad marriage.

So I am left with regrets that I handled things the way I handled them. My family deserved better; I can console myself by thinking it could have been worse, but they did deserve better. I was capable of giving them better, but I didn't.

I've never lived with anyone else before or after my marriage. I've always been a loner. I don't know what is satisfying about coming home to a big house and sitting down and looking at furniture, but I find it satisfying. When I buy a house, I need to get one that is good for entertaining, knowing that, quite possibly, not a soul will ever come through its doors.

It's possible I don't belong in a normal relationship. My father's mother had said to my mother, 'Brian isn't the marrying kind.' Maybe there's quite a bit of that about me, but I need to be careful that I'm not saying that to excuse where I've ended up.

I am where I am because that's where I want to be. Sometimes I step back and notice what a pathetic spectacle I make sitting in my mansion, flicking through a magazine and half-watching the Living Channel. Then I might flick over to CNN for a bit. But I always end up back on the Living Channel. I wish I knew what it is that's so fascinating about watching morons deciding whether or not to buy a castle in Spain.

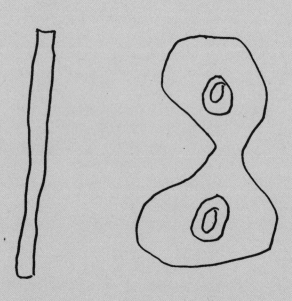

I couldn't ask my mother to draw a penis as I don't think
she'd remember what one looks like

CHAPTER 18 FACE TO FACE WITH AN UGLY PENIS

> **THE IDEA WAS THAT I WOULD BE THE RIGHT-WING CURMUDGEON AND PAM, THE FORMER ALLIANCE MP, WOULD BE THE LIBERAL LOON. I THOUGHT IT WAS A BRILLIANT IDEA BECAUSE I WAS ALWAYS LOOKING FOR SOMETHING NEW TO TRY, SO IT WAS THE NEXT CHALLENGE. PEOPLE DIDN'T REALLY UNDERSTAND IT. IN FACT THEY OFTEN COULDN'T UNDERSTAND IT BECAUSE PAM AND I ENTERTAINED EACH OTHER SO MUCH WE SPENT A LOT OF OUR TIME LAUGHING.**

FOR ABOUT TWO YEARS I was a guinea pig in a broadcasting experiment on Radio Pacific's breakfast slot called *The Morning Grill*. That slot seldom stayed the same for long, as various hosts and combinations were tried.

I had been doing nine till noon at Pacific in Auckland when Pam Corkery was doing breakfast on her own, and I used to come into the studio near the end of her show and we had reasonably amusing on-air conversations. This gave someone the idea that perhaps this could be stretched out for a whole show. The idea was that I would be the right-wing curmudgeon and Pam, the former Alliance MP, would be the liberal loon.

I thought it was a brilliant idea because I was always looking for something new to try, so it was the next challenge.

People didn't really understand it. In fact they often couldn't understand it because Pam and I entertained each other so much we spent a lot of our time laughing. One of our priorities for a news story was whether or not it made us laugh. For some reason we found anything to do with kiwifruit hilarious.

She said things that made me laugh, I said things that made her laugh and her laughing made me laugh more. Sometimes it was uncontrollable, and we knew it was uncontrollable and that it had got to the point where it couldn't possibly be entertaining. But we couldn't stop and tears were pouring from our eyes.

Often people tuned in to the sound of our laughing, listened briefly to our laughter and then, probably in pursuit of something that came closer to a traditional definition of news, tuned out again.

Occasionally we behaved like the mature broadcasters we weren't, but a fundamental problem was that the show was ahead of its time. No one had experimented with two hosts in this way, unless you count National Radio's *Morning Report*, which of course, I don't. It was also stressful because we are quite inconsistent in our views. She never knew exactly which way I would go on something and I never knew exactly which way she would go on something. The only real difference in our political beliefs on social issues was how you funded it. We basically wanted the same things, we just disagreed on how you achieved the funding for them.

She was very liberal until she lost patience with someone and I just automatically lost patience with people. It was the intolerant meeting the intolerant.

Some of the things I hate

1. Other drivers.
2. Subtitled movies. Just get a book.
3. Op shops. I find clothes impregnated with the skin of dead people very unappealing. Op shops smell like morgues.
4. Plumbing that doesn't work (prevalent in many European and African countries). If you're going to the trouble of piping it in, make sure its functioning. It's better to live in a dung hut than a palace with overflowing toilets.
5. Public holiday surcharges. If you can't afford to pay your staff, don't have any.
6. Pious businesses that have decided you can carry a handful of tiny little items home without the convenience of a plastic bag. Why don't you just shut your businesses down and become environmental campaigners?
7. Forced donations. If it's forced it's not a donation, it's a tax.
8. Councils. They're just arse.

ARSE!

These are a few of my favourite things

1. My Napier bach. After a lifetime of trying to surround myself with opulence and wealth, I love this hokey sixties bach next to the ocean just north of Napier. It's in a street that time forgot, Colleen on one side, Paul on the other and the Hopkinses down the road are the best people, and being there brings me perilously close to relaxing.
2. Concrete. Prepared properly it will seldom, if ever, let you down.
3. Candles. In a male, a possible homosexual flag.
4. Furniture. I love thinking about, talking about and buying furniture. I know, another warning flag.
5. Flags/flagpoles.
6. Gardens. Jesus is my gardener, he selects the plants that will flourish in my garden and cares for them; the rest, I cover in concrete.
7. Boats. The constant threat of death appeals to me. I could talk about boats until you slip into a coma.
8. Plinths. If it's worth buying, it's worth displaying. This book is a sort of plinth to my memories.
9. Low-wattage light bulbs and lots of them. If you can read this with ease, your wattage could well be too high.

We were seriously under-resourced. For some time we didn't even have a producer and had to set up all our own interviews, which is a time- and energy-consuming process that means you have to work intensively at both ends of the day, which affects your performance.

Management thinking was that with two hosts we only had to work half as hard. But look who the hosts were! In reality we had to work twice as hard.

They did find money to put pictures of us on the backs of buses. I was entranced by this. I had never experienced anything like it. Whenever I saw myself on the back of a bus I stopped and stared. My father made one of his spontaneous visits while these were around.

'I was driving down Khyber Pass behind a bus with an enormous picture of you on it,' he said. 'I've done a lot of things in my life but I've never been plastered on a bus.' That acknowledgement was as close as he ever got to showing me he might be proud. He died not long after, at the end of 2001.

Our ratings weren't great but they weren't falling and we hadn't taken over from a ratings winner. We were always going to be lagging behind the news monolith that is Newstalk ZB, with whom we were in direct competition. In radio, when you do something different, it can take years for the audience to get it and come along with you. When folksy old 1ZB became Newstalk it was an abysmal failure to start with and it took enormous courage for them to persist with the change of format. Now it has been at the top of the Auckland radio market for years.

In our case it was obviously going to be some time before the nation took a pair as raucous and contentious as we were to their hearts, lovable though we thought we were. And even longer before our remuneration became commensurate with our talents.

Pam is one of the kindest people I know. In fact she is almost as nice as Arch Tambakis was vile. She is an absolute perfectionist up to the point where she says, 'Fuck it. I don't want to do it anymore.' She was operating at a much higher level than anyone else at Radio Pacific. She is a world-class broadcaster but she didn't have world-class support. In the States she would have been paid an absolute fortune and have a cult following. She would have been picked up for work every day in a chauffeur-driven limousine.

It was hard for us because we weren't really that different under the skin. In the end we did a lot of things simultaneously. We were complementary when it came to knowledge — each of us knew lots about things that the other one didn't. We're both intelligent and capable people with short attention spans.

To start with, I thought she was magnificently informed on everything but I soon realised she was magnificently informed on something if she was interested in it. I envy people who can read the way she read. She was amazed that I knew nothing at all about certain things. If we were doing something on international affairs, which I was interested in, I knew all about it and found it inconceivable that Pam didn't. Equally, it was inconceivable to her that I wasn't interested in reading the new book by someone we had coming in on Wednesday.

The amount we were paid was a constant source of irritation to Pam. I was quite happy to ride along on her coat tails when she went in to fight for more money. This was usually after a show, so we would both be dead tired. It was worse on those mornings when we had been annoying each other, which we did from time to time. Pam once discovered that some much younger hosts were getting paid more than we were. She did her best to whip me up into a frenzy of indignation about these whippersnappers and I managed to get mildly agitated, which was quite good for me. Whatever we were on, she was determined to get double and considered that would still be meagre recompense.

We walked into our meeting and it went spectacularly badly. It needed to be put out of its misery. Pam had worked herself into a lather and my attempts to calm things down were too little too late. Suddenly she leapt from her seat and slammed her hands down on the table.

'You are fucking killing us,' she bellowed. 'You are sucking the fucking lifeblood out of us. It's a well-known fact that people who work shift hours are dying.'

I knew our conditions weren't stellar, but I had no idea they were life-threatening. The meeting finished soon after that and we left together.

'How do you think that went?' asked Pam.

'I don't think it went well, Pam.'

'I think they know how we feel.'

'I'm sure that's true.'

The overwhelming feeling we had from them was that they weren't at all sold on the idea of the programme continuing, let alone doubling our pay.

Also we didn't have a good reputation with interview subjects from among the small pool you have to work with in New Zealand. Being on the receiving end of an interview — if you could call it that — with the pair of us was seldom pleasant and rarely illuminating. A lot of people refused to come on the show. 'Well the last time I was interviewed on that programme I couldn't get a word in,' they frequently complained.

We survived the usual barrage of complaints. Cabinet minister George Hawkins was an interesting case because I always used to refer to him as Minister Stupid. At one point there was a suggestion from his office that there would be a Broadcasting Standards Authority (BSA) complaint laid unless an apology was given. I was very keen for that to happen. I would have preferred a defamation action because I would have relished the sight of George Hawkins turning up at court in an attempt to prove he wasn't stupid. He'd prove the opposite merely by bringing the complaint.

The man from *Puppetry of the Penis* probably had the worst of it. He came in and demonstrated how he could manipulate his penis, which is not great radio to start with.

Pam began determined to be unimpressed with his penis, and to be honest *I* was unimpressed with his penis too because, perhaps as a result of the act, it was moderately deformed.

It was an ugly penis.

And as he contorted it beyond reason, it became uglier. It wasn't funny and it wasn't entertaining. I had a slight out-of-body experience when I realised I was in a radio studio with a man who had his pants down and his penis in his hand while I sat next to Pam Corkery, who was determined to tear him apart.

The only thing that made Pam more irate than the amount we were paid was having to listen to consultants, who are the bane of every media worker's life. This was an attitude I shared. People who know next to nothing about media and much less about New Zealand and our audiences were regularly shipped over, usually from America, and paid the sort of money we weren't to tell us how to do our jobs.

'What does he know?' Pam said once. 'He is an American, he is some carpetbagger, come from another country to try and tell us how to do what we know how to do better than the rest of the world.' When she said 'we' she meant her and me but mainly her. She treated the consultants like they were trying to impress her with penis tricks. We could have used some guidance on a few things but there was no one there capable of guiding us.

For the time we did that show I spent the larger part of the day sleeping and panicking. Pam and I lived in hope that we would be funded properly and get an extra producer. But it just went on and on and on, and got harder and harder. When it ended, the most common reaction from those concerned was relief.

Pam left first, to a TV job, and I carried on doing breakfast on my own for a while. One of the things that takes on a strange level of importance when you're working early in the morning is the smell of co-workers. Pam, I remember, always smelt nice in the morning, but there was one particular morning where she smelt exceptionally good. So good in fact that we talked about it before going on air. I sniffed her up and down and discovered that the strikingly pleasing aroma was coming from her head. She felt her hair and it dawned on her that she had doused herself in air freshener.

If only our producer Kate McCallum had made the same mistake on another occasion. She was a nuggety young lady with a single-minded doggedness on the job. If you had asked her to get a pen at the moment when someone flew a plane into the Twin Towers and you said, perhaps we should do something about that, she would keep walking and say, 'Not now. I'm getting a pen.'

She was always in before me and one morning when I arrived I instantly noticed an appalling stench.

'Can you smell that?' I said to Kate.

'Can't smell anything,' she said.

It was clear to me that Kate's sensory perception was at a low ebb. I base this not only on her olfactory deficiency but also on the fact that she was still wearing a ballgown from the night before, her make-up was iffy and she had twigs in her hair.

After half an hour it became apparent that the stench came and went every time Kate went in and out of the office. Finally I pinned her to a chair and sniffed her up and down.

'Kate, this stench that I've been referring to all morning is coming from you,' I said. 'What the hell happened to you last night?'

Eventually she admitted that she had staggered home from an event at the yacht club and collapsed on her bed.

'You've been pissed on by a cat,' I said. 'A cat has pissed on you and you have come to work.'

KATE IS A VERY VERY GOOD SORT!

She then sniffed herself and even with her compromised senses had to admit the accuracy of my observation. She had discovered when she came to in the morning that she had collapsed on the cat when she went to bed. She strode home and got changed before returning to work to set up some interviews. She doesn't look terribly athletic but she can move quickly when she needs to.

While I was still doing breakfast with Pam I was contacted by Wendyl Nissen and asked if I was interested in appearing on a TV advice show she was producing called *How's Life?* It ran just before the six o'clock news on TV1 so I saw some of it most nights.

I was immediately enthusiastic. I've never mastered the art of not appearing enthusiastic in order to force up my price or make people work harder to get me. If I like an idea it shows straight away. And I'm quite capable of being enthusiastic and haggling at the same time, though I didn't bother in this case.

Part of me thought that, being television, it would probably never happen, but within a very short time I was being styled. This was a concern I raised with Wendyl at our first meeting because I know I dress badly. Fortunately, this was a show that wanted its presenters to look good so that responsibility was taken away from me and given to someone who could handle it.

The content of the letters we got asking for advice used to worry me, even more so when I found out they were all real and not made up as many people thought. I was surprised that people would write to seek advice for problems which were so obviously solvable. The letters showed that people's lives are desperately boring and ordinary. It used to frustrate me. I wondered how the other panellists could take these problems so seriously. Was that what their own lives were like?

On one of my first shows I was the last person to speak. We had a letter from a woman whose husband was obviously a prime shit. Everyone else recommended counselling. I suggested she poison him. I explained that it could be done because she had his trust and he would not expect it.

'You'll get away with it,' I went on, 'because I'm assuming you've never poisoned anyone to death before. You will be successful, but you do have to be very careful that the success doesn't go to your head and you don't keep poisoning people until you're found out.'

I watched it go to air and when the news started immediately afterwards, I'm sure Judy Bailey had been watching, because she appeared to be a combination of shocked, alarmed and amused. I thought if I could shock, alarm and amuse Judy Bailey I must be doing something right.

How's Life? started to give me a reputation as someone who spoke his mind. I was happy to be typecast in that way because it was a general niche, not one that constrained me. I actually toned things down a bit because I didn't want people to think I was saying what I said in order to be sensational. It merely sounded sensational because what other people were saying was so bland.

The host, Charlotte Dawson, was extremely entertaining. I felt her breasts twice, I think. There was nothing significant in that. Almost everyone was offered the opportunity to feel them, so I took it. The other panellists were nearly all people I had heard of but never met and I enjoyed the experience, though it would be going too far to say I liked them all. But I was amused by them. They seemed to see the show as a doorway to stardom and several became prima donnas. They had agendas and they began scheming to get those agendas met.

I thought it was fine to capitalise on something, but not to scheme to get rid of people to advance your own status. I thought it was probably a better use of time to focus on my own performance.

The other thing that surprised me was the research they put in. I looked at the letters in the green room before we went on because I figured the best TV would come from getting our reactions to the letters. Other people agonised over them and came in with lists of books that people were never going to read.

Panellists were rotated so you got different combinations on different taping days. Sometimes it was like *Survivor* with alliances being formed and plots being drawn up so people could get on more often. Some became convinced they were being deliberately overlooked. And if a new face turned up, everyone's first thought was how much of a threat they were going to be.

When the show was cancelled — for reasons that remain mysterious because I think it was a good, useful, cheap and entertaining show that I know rated well — I was one of the few people on it who wasn't devastated. The others were stunned. They lost all sense of proportion. They couldn't imagine anyone not loving their show. And them in particular. They were planning to take a live version on the road. They were going to write advice books. As far as I was concerned it was great fun but it was just a little bit of my life. I was unconcerned because I have never seen any of my jobs as a career. *How's Life?* wasn't meant to be a stepping stone to anything, though I believe Pam Corkery was once heard to comment that in my case it had created a monster.

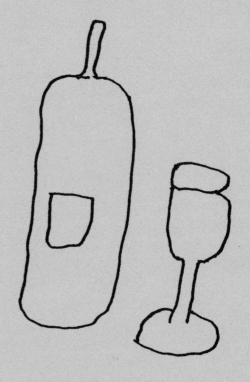

Wine

CHAPTER 19
HAD ME FOR
BREAKFAST

> **THE MEDIA HAVE ALWAYS OPERATED, AND CONTINUE TO OPERATE, ON THE SYSTEM KNOWN AS SWINGS AND ROUNDABOUTS. THERE'S NO BETTER EXAMPLE OF THIS THAN THE PROFESSIONAL RELATIONSHIP BETWEEN ME AND BILL RALSTON, WHO USED TO FILL IN FOR PAM AND ME IF WE WERE EVER AWAY AT THE SAME TIME.**

THE MEDIA HAVE ALWAYS operated, and continue to operate, on the system known as swings and roundabouts. There's no better example of this than the professional relationship between me and Bill Ralston, who used to fill in for Pam and me if we were ever away at the same time. His primary role was host of the show after ours, and he and Pam would often share a cigarette together during breaks. Not much later, when I was doing Pacific breakfast on my own, Bill had become head of the biggest news organisation in the country — TVNZ News and Current Affairs.

One day he rang me and suggested we catch up.

'How about we do lunch at Prego?' he said.

I had read about Bill Ralston's lunches, which were reputed to be magnificent. He arrived at the restaurant in his customary shambolic fashion. Bill has a distinctive gait, a slight hunch as he constantly runs his hands through his pockets checking for his cell phone, or his cigarettes or matches, where is my wallet, do I have my credit card — not unlike an Australian warding off flies.

'I am revamping *Breakfast*,' Bill said after we had both ordered. Alison Mau was doing it on her own at that stage. 'How would you feel about doing *Breakfast* on Television New Zealand?'

Before I could say yes — and I was never really going to say anything else — he interrupted to tell me about a new company edict forbidding the purchase of wine costing more than $60 a bottle. He was unconcerned because the edict said you could buy as many bottles of wine at $59.99 as you liked and, good journalist that he was, Bill had done his research and discovered some particularly good ones. We spent at least $119.98 on two bottles of wine — which was a large amount for me — and by the end of bottle number two the deal was informally agreed.

I spoke to Brent Impey, my employer of sorts at Pacific, about it. He was not impressed. He liked to repeat the axiom that radio is the bread and butter on the table and TV is the icing on the cake. There is some truth in that. Long careers in broadcasting are more likely to be on radio than on television. He managed to fill me with uncertainty about the wisdom of going to TV.

'Don't piss anyone off in radio, because you could well need to come back to this,' he said, hinting that every week at TVNZ could be my last.

I ignored Brent's warnings and within a few weeks I had resigned from Pacific yet again and was having lunch with my new co-presenter, Alison Mau, who I met for the first time at Andiamo, just a few restaurants down the road from Prego. Our on-air relationship was one thing I could see I wouldn't have to worry about — she was always a lovely, considerate colleague.

Brent was spot-on in the end.

I had only a few days at TVNZ and quite a lot to learn before I went on air. Among other handicaps, I had never read an autocue before. Doing that was a big part of the *Breakfast* job description.

I've never worried about my ability to do anything, but I always worry about my ability to be bothered doing it well. I didn't know a lot about what the new job entailed, apart from the fact that I had to get up early and go to the studio. I didn't understand how the rundown worked; I didn't understand how computers worked beyond what is necessary to function as a human being in the twenty-first century; I didn't need or want to know what the people in the control room did.

When I ascertained very early on that mastering the autocue was the one essential, I committed to getting the hang of it. Most people can manage it, but they are not dyslexic and this was a key difference for me.

When I did other jobs that required me to read out loud I always had time to study the material before delivering it. Even with late-breaking news, on the radio, there are usually a few moments where you can scan something and work out what the words are — especially when no one can see you.

With an autocue, however, you can't see more than a few words ahead and you are at the mercy of the operator who controls how fast the words scroll by — in some situations operators have been replaced by a button the host presses with his or her foot to control the autocue. As yet, this innovation has apparently not seen a mass influx of dyslexics into the industry.

But the strategy I had honed over the years through panic and necessity was no longer going to work, at a time when I most needed it. I had to try to get as much script as possible to study before we were on. Right up to my last day on air, I read as much as I could in advance. One of the biggest problems with dyslexia is that it sucks your confidence away, which exacerbates the problem. I've managed to gain confidence by creating some skills, so at least now my only challenge is the dyslexia.

It was always the little, odd-looking words that I stumbled over. 'Philanthropist' and 'bovine spongiform encephalopathy' gave me no grief whatsoever, but I could stare at 'query' for ages trying to work out what it was.

I got good at bluffing. There are other strategies, such as changing the subject to avoid using an unrecognisable word you see coming up. While your co-host is otherwise engaged, you can have a crack at figuring it out.

The network also tried to give me computer training early on and put me in a room with computers and a lot of young people. My attitude was that this was far beneath me, and I have an inkling that I might have let that show, so I learnt nothing there and continued to learn nothing about computers during my entire time at TVNZ.

We used an editing system called Quantel and I have only started to pronounce that properly since leaving the organisation. I deliberately mispronounced it because I reasoned that if they thought I couldn't even pronounce it, they would never expect me to operate it.

On my first day in the building, not long before my scheduled debut, the producers sat me down to run through a script on autocue, and I completely mangled it. I couldn't make sense of the words or why they were moving the way they were. And as soon as I started to stumble, the scrolling stopped. There were four words on the screen and I couldn't say 25 per cent of them.

There was doubtless some consternation in the control room as the realisation that their new presenter could not read out loud dawned on the production team. And they were stuck with me — thanks to Bill, my employment was a done deal. There was no trial period.

Simon Dallow was hurriedly brought in to train me. I sat on a cushion — slightly elevated to bring my eye level within the vicinity of the statuesque Alison's. 'I can bluff my way through nearly everything,' I told Simon. 'I just want you to give me some tips on autocue and that.'

Simon stood back and looked at me for a while with his finger on his chin.

'Are you entirely happy with the way you are sitting?' he finally said. Then I was really worried. Not only could I not read, apparently I didn't even know how to sit down unaided. So much to learn in such a short time. The job had two parts — reading and sitting — and I really thought I had sitting nailed. I was beyond any help Simon might have been able to give me. Of course, the other thing about a new job is the people you meet and the new friends you make. I had been at TVNZ for a very short period of time when I had a run-in with Paul Holmes. I had said something critical on Radio Pacific about a *Holmes* show in which he interviewed Julie Christie in a way that seemed to me unreasonable. It may not have been him; it could have been the way it was produced. But in the end I had no idea who was right or wrong. I just felt sorry for her — and that's not an easy emotion for me to summon up.

The interview contradicted one of my fundamental beliefs about the profession: the way I saw it, my job was not just to ask the questions but to make sure that the interviewee answered them. It was not my job to determine that the answer wasn't good enough.

'Why do you keep interrupting?' people would frequently say in my interviews.

'Because you are not answering the question and I will keep interrupting until you do,' I said. But that was as far as it went. The viewer or listener could decide for themselves whether the answer, when it finally came, was adequate. Occasionally, if I judged an answer to be particularly appalling I pointed that out and gave them another opportunity to respond.

Critics didn't like the interrupting. They claimed they only wanted to hear what the interviewee had to say. But I didn't interrupt unless they were avoiding the question.

It was on these grounds that I criticised the *Holmes* interview. He took exception to my criticism. It was about day two of my tenure at TVNZ. I was sitting in the middle of the newsroom, staring at a computer and wondering how to switch it on.

Suddenly, Holmes swept across the floor in my direction and went ballistic. The entire newsroom fell silent. Towards the end of his tirade he said, 'Do you think I'm stupid?'

'No, Paul,' I said, 'I know you're not stupid, but you looked stupid on television the other night.'

Fortunately the newsroom offices have sliding doors, which means they are much harder to slam.

I made it through my first broadcast and soon came to terms with the autocue and other encumbrances. *Breakfast* was the best programme at the worst time. Apart from the hours, it was ideal for me because it gave me so much licence but with a great deal of structure and support.

My alarm went off at 4am and I got in anywhere between 4.30 and 5am, never later. I never felt like waking up. I'm not a morning person, I'm a night person. The only thing I disliked more than having to get up straight away was having to go to bed early. I didn't do it begrudgingly, because I loved the job and I was paid a very small fortune to do it. But it was an odd job that had you in an underground bunker having make-up applied at nought o'clock in the morning when everyone else was still asleep.

I always went straight to my dressing room and stood for a moment pondering why, no matter how many shirts and suits you have, you always look the same. I didn't wear a tie because I don't like ties and who wants to wake up in the morning to someone looking like an accountant? Even people who are married to accountants don't want that.

I touched the suits that I touched every day and never wore. Then I pulled out shirts and failed to make a decision about which to wear before going into the newsroom to entertain whoever was there, no matter what mood I was in.

My aim was to avoid actually knuckling down and looking at the programme. People thought I was wasting their time but really I was waking up and trying to get interested in another day. Then I opened the programme up and saw the mistakes and everything that was going to go wrong.

Then back into wardrobe where I chose a shirt I had worn dozens of times before, even though I knew lilac didn't suit me but at least it was slightly different.

Despite the fact I was well catered for in the styling, make-up and hair departments, I used to sometimes, for almost no good reason, do my own hair at home because many years earlier I had purchased a Warh hair-clipper set and didn't want to waste my investment.

One disastrous Sunday afternoon, I attempted to style my hair in a number two, but the plastic number two comb detached itself from the shaver, resulting in an inch and a half wide number nought over my right ear. My choices were limited. Did I go in completely bald or find a way to simulate a tuft of hair? I chose the latter option. By dibby-dabbing some Kiwi nugget I was able to create the illusion of the existence of hair in the offending patch, from a certain angle only. Like the rest of me, my hair was able to bluff its way through a career in television.

After wardrobe, it was into make-up and then into the studio with my folder of bits and pieces and my mind full of things I might say or do. Sometimes the stuff I ad-libbed took up as much time as what was prepared.

We were constantly chasing time. We were also worried

about not filling the time. I thought we should have a two-minute timeless piece of story we could keep to play if we did ever go short, but that never happened.

Some people on the show needed one event to follow another exactly as planned. Sometimes things collapsed hopelessly. I could feel it happen. I would launch a story and the autocue operator would stop and look for it because he didn't realise it was an ad lib. And by the time he worked that out he had forgotten at which point I had left the script so couldn't find the right place for me to get back on track. Those were golden mornings.

Meanwhile, the producer was wondering how we were going to get the ad break in and what we would do with the guest who was sitting in the green room when he finally got on for the 12 seconds that would be left for him.

The day before, I never wanted to know what was on the next morning's show. I didn't turn on the computer to check the programme before going to bed. I followed the news in detail and thought that was enough for me to be familiar with anything that came up. And if not, I had the producers' notes and my own brain to get my head around a story in time to be on air. Otherwise the job could take up 24 hours a day. Also we reacted to things, so something could easily happen to throw away all our best-laid plans.

All my co-hosts used to read at night to work out what was likely to be on the show the next morning. As soon as a programme was finished, it was dead to me. And until the next programme had started, it was dead to me too. That's the only way I could survive with that much television, really.

'Oh, you're lucky you've got the rest of the day to yourself,' people said when they saw me in the lift at 9.30.

'Yes, I'm going to go home, where I'm going to curl up in the foetal position and bang my head against a wall until it's time for me to watch the news and go to bed.' That was a slight exaggeration.

It helped my attitude that I am blessed with a good understanding of my place in the great scheme of things and understand much better than most people how insignificant I am. I wasn't going on television to try and change people's minds. I've travelled a lot and seen an awful lot. I know that we're all breathing the same oxygen but that if any one person stops breathing it's not going to make a huge difference at all. If you can make someone laugh, now that's an achievement. If you can make a thousand people laugh, that's brilliant. But if you go on breakfast, on radio or television, with the hope of changing the world not only are you not going to make anyone laugh, but you're wasting your time.

I was a breakfast television host. I wasn't there to negotiate a free-trade agreement or indeed stand in the way of a free-trade agreement, which was one of the more hysterical allegations thrown around at the time I resigned.

People are busy at the time *Breakfast* goes to air, rushing around getting ready for their days. I had ways of making them watch. 'God, this is interesting,' I said sometimes, knowing they were in the kitchen and I had to get them into the lounge where I was. 'Hey, that was cool, can we play that again?' was another line I used to wrangle the little rascals.

The show was designed for busy people who gave it a moment of their time. I wanted to let them have a bit of a laugh, make them see another side of an argument or at least broaden their vision a bit and challenge their prejudices. Sometimes I pushed very hard for us to make great television. Other times I thought: 'Too hard. Let's just do our best.'

When I was fired up, at our post-show meeting, I would hit the ground ranting. It was 9.15am and I would pour some cheap wine — making people drink early in the morning is a good way of cutting through the lethargy — and get stuck into what was wrong with the show. I got especially infuriated if there was a big overseas story and we only covered it if we could find the New Zealand angle. America was full of Americans who knew all about American stories, but we had to find the New Zealander on holiday who had been caught up in whatever it was before a story was allowed on our programme. Then we had four minutes with someone who knew nothing when we could have had an expert who would have been a lot cheaper to find and told us something we didn't already know. Having a New Zealand angle does not necessarily make something a story.

Also, when something really big happened, I thought we should go to blanket coverage instead of sticking to our rundown because it was there and merely interrupting with all the updates. There is nothing more compelling to watch than a story unfolding before your eyes.

As important as going that extra mile to get something good is making the most of what you've got sitting next to you. A bad interview with good talent is so much better than a good interview with bad talent. I have seen interviews that qualify as tragedies because a ham-fisted interviewer is not getting the best out of a wonderful subject. Often people are brought on not because they will get a chance to shine, but because the network wants a chance to shine. They congratulate themselves on getting someone ahead of their competition and then fail to get anything out of that person. They often misuse their own people, too. A link and satellites are organised. The reporter is flown over, someone finds a flak jacket in his size for him to wear. And he stands in front of the camera and doesn't tell you much more than that it is Wednesday.

I was accused often of having a National Party agenda because I had stood for the party and said I voted for them. Both those things are true but I never wanted to sway anyone to vote the way I do, although in a perfect world no one would vote for the Alliance or the Greens. If you're not going to challenge people then your political beliefs aren't an issue. You're just asking a series of questions for which there is no pressure on anyone to tell the truth or even answer. They get to say as much or as little as they want. Nothing is expressed in those interviews. They are just propaganda.

A lot of people didn't understand all this, but enough did and the show's ratings went up over time. The ratings were also boosted by those people who watched to have their prejudices about me confirmed. Hopefully they will be reading this book now and tasting blood in their mouths as they realise they are the stupid people I am talking about in words they can barely understand.

Not only did *Breakfast* become a programme that people enjoyed watching, it became a programme that showed the opposition there was money to be made by doing so. TV3 launched *Sunrise* and gave it a damn good go. It wasn't amateurish — I thought their set was better than ours. In a cheap way they spent a lot of money on it and they failed. It's an achievement to see off the opposition in any market, especially when the opposition are putting up a good fight, which they did.

For the most part, people watching TV will see what they want to see and hear what they want to hear. I had a wonderful example of this once when I was driving home after *Breakfast* and had Leighton Smith's show on. There must have been something wrong with the car radio.

'Did you hear Paul Henry this morning?' asked a caller. 'Did you hear the interview with John Key? He is in Labour's pocket, that Paul Henry.'

That was a refreshing change in some ways but mind-numbingly illogical to anyone who knew anything about me. I had given the Prime Minister a tough time that morning, which

I did whenever the topic required me to, so I thought perhaps this caller had not seen *Breakfast* before. Deep down I knew, of course, he watched every day with his extreme personal political prejudice prickling, waiting for someone to jiggle one of the little antennae. But Leighton Smith managed to surpass him in absurdity.

'Like all broadcasters,' said Leighton, 'he's a socialist. They're all socialists.'

Given my aim has always been to make sure listeners and viewers know where I stand so they can make up their own minds about what I say, these assessments suggested I had failed dismally.

People asked me frequently who I voted for.

'I vote National.'

'Ah ha, ah, I thought so. Well, that's obvious, isn't it?'

Not really, if you needed to ask.

The other thing about having a tendency to support one party is that, in my case at least, I am more likely to have a go at them because they are in a better position to let me down.

People asked me if I was the same in real life as on television. Obviously not — television is not real life. You sit in a studio in front of cameras under lights with make-up and a suit on. But in all of my dealings with people I come as close to being me as I possibly can. On the other hand, I know people who have well-honed senses of humour but appear to be totally devoid of personality when they appear on television. There are too many people on TV without personality, and there are too many people watching who want that.

Why would you want someone in your living room whose views you don't know or understand because they keep them to themselves, or who is so stoic in demeanour as to be comatose. They are just telling you the time. 'This is the Prime Minister and I'm going to ask him a question and when that's finished I'll tell you the time again.' What a load of bollocks. I would never want to do that.

If your primary concern as a broadcaster is to produce something safe, then you're not broadcasting, you're running through the motions. The best TV is what happens when everyone — audience, host, viewer — has the feeling things could get out of control. My co-hosts would frequently be keen to get out of that interesting zone of tension, but I used to fight to keep us there just a little bit longer.

I wouldn't have been the easiest person to work with because I'm quite full-on and I do command my space. But all my co-hosts were talented professionals — Alison, Kay Gregory and Pippa Wetzell.

I worked with Pippa more than either of the others as a co-host and fell in love with her, as anyone would. I adore her. Her edge as a broadcaster is that she is the girl next door, and you can't manufacture that. You can learn polish and other aspects of your craft, but the only way you can be the girl next door is if you're the girl next door.

When we weren't planning to sabotage free-trade agreements or install a National Party government for life, we mainly talked about our children. With her family being much younger than mine, I had the opportunity to tell her about all the mistakes I had made and what she should avoid doing. We couldn't wait for an interview to finish and an ad break to come on so we could pore over the latest photos of her girls, Brodie and Cameron.

When I started receiving a lot of very enthusiastic mail, I thought it was extraordinary that so many people loved me so much. Then I discovered someone was opening my mail and filtering out the negative letters. 'I would really rather not get any mail at all,' I explained, 'because I don't want to have to be answering it,

Friends

The following is a list of well-known New Zealanders who I absolutely trust would instantly drop everything and come to my aid in this, and almost all emergency situations: For some extraordinary reason I find myself handcuffed to a table in the kitchen at a bar mitzvah. I need a distraction, a hacksaw and a discreet ride home.

The list
- Annabelle White, cook
- Darren Hughes, ex public servant
- Peter Williams, Queen's Counsel
- Pam Corkery, madam
- John Banks, Honourable
- Pippa Wetzell, mother
- Diane Forman, ice-cream maker

These people I know for a fact I can count on. I would have liked to have named the Topp Twins — I count them among my very best friends; however, as I have met them only three times, I'm not sure it is reciprocated. Shane Cortese — he's the loveliest man but would probably be on stage at the bar mitzvah anyway, and Bill Ralston, not only a great guy but as he wouldn't remember anything the next day I wouldn't owe him back. Bonus!

I'm tempted to add Phil Goff's name to the list. He seems like the sort of person who would attempt to help anyone in a crisis, unlike Bill English who, I suspect, would immediately alert the media.

but if you're going to be sending me good letters, send me the bad letters too. Nice ones are no use to me whatsoever.'

I was used to hostile audience reactions — I got bullets in the mail when I was doing radio. I got those reactions because when I thought something I said it, although I always slightly tempered what I was saying based on the company I was in.

In broadcasting, once something has gone out, it's out there and you live with it. If there's something you can learn from it, do that; if there's nothing then just forget it straight away. When people would feast over some comment I made, it seemed extraordinary to me. As far as I was concerned it was electronic fish and chip paper. Sometimes when I was ploughing through another mountain of complaints, I found myself wondering if the complainants were amputees who had been strapped to their chairs and couldn't reach the off button. Either that or they were so poisoned by their own prejudices that they couldn't recognise a joke when they saw one.

It's such a contrast with the US where some of the most highly paid broadcasters are people hardly anyone agrees with — in fact you would hope no one at all agreed with many of them.

I knew I could be what the critics were saying they wanted. I could come in every morning and read the autocue — barely — and go home. Then in the evening I could accept all the invitations to functions and enjoy the free food and drink. But I couldn't take money to do those things.

Big international stories were still close to my heart and among the highlights of my time at *Breakfast*. We were on air when Michael Jackson's death was announced and we extended our coverage. That was one of those rare occasions, like the Twin Towers, when you feel the whole world is looking in the same direction. But those days were the exception because of where we came in the daily news cycle. Not much happened in New

Zealand between the late news the previous night and us going to air in the morning. A lot happened overseas, though, and we got to bring those stories to people first, which was a challenge.

Most days our job was to make shit shine. Television is different from radio for obvious reasons, but one of the biggest is that there are so many components that can bring it down — the sets, the lighting, your clothes. And with a big machine it's hard to change direction at short notice. On radio we could decide to drop someone and replace them with someone more interesting at the last minute because they only had to be on the phone. There is a big difference between ringing someone up in the morning and saying, 'Can we talk to you for five minutes?' and ringing them up and saying, 'Can we send a taxi around? Can you get dressed? We'll have make-up for you at this time and put you on TV'.

I was allowed to travel occasionally for *Breakfast* if the story seemed to warrant it. Like a lot of people I was fascinated by the rise of Sarah Palin. I was in the US to cover the Obama election and thought it would be fun to go to Alaska and look at her house. I was treating her rather like I did Pol Pot — I wanted to see how close we could get before someone tried to shoot us. I had a cameraman and a producer with me, and we had rented a big black vehicle which looked to me like it could have belonged to the Secret Service. We drove up to her neighbour's house, where I thought security would not be quite so tight.

'I'll go up and knock on the neighbour's door,' I told the cameraman. 'You follow me with the camera, and we'll be able to see over the fence.' But it was a very high fence and we couldn't see anything. We also learnt later that the Secret Service had rented the neighbour's house.

I wasn't satisfied. 'Let's drive up to Sarah Palin's house and see how far we can get,' I said. 'If anyone stops us we'll plead ignorance.'

We took the disc with what we had shot so far out of the

camera and put it away because we knew it would be confiscated when we got into trouble. I did a commentary as we drove up. There was a Trespassers Will Be Prosecuted sign, which was fine — once someone told us to leave, we would leave. There was thick bush on either side of the driveway and we suddenly felt very remote. I knew it wasn't going to be easy to back out of here at any speed once the Secret Service started firing.

But suddenly the driveway opened out into a large area that was full of big black official police vehicles. And there was Sarah Palin's house — quite an ordinary dwelling, festooned with US flags. We had got a lot further than I expected. Suddenly all the doors on the vehicles opened and armed troopers poured out. 'What are you doing? Can I help you? You've got to go', they variously barked. Talk about mixed messages.

'Oh, we've just come to see if Sarah Palin is in. We're from New Zealand,' I said as our cameraman continued to shoot. 'We're from New Zealand' is another way of saying 'We are too stupid to kill'. For some reason the trooper in charge didn't ask for our camera or footage.

'We'll go now, then,' I said. And rather than back up I did a laborious 19-point turn in the driveway, during which the cameraman held his camera so it looked like he wasn't shooting but moved it around so he got every angle possible. And as soon as we had finished the turn, we drove out and kept going. We fully expected someone to come after us, but they probably realised we were harmless. Also it didn't look good for them that we had got that far. Why weren't they at the other end of the driveway?

I also went to New York and spent a couple of days with Helen Clark, for a story. We have had some real humdingers over the years and this meeting was facilitated by Darren Hughes, who is a good friend to both of us. She gave me great access. We didn't just sit in her office. We went to her local breakfast place and interviewed her while she ate, then we did go to her office and I inspected her knick-knacks closely. She came out with me for the day and I took her to some New York sites that she hadn't had time to see. We went to the Statue of Liberty and wore the funny hats.

She recommended a play to me. She knew I was interested in Africa and there was a play off Broadway called *Ruined* which was about Congolese prostitutes. She had seen it before but wanted to go again and organised tickets. I had to pay for mine; she's still a socialist. Darren Hughes came too and it was a great play. We couldn't get three seats together so she had me sit next to her — probably because she's sat next to Darren lots of times. She has fantastic interval technique. Just before interval, which she must have remembered from last time, she said, 'Just follow me, it's almost intermission, we've got to go and get a drink.' The moment the lights went up she charged out dragging me behind, and we were first at the bar. Then we went out and had a pizza and a Chianti. She was brilliant company and it was illuminating to see her world through her eyes.

I asked her which politician she considered to be the nastiest she had ever encountered. After some negotiation we agreed we would both write the name of the person we thought met that description on a piece of paper and then exchange them. Which we did and, indeed, we had both written the same name. We had a wonderful conversation about the way I had treated her and other politicians. There was one she felt I had always treated unfairly and she made me promise to have a wine with that person and bury the hatchet and I really must get around to that one day.

A very different, more personal highlight — in fact I've often wondered if I was the only person who was even slightly interested — was when Jeff Wayne came on the show. His album *War of the Worlds*, which came out in 1978, was huge.

I was surrounded at *Breakfast* by cultural illiterates — people under 40, in other words — who had never heard of Jeff Wayne or his masterpiece.

'Oh God, this really is scraping the bottom of the barrel,' one said when he heard Wayne was coming. 'Who is Jeff Wayne?'

Occasionally I lectured them on the importance of people they had never heard of, who were coming on the show solely because I wanted to meet them. At those times I could read their minds. They were thinking: 'Please, don't let me ever get to be as old as him.'

I remember being invited to the Wellington planetarium when I worked for the old National Programme, many years earlier. The record company were launching something they said was truly magnificent; it turned out to be Jeff Wayne's masterpiece. At the same event the record company introduced us to a young girl they said would be the next big thing in New Zealand. I think I fell in love with Sharon O'Neill that night, largely because she was wearing almost nothing at all. Anyway, here was an opportunity to have not only Jeff Wayne in the studio, but also Justin Hayward the singer of the number-one hit 'Forever Autumn' from the *War of the Worlds* album. In the end the interview was brilliant and Hayward sang the song live in the studio with a DVD background played on the green screen. It was television gold, as I used to say. Much in the same vein, I instantly said yes to an interview with Prunella Scales, not because of what she was doing in the country but because she was, and will always be, Sybil Fawlty to me.

The real achievements of the *Breakfast* years, though, were things like getting a letter from someone who said his wife had just passed away after a long illness and she had spent her last six months laughing at me.

Another high point was after I had a tirade on air about people stealing the magic from their children's eyes too young. I haven't forgotten the magic from when I was young. My kids were among the last ones to realise that Santa Claus may possibly not be completely legit, because there's still doubt in my mind. I kept the magic alive in my kids' eyes as long as possible, and I still try to instil it in them now.

This morning, I talked about a dairy I had gone into where there was a little boy with his hands pressed against the glass looking in at the lollies. 'Hurry up, hurry up,' said his mother. 'I haven't got all day.' The kid just wanted to choose. There was a 50-cent piece in his hand and it was the most money he could ever imagine. I wanted to take that mother out of that shop and read her the riot act. Instead, I read the riot act to her and to any other person watching on air.

'Why do you have children if you can't capitalise on the magic of a situation like that?' I said. 'Just remember what it's like to be a kid.'

Later, I got a letter from a child, sent in by their mother. He or she — I can't now remember which — had been in a dairy choosing lollies and for the first time they could remember Mum just stood there waiting patiently while the child ummed and ahhed over the best choice. Afterwards the kid asked about this out-of-character behaviour and the mother said she had heard my comments on *Breakfast*.

'That's what I do,' she said, 'I steal the magic from your eyes.' The pair of them had written to thank me for putting her right. Those are the biggest achievements.

Breakfast should have been enough work for any person but twice during my years there I did the drive-time show at Radio Live — the old Radio Pacific. Working at both ends of the day was a nightmare. Radio Live made it as easy as possible — all I had to do was roll in at the last minute and be myself for about two hours. It was talk, not talkback. The offer was hard to resist, not because of money, which had nothing to do with it, but because I have always preferred radio and I missed it.

I love radio's intimacy as a form of communication. In my mind there is always only one listener and I am talking directly to them. I had been taught that at the BBC — you have a listener, imagine what that listener looks like, imagine what they're interested in and everything you say you're just telling that one person, because people listen to radio individually. There is an intimacy you don't have with any other medium, except perhaps a book you get thoroughly engrossed in. In a radio studio there are one or two other people, not multiple camera operators and a control room of crew looking after innumerable obscure technical details.

The difference is acknowledged in subtle ways. Usually when TV networks promote themselves, they play up the huge number of people involved in getting your show to air. When radio stations promote themselves they emphasise the individual on-air personalities.

When I started at the Radio New Zealand station in the Wairarapa, their branding line was 'In touch with your community'. I thought that was the most out-of-touch thing they could say. Surely they should have been saying 'In touch with *our* community'.

TVNZ were very good about me doing the drive show, even though Radio Live and their competitor TV3 had the same owner, CanWest. The first time I did it, Bill Ralston was head of news and current affairs, and he could see the value in the cross-pollination. However, it didn't sit entirely comfortably that my programme ended when the simulcast of *3 News* began on Radio Live. 'See you on *Breakfast* tomorrow morning at 6am,' I said, and then the programme went to *3 News*. In the end the arrangement fell foul of the commercial politics and TVNZ asked me to stop, which I did because they were my primary employer. Brent Impey wasn't impressed and repeated his line about bread and butter and icing.

But things changed, and I went back for another year of drive-time radio later. On that occasion, the wheel had turned full circle and Bill Ralston was no longer head of news and current affairs at TVNZ but filled in for me on Radio Live occasionally. It was no easier and I was frequently reminded of how small the country is. I was also filling in on *Close Up* occasionally at that point, which meant some days I did breakfast TV, drive-time radio and prime-time TV. This reached its most absurd point when Richard E Grant was visiting the country and I interviewed him on all three shows. He felt as if he had come here just to see me. I made it a point of pride to have three different conversations and we managed because he is a fascinating character.

I take my hat off to Paul Holmes, who did breakfast radio and prime-time nightly TV for so long. You cannot do it unless you're thinking all the time. You can't miss a beat. You have to know what's happening; you have to be on top of the planning of the programme. It was so hard. Ultimately the split shift and having to peak at least twice, occasionally three times, a day wore me down and I restricted myself to *Breakfast* and filling in on *Close Up*, which was the job I really wanted.

Mount Everest

CHAPTER 20
CLOSE UP AND PERSONAL

> **" AS IS MY PRACTICE, I ASCERTAINED FIRST HOW LITTLE WORK I WOULD NEED TO DO. I DIDN'T MIND THE TWO WEEKS OVERSEAS BUT I DIDN'T WANT TO BE SHUT IN A STUDIO BACK HOME DOING VOICEOVERS AND LOOKING AT EDITS. ONCE I ESTABLISHED THAT WOULDN'T BE NECESSARY, I AGREED. "**

ONE OF THE OTHER things that sowed the seed of my hosting *Breakfast* in Bill Ralston's mind was my episode of *Intrepid Journeys*.

With the exposure I had got from doing *How's Life?* on TV, producer Melanie Rakena rang me one day and asked if I would like to make one of her *Intrepid Journeys*, to Nepal and Tibet. I was keen because I had never been to either of those places and all New Zealanders are slightly interested in them because of their connection with Sir Edmund Hillary.

As is my practice, I ascertained first how little work I would need to do. I didn't mind the two weeks overseas but I didn't want to be shut in a studio back home doing voiceovers and looking at edits. Once I established that wouldn't be necessary, I agreed.

I played up the deprivation during filming, because it was at the low level compared with a lot of what I had seen. I didn't want to spend the entire journey saying, 'Well, I've been in countries like this before and quite frankly this is luxury.'

I was the perfect specimen for a study of oxygen deprivation because I was in appalling physical shape anyway. We stopped in Kathmandu to buy oxygen. 'I should be listening to this,' I said as the seller was explaining to me how to use the oxygen. Instead I glazed over. 'Oh I see, yes, then you just do that. I think I've used one of these before,' I said, just wanting him to shut up so I could get going. Little did I know that this was going to come back and bite me on the arse in a few days.

We went through Nepal into Tibet. You can't go that close to Everest and not retrace at least some of Hillary's famous footsteps. We went very quickly up to a high altitude and there I developed quite the headache. The next morning the headache had been joined by several more.

A few days into the journey, we planned to stay in a temple on the slopes of Everest but by then I was templed out. Everyone else was very excited because, of course, this was the best temple in Nepal, just like all the others we had seen, and we were going to climb up the steps and sleep on its floor. I am not a prima donna. I can put up with all kinds of deprivation. So if I don't want to do something it's because I don't want to do it, not because I'm having a diva fit. And I did not want to sleep in, talk about or even look at this temple.

'Do you not think it would be much better for us to go and spend the night at Everest base camp?' I said. That would be exciting, especially as I was still wearing jandals.

'You'll have no indemnity,' our local contact said. 'Our people stay at the temple because this is a really important one to see and we can't imagine why anyone wouldn't want to see it. You're going to have to sign a waiver if you're going to go up to base camp.' I would've agreed to anything not to have to go inside another temple, so we signed the waiver.

Base camp was about eight kilometres away. You couldn't drive but could hire a donkey and a cart. I had to be sensible and exchange my jandals for a pair of bright orange sneakers.

I still had my headache and didn't think the sight of me in a donkey cart with a sore head would make for great television so decided to walk while the others rode. Eight kilometres is a long distance for me on the Auckland waterfront. Up a mountain in the Himalayas, ascending 250 metres over its length, it's extremely challenging. You could do a whole documentary on that. It took hours. The others, with their fancy oxygen and their anti-altitude sickness medication and their generally high level of fitness could probably have run it but I struggled with every step. My brain played tricks on me. When I stood still I felt fine. Then I walked a few steps and started gasping for breath.

Eventually we reached base camp. It was late and cold and a very nasty wind was starting to blow. We stayed in a big tent that had a sign on it which read 'Hotel California'. This was paid accommodation, a shelter put together out of lots of old canvas. Inside were a big pot belly stove and a lot of Sherpas sitting around telling amazing stories. There is nothing in New Zealand as high as this location and I fell rather than walked into the tent, but I was very proud of having made it. Just before I collapsed someone opened a flap in the tent and I saw the peak of Mount Everest. 'That's good,' I thought. 'I can die now.'

I started taking oxygen the next day. I sat with the ten moving parts necessary to make the equipment work and bitterly regretted not having paid more attention to the introductory lecture before I managed to get the oxygen flowing. My headache began to recede. I caught the donkey on the way back.

There is a strong feeling that China is responsible for a lot

Jandals

I have a tip to any traveller: no matter what country you're going to, always pack jandals. Jandals are the best bloody things, even just so you don't risk a variety of fungal infections when having a shower. There have been countries where jandals have saved my life. There are lots of times when you can't put your feet in shoes, because they're filled up with shit or your feet have swelled or you're so dirty and sticky. But you can always put on your jandals.

of damage to Tibet and the people's way of life, but as far as I could see these lives were wretched not so much because of the Chinese but because of the Buddhist monks who oversaw preposterous religious practices that seriously impeded people's ability to lead a decent life. Tibetans who should have been out working to feed their families were crawling on their bellies to carry a sliver of gold to a temple as an offering. I could not see what kind of God would be impressed by that. The Dalai Lama's home is bigger than Buckingham Palace, in a country full of impoverished people.

The Chinese have done appalling things but I wasn't convinced that theirs was the greater evil. Many of the monks have been imprisoned by the Chinese, but if that keeps them out of circulation so they can't lord it over peasants that's a good thing. And while I could sense animosity between the monks and the Chinese, I didn't notice any between the Chinese and the secular population.

Back home, having been given the job of hosting *Breakfast*, the job I really wanted was *Close Up*, the current affairs show in the 7pm slot that had been Paul Holmes' fiefdom for many, many years before he vacated it and moved to Prime. I was perfect for it. I was just what it needed. I made sure I would get it by telling every person I met that I wanted it.

When Paul left, rumours immediately began circulating that Bill Ralston had me lined up for the evening slot. The rumours were absolutely correct. He was on the phone the day Holmes went, discussing my involvement in the programme that would replace *Holmes*. Susan Wood had been the regular fill-in during Holmes' absences and carried on with the renamed show. For a while management toyed with the idea of having two co-hosts. At one stage they were looking at three, with one host always out somewhere and the other two in the studio. In the end it was decided I would be the official fill-in and Susan Wood would do the show. 'Official fill-in for Susan Wood' — it didn't make a stunning business card.

I have never been interested in the politics of my jobs and there was quite a lot of politicking around this show. I don't insist on things very often. If someone gives me the impression they don't want me to do a job, my interest ends there. That's fine. I certainly, to misquote Groucho Marx, wouldn't want to belong to a club that didn't want to have me as a member.

Suddenly, not only was Mark Sainsbury the permanent fill-in, but the role, which I had been juggling with five mornings of *Breakfast* a week, was a full-time one. Mark did another programme for a little while — a short series of chat shows where he talked to people who either weren't interesting at all or were interesting when you heard the answer the first ten times but not the eleventh and subsequent times they had been introduced — but his job was really fill-in on *Close Up*. I was now the fill-in's fill-in and my business card, while running out of space, was no more impressive. Then Susan resigned and there were only two people up for the job. It was *inconceivable* to me that Mark would get it ahead of me. And, naturally, Mark got the job.

The selection process included one informal lunch with Bill Ralston at his house and then an official meeting in his office. Present were Bill, the head of television, Jeff Latch, and someone from HR. I still don't know why the HR person was there. Were they worried Bill and the head of television would try to molest me halfway through the interview?

'What would you like to do with the programme?' I was asked.

I had seen in the paper a couple days before a photograph of the Governor-General, Sir Anand Satyanand, welcoming someone into Government House. Everything was lovely in this photograph but on a table in front of the Governor-General and Lady Satyanand was a plate of hundreds and thousands biscuits. It struck me that, no matter how much you may enjoy them, you cannot claim that those are classy biscuits. No one wants to go to Government House and have an orange hundred and thousand stuck in their teeth, which is inevitable because they never all stay stuck to the pink icing.

'The one thing Paul Holmes did very well,' I said, 'was that he made his programme more than just a series of disparate items with someone linking them. Holmes was the programme, and his comments on stories — the introductions to stories, the interviews — were crafted. And when Holmes was at his best they were crafted brilliantly. You need people to watch so that even when they're not particularly interested in one element they will keep watching because they know it's part of this rich tapestry which is half an hour of their life, five nights of the week.'

I then described the affair of the hundreds and thousands biscuits and pointed out that it was exactly the sort of thing that, while not news or even remotely newsworthy, got people talking and therefore helped make them loyal viewers of the programme. What biscuits should the Governor-General be serving?

The other thing you need with a show like *Close Up* is to tear someone to shreds once a week. It has to be justified but it has to be done. There will always be someone who should be held to account for some wrongdoing and that programme should be making people accountable. People will watch the show every night if they know there is a possibility they will see that.

'It's only the two of us,' I said after more pointless chat. 'It's just a matter of choosing one, isn't it? You know what we both can do.' And knowing that, there was really only one choice for them to make, as far as I could see.

'What do you imagine the job would pay?' I was asked. Oh good, I thought, I've sold another roof.

'It's pretty well known what Susan Wood is getting now,' I said, because it had been the subject of an employment dispute when TVNZ tried to reduce the amount. 'And it's pretty well known you don't like paying it, so I imagine it would pay less than that. I am also of the opinion that if this job is done properly it is without doubt a $400,000 job. And surely properly is the only way you'd want it done.' Susan was getting $450,000. They teetered on the brink of laughter. 'Is this the point,' I said, 'where I'm supposed to say that I'll do it for much less or I'll do it for nothing or I'll do it and I'll clean your cars for you too?' That didn't go down well.

I left the interview with the clear impression I had the job. When I was informed that Mark had it, I was told I was a bit 'off the wall'. I certainly hope I am. That is what audiences want. They want a bit of excitement, something unusual and different. But all was not lost. When Bill rang to give me the news, he asked if I would like to be a permanent fill-in. I am not a thrower out of toys from my cot, so I agreed. At least it kept me near the show should, God forbid, anything happen to Mark. It also gave me the opportunity to continually demonstrate to people how much better I was at it. The fill-in position, of course, now went back to being a part-time role.

This left a little time for other pursuits. While making my *Intrepid Journey* years earlier I discussed another idea with the director, Petra Brett-Kelly.

'Isn't it extraordinary how wherever you go in the world you bump into New Zealanders?' I said. That led to the idea of tracking down and filming New Zealanders in the remotest parts of the planet. Again it looked like far too much work so we had to refine it to a point where my energy expenditure would be minimal. Petra went away and set it all up. It was really her gig. We planned on four hour-long programmes, each about two countries, and ended up visiting seven — Afghanistan, Sudan, Uganda, the Arctic Circle, Kazakhstan, Cocos Islands and the Amazon.

Despite my best efforts, it was a lot of work. It took a year to film, juggled around *Breakfast* and other commitments. We never knew until we got to a place just how good the talent would be and how much story they would have to tell.

When we set out, I thought, if these New Zealanders are in these places, how hard can they be to reach? I hadn't factored in that they had all the time in the world — they weren't stealing some leave from their early morning TV presenting jobs. We were there with them for a week or two and in that time we had to see and understand their entire world. We were under a lot of pressure to get the right stuff and get it quickly.

Getting to the Hindu Kush in Afghanistan was a good example of the difficulties. We had to fly into Kabul, travel from there on a light plane into the mountains and then trek for three days on horseback over passes that were only just passable. I'm not a horseman and our steeds were mean beasts largely trained for *buzkashi*, which is like an incredibly violent form of polo using a dead sheep instead of a ball. The trails were so bad even the horses slipped on them. When that happens, you have a good chance of finishing your life underneath a horse so if that looks likely, you get off and walk. I asked Jesus to take me to his bosom several times.

'Do not make me go through this and then kill me in a week,' I said. 'If I haven't got long to go, just take me now and make this trip worthwhile.' But he remained as unresponsive as ever.

We got to a village where we had to stay in a house made of dung. It had no windows because it was so bitterly cold in the region, just an opening wide enough for a horse to walk into. That was where the horseman and the horses stayed. The top horseman and I, being the guest, stayed in another room made of dung where a dung fire was emitting a cheerful dungy glow. When I shone my torch I could see dung particles floating in the air. If I put my finger in my nose I found fresh dung inhaled on my last breath.

When it came time to go I insisted on an alternative to life-threatening horses. If that wasn't possible I would stay on. 'I'm sure I can afford to buy a bach here,' I said. 'I can grow a little opium and have a much better quality of life than if I have to get back on one of those animals.'

For various reasons we ended up chartering a plane to get us out. The air strip was a reasonably flat part of a steep mountain range. We had to pay villagers to shovel the snow off but the plane couldn't get over the mountains that day. The next day we made another attempt but it snowed overnight so we had to pay the villagers to get out their shovels again. They were very happy about our plans. It was a spectacular location, and the programme shows that, but for us at this stage it was really the world's most beautiful prison. I have seldom heard as wonderful a sound as the distant drone of our plane as it finally approached on the third day.

In the Amazon we met a New Zealander who was working for Greenpeace. I have quite a low opinion of Greenpeace because I think it has completely lost its way. When I spoke to Dave McTaggart about it, he was entirely disenchanted with the organisation he had helped found and he ended up leaving it in a very famous and public way. So it was interesting to go up the Amazon and meet true fighters.

They knew exactly what they were fighting for. They could see it out the window. Every second night gangs of people would harass them or try to sink their boat. It was very interesting to be there and experience that more raw and genuine side of Greenpeace. These were young, brave people. They were also very attractive and there was major sex happening every night. They'd start by hosing each other down on the deck and then have sex with each other, probably another little hose down and then off to bed with someone else. They were worthy and they were young and they were attractive and this was an exciting adventure. OK, so not all of them.

One of the problems with a show like *Ends of the Earth* is that I have a horror of selling people short. I don't want to go somewhere and miss something or not convey to people just what it is like being there. But practicalities and the limits of a commercial half hour or hour work against that. You can't keep saying it is cold; you have to show people that the hairs in your nostrils froze the moment you put your head outside. When we were in the Amazon, there was a tree completely seething with ants. You couldn't film it because they were packed together so solidly it just looked like a tree. I really wanted to show the ants to people.

'I'm going to put my hand on there and you film it as they climb,' I said. It was like a cloud of brown going right up my arm. I hadn't thought it through. I didn't realise I wouldn't be able to stop these little bastards once they started running up my arm. At least they weren't biting me. They only started biting me when I tried to get them off. But it was an amazing piece of film which I think we didn't use in the end.

TVNZ wanted to commission another series. I laughed. I would quite like to spend six months living with Bedouins one day. That would make a good hour of television.

My multi-tasking reached its apogee one nightmarish weekend where I did *Breakfast* on the Friday, *Close Up* on the Friday night and then filled in for Simon Dallow doing *Agenda* on Saturday morning. It was ludicrous. Even I could see that. I reminded myself that I had never wanted to be a fill-in on *Close Up* and Mark appeared intent on staying so I asked my employers to find someone else to fill in.

One show I was happy to make time for while also doing *Breakfast* was *This Is Your Life*, which was an outside production done by the legendary Julie Christie.

'Paul, it's Julie Christie here,' she snapped down the phone. 'Have you got a minute?'

You always say yes to Julie when she calls you. You stop whatever you're doing to take the call.

'Yes, yes, of course, Julie,' I said, pulling the car over to give her my complete attention.

'Oh, someone's come in. I'll phone back,' and she hung up.

Eventually we spoke. She was planning to do four episodes of *This Is Your Life*, the show that profiles a celebrity by surprising him or her and having friends and family from over the years come into a studio to talk about them. She wanted to know if I would be interested in hosting. I had been a fan of the show since I used to watch the English version when I was a little boy. It's old-fashioned TV, but a flagship show and the chance was too good to pass up. To a certain degree I'm the sort of person who finds it very hard to say no to people, and if it sounds to me like something that will never happen, which this did, I always say yes and then it immediately goes out of mind.

A lot of people think that Julie is officious but it's simply because she is doing a million things at once. She is always late. She doesn't walk. She stomps, not just because she is from the West Coast but because she is always late and always rushing to the next thing. She has made money in an area that is notoriously hard to make money in but she is also a lot of fun.

This Is Your Life is a hard programme to pull off. Your subject is always going to feel off-centre because they have been taken by surprise. They would be nervous about being on a show anyway, but it's ten times worse when the show starts with them finding out for the first time that it is happening. They are also going to be nervous about who is going to appear from their past. What if they don't recognise the people? What if the people turn out to include several illegitimate children? What do we know that they would rather we didn't? *This Is Your Life* could be The End of Your Life. The reality is that it's a celebration of a life and everyone wants it to be a joyous occasion.

On the other hand, there are the guests who are in on the secret and feeling very celebratory. They are seeing people they haven't seen for ages. They are enjoying themselves. Many of them have enjoyed themselves too much with the hospitality afforded them. As a host you can end up trying to walk a line between a shell-shocked subject and a guest who's so pissed they can barely walk. You are also working with a script that has been finalised just minutes before the programme begins. On my first show, with Jonah Lomu, pages were being slipped into my script during ad breaks. My knowledge of rugby being what it is — none — I was sure I missed little nuances that an expert would have picked up on. I also had grief from guests who would launch into a story that we had someone else lined up to tell three guests later. It's not a hard show to do averagely but it is a very complicated show to do well. It's like juggling fish.

After all my years in TV, I still learnt a lot from working with Julie. We walked into the studio the day before the first show, when the set was going up. She stopped in her tracks and she looked up.

'That is not a star curtain,' she said and called someone over. 'Hey! I said star curtains. They're not star curtains. They are black cloths with twinkling lights hanging down. A star curtain is peppered with lights, just unpredictable patterns of lights. That's not a star curtain. I don't want it, take it down.'

A normal producer would have looked at it and thought: 'That's not what I asked for. Oh well. Too late to change it.'

On another occasion she came on the set, which was

dominated by the biggest plasma screen I had ever seen.

'That's too low, have you put that in place yet?' she said.

'Yeah, yeah, it has to go there because it's so heavy,' said the set designer.

'It's too low.'

'But it's so heavy it has to go there.'

'But what's the point having it, if it's too low? Why don't you go up there and sit on the seats, which is where our audience are going to be, and see if you can see the bottom of it. Maybe we only need a plasma half as big because we can't see the bottom of the plasma from where the seats are.'

Again she insisted on something that other people would have let slide.

'Are you telling me it is impossible — not hard, not very hard, but are you telling me it is impossible to raise that plasma screen?'

'It's not impossible . . .' said the designer, a phrase he would live to regret having uttered.

'Right then, I'll be back in an hour and it will be where I want it and where I'm paying for it to go.' And it was.

The logistics of getting your subject in place and keeping the whole project a secret from them when almost every person they have ever met in their life is in on it are enormously complicated.

When we had on Mark Inglis, the double amputee who climbed Everest, we went down to surprise him at home in Hanmer. We didn't go down the day before. We went down on the day of the show, which meant we had to get him immediately to Auckland in as short a time as possible. A car took us to Mechanics Bay, where a helicopter was waiting to take us to Ardmore where we got on a private jet that flew us to Christchurch where another helicopter was waiting to fly us to a paddock where there was a car that drove us to Mark's shed where he was tinkering away on a bike. His wife

Right:
Outside Homebush.
Maria had just replaced
the drapes. Left to right
— Lucy, Sophie, Bella.

Below:
In their Sunday best —
Sophie, Lucy, Bella.

Above:
Homebush from the air.

Below:
Lucy mowing the lawn.

Above:
Lucy sitting in the only building I have ever built myself from scratch.

Right:
Bella fascinated in a conversation with me, 1999.

Below:
My massive campaign machine. Sophie stands between the stuffed figures of Jenny and Burton Shipley.

Above:
With Deputy Prime Minister Wyatt
Creech, outside Masterton Hospital.

Left:
With Jenny Shipley, when clearly
we still thought we had a chance.

Below:
Sophie and me, 2009.

Above and right:
Lucy on the way to
Kisoro, Uganda, and
with snake charmers
with poor eyesight in
Tanzania.

Below:
First catch in the
Arctic while filming
Ends of the Earth.

Right:
With Helen Clark,
not sure where.

Below:
Bella and my mother,
dressed and ready to
jump off Sky Tower.

Above:
With Bella, 2011,
just before she left
for a year in Kansas.

Right:
Lucy on the day she
graduated as a nurse.

Left:
Pam and me looking like
the back of a bus.

Below:
With cameraman Peter
Day, taping for Breakfast
in Camden Rd, Bristol.

Bottom:
With Pippa who I love,
in Napier.

was running out of excuses to keep him in the shed because he had been planning to go for a ride.

I went through the script on the way down, trying to learn it. I don't think I've ever seen anyone so surprised. Like most people he knew there was an episode of *This Is Your Life* on that night and he knew — though it had crossed his mind that it might happen to him one day — that it wouldn't be him. How could it? He was in his shed in Hanmer and the show was on in Auckland in a few hours.

His wife whipped out the overnight bag she had packed and secretly hidden underneath the bed. Next minute, he was in the car, at the paddock, in the helicopter, at Christchurch, in the private jet, in another helicopter back to Mechanics Bay and then sitting down for half an hour in the green room while I was getting made up.

At every one of those stages — a flat tyre here, some fog there, the whole thing could have fallen to pieces. When I left TVNZ I was due to do another episode of *This Is Your Life*, with Peter Leitch, the Mad Butcher. We talked about letting me do the one show while suspended but I didn't think it was a good idea. They considered a few names and in the end got Paul Holmes.

I REAIY LOVE
PETER LEITCH.

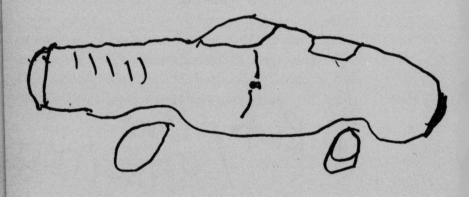

Aston Martin

CHAPTER 21
THE END

"ACCEPTING THE AWARD I READ OUT A LETTER THAT WAS NOT UNTYPICAL OF THE MAIL I RECEIVED FROM PEOPLE WHO DID NOT SHARE WHAT THEY ASSUMED TO BE MY VIEWS. IT GOT A HUGE LAUGH AND AFTER THE CEREMONY PEOPLE WERE ALMOST QUEUING UP TO SEE IT. IT WAS, BY ANY STANDARDS, A SPECTACULAR PIECE OF MAIL . . ."

IN SEPTEMBER 2010 I won the *New Idea* People's Choice Award for most popular television personality. Accepting the award I read out a letter that was not untypical of the mail I received from people who did not share what they assumed to be my views. It got a huge laugh and after the ceremony, people were almost queuing up to see it. It was, by any standards, a spectacular piece of mail:

'You are the most insulting, little self-conceited little mongrel prick on TV. I would love Susan Boyle to shit on your ugly face, Pamela Anderson to give you Aids, David Hasselhoff to punch you on the nose, preferably before Susan shits on you. You fucking poofter pommy mongrel prick. Die you cunt.'

We all had a good laugh on the night. Linda Topp souvenired the original. Despite coming so late in the year, the clip of me reading the letter was the most viewed New Zealand YouTube item of 2010, reaching more than 350,000 hits that year.

I've referred previously to how quickly fortunes can change in the media. A spectacular number of things can go wrong during two and a half hours of live television every morning. In my case, many of them have ended up on T-Shirts.

The Susan Boyle incident was typical of how I offend people who live and breathe in order to be offended. People who like to be offended tend to congregate together and multiply. They sit in front of their TVs like little ticking time bombs of potential offence waiting to explode.

When I watched the clip of Susan Boyle singing and being interviewed and then read an article on her and the difficulties she had in a magazine, I said on air it was official she was in fact retarded.

Other members of the media, better informed about today's acceptable terminology than I, have got away with assessing Boyle's situation by saying she has a 'condition' or faces 'special challenges'. When I was a boy the word used to describe people in that position was 'retarded'. Apparently it has since ended up on the banned list and no one had told me. But for people to extrapolate from the use of that word that I in some way had it in for handicapped people, as I was accused of doing, was too bizarre.

I realised the word was slightly old-fashioned but I don't have time to agonise over such phrasing. I established this policy sometime prior, during a radio interview about kindergartens.

'What do kindy teachers make of this?' I asked.

'Actually,' said the kindy teacher, 'if I could correct you, we are early childhood educators.'

'Are you busy?' I said.

'We're always busy,' she said.

'Well, I better let you get on with it then,' I said and hung up on her. Retarded was obviously on the same list as 'kindy'.

In the wake of the Susan Boyle remark, the offence time bombs had contacted relevant organisations who worked with disabled people, which had then written pro-forma letters of complaint and distributed these to their members to forward to TVNZ. I was contacted by a couple of people who were members of one of these organisations.

'We thought you might like to know we've been phoned and instructed to be offended,' they said. 'We've been told that you are against our people and that you're going around calling people retards.'

Other incidents caused me as much trouble without getting quite as much public exposure. During Helen Clark's last election campaign as Prime Minister I was talking to our political editor Guyon Espiner about how the ratings had been consistently going down for Labour and all of a sudden there had been a bit of a lift, and rightfully so because National were dropping the ball left, right and centre.

'Are you telling me that, after all that has happened,' I said to Guyon, 'there are people thinking, "I don't know. I know I was saying last week I wasn't going to vote for Labour but now I think I might"?'

'It seems that way,' said Guyon.

'Oh God, will this reign of terror never end?' I said. And Labour was obviously so worried about how badly they were doing that there was a suggestion of a Broadcasting Standards Authority complaint over the comparison to the excesses of the French Revolution.

At the same time, I was told by a couple of Labour MPs that they almost pissed themselves laughing when they heard it.

And when they found out there was talk of a complaint they put the kibosh on it very quickly. It would have made them look ridiculous. It's called humour!

Another political complaint that never made it all the way involved Murray McCully as Foreign Minister. Because the political talent pool is so small and the expectations are so low he a) has the job, and b) is seen to be doing it adequately. If Winston Peters and Murray McCully can do a good job as Foreign Minister, who couldn't? Why don't they get Susan Boyle? To me Murray represented everything that was wrong with National being in government. Here he was again, back at the top after all these years, shuffling around in those suits. I always used to refer to him as silly old Murray McCully, even when I was interviewing John Key.

'Are you going to get Winston back or will silly old Murray McCully be Minister of Foreign Affairs?' I asked, and he didn't pull me up on it, which was to become something of a habit with him.

Murray McCully wasn't happy, however. He is also much smarter than George Hawkins. He recognised it was going to be hard having a go at me over the use of 'silly', but he complained about the use of 'old', based on the fact that he was only marginally older than me. He was able to get some mileage out of the complaint but it didn't go to the Broadcasting Standards Authority. He did have a point re our similar age.

I think I have the record for generating more BSA complaints than anyone, but I don't have the record for complaints being upheld, because I knew where the lines were drawn. You can cross a line in good taste or good judgement, and I frequently did, long before you cross a line that will get you into legal trouble. The best broadcasting takes place on the line.

I hope that anyone who has bought — or probably borrowed — this book hoping to read what I have to say about things like the Greenpeace spokeswoman Stephanie Mills' moustache 'affair' and then scorn my 'attempts to justify' such incidents will be disappointed. I don't need to justify anything. If any of those people has a genuine interest in being informed, I would encourage them to go online and look for the original broadcasts where they will invariably find that what happened differed considerably from what was reported.

The occasion on which I upset some homosexuals by saying that it was 'not natural' for gays to adopt children is typical. Most reports ended there. They did not add that I backed it up. I said same sex adoption is not natural because it does not occur in the animal kingdom. I went on to say that homosexuality itself is perfectly natural, and I know that because it is displayed widely in other species. I talked about animals that I know for a fact have been caught in homosexual acts. My point was that you can't argue with the way nature organises things.

The people who complained did not want me to be reasonable. They wanted to have their own prejudices reinforced.

I must, however, since they were front-page news for months — not days or weeks, but months — and led to my resignation, discuss my on-air comments about Sheila Dikshit and Anand Satyanand.

Sheila Dikshit is the chief minister of Delhi and has a funny name. No one can deny it is a funny name. Attempts at such denial are futile. Nor will I attempt to deny that I made fun of it on air. Many of the people who purported to be incensed by what I said, I know, had themselves made fun of it privately. How could you resist? I made fun of it because it made me laugh and because it wound up our *Breakfast* newsreader Peter Williams. The humour inherent in the name was magnified for me because at the time she was having to front up to defend Delhi's preparedness for the Commonwealth Games, when there were reports that the plumbing facilities were less than ideal.

There were murmurings of complaint after my comments and members of the BSA had to wake up and take a call or two, but that was it.

Many people, including Peter Williams, claimed that the name was pronounced Dicks-it. It is not. In any news video from India that involves her, the name is clearly pronounced Dick-shit. Australia's *Sunrise* programme had noticed what an interesting name Ms Dikshit had some time earlier. They interviewed her and at the end of the interview, the journalist said, 'Can you just tell me how you pronounce your name?'

'Sheila,' she says, 'as in Sheila, dick shit.'

'Can you say that again?'

'Dick shit.'

I did not — never have and never would — deliberately mispronounce her name for comic effect. I didn't need to.

Timid non-Indian news organisations, among them TVNZ, insist on mispronouncing her name to avoid the comedy inherent in it. I think that's hugely insulting. One of the basics of journalism is to get people's names right. To deliberately mispronounce a person's name because it is unpalatable is offensive.

I got a lot of feedback about this and a surprising amount of it was from Indian people telling me that they had been laughing at her name for years.

It would almost certainly have been tossed on the pile with my other alleged misdemeanours from over the years had I not asked the Prime Minister, John Key, some days later about selecting a new Governor-General when Sir Anand Satyanand's term came to an end.

'Is he even a New Zealander?' I asked. 'Are you going to choose a New Zealander who looks and sounds like a New Zealander this time?' It was a cheeky way of asking what sort of person he was looking for.

When TVNZ PR person Andi Brotherston said in the following days, unhelpfully as it turned out, 'Paul says what a lot of people think but don't say', she was actually close to the mark. A lot of people don't register that someone of Indian descent and with an Indian name is a New Zealander. I am not one of those people but I wanted in my roundabout way to point out that this was a point of view that existed in the community.

Of course I know that Governors-General now have to be born in New Zealand. I wasn't saying that Sir Anand wasn't a New Zealander or that he wasn't fit to be Governor-General.

I thought no more about it until I heard some talk on the radio about the fact that I was a racist because I had said that unless someone looked and sounded exactly like me they weren't a New Zealander. This person claimed I wouldn't countenance a woman as Governor-General, which was doubly ironic because had we not run out of time I was going to give the PM my short list for the position, at the top of which was the Auckland City Missioner Dianne Robertson, for whom I have an enormous amount of respect and admiration. I assume she is a New Zealander. I think someone who gives their life to helping the destitute and homeless, and has smarts, is just what we need as Governor-General.

As usual most of the people who expressed strong opinions about what I had said hadn't seen the broadcast. As far as TVNZ was concerned, in the early stages of reaction there was not a lot to worry about. I had never been sat down at any time and asked to tone things down. The only feedback I ever had from management was that things were going well, thank you very much. I was never encouraged to be more outrageous, but I was trusted and left to perform.

I know people at management level came under pressure

at times to rein me in. They had a right to do so because they were paying me, but if they had I would have left long before because that was not how I worked. So they let me carry on. But in a quiet news week the *New Zealand Herald* made a big story out of the Satyanand interview and resurrected the Sheila Dikshit comments. And when a massive public outcry arose, calling for my dismissal, all of a sudden, management were very quick to advise me and counsel me, but it was too late. I have no ill feeling towards TVNZ nor to those mindless individuals who got worked up into such a lather. Not the least of the ironies in the whole affair was that I was able to entertain even them. I'm glad I subjected them to me for as long as I did.

The *Herald*'s coverage created the perfect storm from which it was very hard to see an easy way out, especially when the Dikshit story was picked up around the world. That was awkward. Suddenly there was a feeding frenzy with me at the centre. It was talkback catnip — hosts didn't need to come up with a topic of their own for days.

I spoke to TVNZ. We agreed that an official apology was needed to put the lid on the whole thing, and that was planned for the next morning. I had no qualms about apologising for hurting anyone's feelings. I never intend to hurt people, so I'm always happy to apologise on the odd chance that I have genuinely hurt someone. But I will never apologise for outraging anyone.

On the evening of the day it blew up, I had to go to a fundraising event on behalf of the first Christchurch earthquake. The Prime Minister and various Ministers of the Crown were there. Some people were surprised that I had turned up because I had been keeping a low profile and refusing all comment.

The first person I saw was one of the TVNZ board.

'Oh God, what kind of a day is this?' I said.

'I've suffered slings and arrows for you today,' they told me.

'But it'll be fine. Don't worry, it's just another storm. Everything's cool.'

Numerous MPs slapped me on the back and told me not to worry about it. This was informed advice because I knew what I was going through was what they lived with every day.

Pita Sharples put his arm around me and gave me a big manly hug.

'You're one of us now,' he said, meaning I think, someone on the receiving end, not just dishing it out. I was touched by that. Two days later he was publicly calling for my sacking.

John Key walked in. Normally he would have come over and talked to me but he just moved past. I was talking to Gerry Brownlee at the time, and it was noticeable that he acknowledged Gerry and just kept on walking. I fully understood that and had no intention of embarrassing him by going up and talking to him.

The next day I read a statement on the show:

'I'd like you all to know I have the greatest respect for Sir Anand Satyanand. I don't know him personally, but I understand his reputation is beyond reproach.

'He is highly respected in both judicial circles, as a former judge, and as the Queen's representative here in New Zealand. He has done a very fine job as Governor-General and I am sincerely sorry if I seemed disrespectful to him. That was not what I intended, and I certainly didn't intend to sound racist. It was wrong for me to ask the questions that I did.

'Sir Anand was born in New Zealand. His lineage, as far as I can ascertain, is far more dignified than mine, which makes him a better candidate for Governor-General than me.

'Most people think I'm British, but the truth is much, much worse than that. Like the Governor-General, I was born in New Zealand, however, I am at least half what they colloquially call in Europe, a gyppo.

'So, let me make it quite clear, I will never apologise for causing outrage, however I will and do apologise sincerely for causing real hurt and upset to anyone, no matter what their background, who works to make this country a better country.

'So, in that spirit, I apologise unreservedly to Sir Anand and his family. He is a very distinguished man and I am a gyppo television presenter.'

That just seemed to fire people up more. When the pro-gramme ended I was called upstairs to see the head of news and current affairs, Anthony Flannery.

'This is gaining momentum and we need to find some way of stopping it,' he said. 'We need to go and have a chat with Rick.'

At 11am we went to see Rick Ellis, TVNZ's chief executive officer. I was surprised that when we got there the decision to suspend me had already been made. We talked about it briefly and I could see that for TVNZ it was a good idea.

'Why don't I just walk out now?' I said. 'I won't go back into the newsroom, I'll head out and I'll go to Napier and hang out at my beach house for a while.

'Let's actually dock my salary,' I said. I was getting quite enthusiastic. We made it clear I would be suspended without pay so they could say that. I didn't even take holiday pay, a considerable amount of which I had due.

Before I went to Napier I had to come back home where I was confronted by journalists from the *Herald*. They were on my property, having passed 'Unauthorised Entry is Prohibited' signs, and come down a private right of way. I went in and they knocked on the door moments later.

'I've got no comment,' I said, 'I'm not interested in saying anything.'

A few minutes later I walked out and the photographer was back on my property taking pictures.

'You're trespassing,' I said. 'Leave.'

I went back inside. After another 20 minutes I drove up to

the top of the private road leading to my house — the road I own part of and pay the rates for. And the photographer and two journalists — the fact there were two told me just how slow a news week this was — were still there. Now I was annoyed. I told them to fuck off. I went inside and rang the *Herald*.

'I don't want any of those photos used,' I told the editor. Of course, they were used along with an account of my tirade, with no acknowledgement of the fact that the tirade occurred because they were trespassing and had ignored my requests to leave.

While there, they had interviewed all my neighbours so can rightly claim to know them much better than I do. I can't imagine what they hoped to learn or what questions they asked: 'So, have you seen Paul Henry being racist much?'

They had also been to my local dairy. I'm not sure, because I have never asked them, but I think the people who run it may be of Indian descent. The journalists — and I can see them congratulating themselves on their cleverness when they had the idea — went in to ask the couple how much racial abuse they receive from me in an average week. Unfortunately, though I don't go in there very often, I get on very well with the pair. The husband sent me an email telling me the story. He was highly amused.

I was on the front page for the whole week. TVNZ led their news with the story. TV3 led with it. TV3 were very measured in their handling, although when you've got screaming banshees demonstrating outside TVNZ, you don't really have to sensationalise it.

Other people were very kind. I got offered flights away to take a break. Someone else put his super yacht at my disposal. 'The crew is on board,' he said, 'best wine in the fridge, just go.'

I didn't comment because I was suspended. I was still an employee of TVNZ so it was not my place to do so. I had an unimaginable number of calls and texts coming in on my cell phone, nearly all of which I didn't answer. Napier was good for giving me some distance and perspective. It was a shame the rest of the country couldn't have been there.

A couple of days later TVNZ rang and asked me to come in again because it didn't look like things were going to die down.

The Foreign Affairs official who volunteered an apology to India without any official sanction managed to inflame matters further. New Zealand had not been asked for an apology and, indeed, should not have made an apology at government level. I thought that was rich given people in India had been burning a New Zealander in effigy the week before — Mike Hooper, the Commonwealth Games chief executive who had questioned Delhi's readiness to host the Games.

But someone had decided that my comments threatened a pending free-trade agreement with India. I find it hard to believe that a hard-headed Indian businessperson would have boycotted New Zealand for the sake of Sheila Dikshit.

We planned to meet at Rick Ellis' house on a Saturday morning. At the last minute I got a call to say the meeting would be at TVNZ because 'the media are staking out Rick's house'.

For TVNZ, I knew, there were just two options, both awkward. They could let me go and alienate all those people who wanted me to stay. Rick Ellis had shown me a pile of emails a foot high, apparently just one of several, demanding that I be retained. They weren't just from fanatical Paul Henry fans, but from people who were saying things like 'We actually think he probably did overstep the mark this time, but you don't suspend someone for saying something like this. We're intelligent enough to be able to understand that not everyone is going to say the right thing.'

The other option was to keep me on and drive the crazies even crazier.

I would never want to work anywhere where they didn't want me. I am not a hoop jumper. If I was told I had to cross a road in order to keep a job, I would not cross that road. There were a few other factors to consider, not least the pressure on my family. I could, on one level, stand back and enjoy the entertainment value of the whole scenario, but there was no way I could enjoy the death threats to my mother and my daughters.

Letters had been passed on to the police, one of which specifically mentioned my mother, where she lived and her name. It also mentioned my daughters and the throwing of acid. It was almost more of a threat to them than to me. There was another occasion when the press were outside my mother's rest home, which I found unsettling. Given that I was not going to jump through hoops to keep the job, and that I had the idea of leaving in the back of my mind anyway, the decision was not hard to make or accept.

My youngest daughter, Bella, was turning 18 at the time and having a celebration at a bar in Queen Street. I was advised by TVNZ and the police not to go because, irrespective of any threats, the moment anyone saw me they would ring the media, photographers would turn up and the evening would cease to be about Bella and be about her annoying father instead.

I thought about the matter overnight and we met again on Sunday.

During my career I had never once gone to a meeting about my work with a lawyer or agent or anyone at all. I have been very relaxed about my work conditions and handled things myself. I have never had a 'support person'. HR people know to keep their distance from me. But this time, because everything was going so fast and the circumstances were so exceptional, I took a lawyer and a friend.

In light of everything, the only option I had was to resign. For it to be of any use to TVNZ, it had to be done quickly to make them look decisive and so it could lead the news that night. Journalists had seen me go in and they were blocking exits. It was a very long meeting, but it was extraordinarily amiable.

At one point, I noticed Rick had a paper bag on his desk.

'What's in there?' I asked, and he took out a muffin which he carefully cut into eight pieces and shared among everyone there. We were all hungry.

There was a feeling around the table that something was happening that no one wanted to happen. Everyone was trying to snatch a little bit of victory from the jaws of defeat. In a negotiation like that, the two sides would normally be entirely at odds but there was so much common ground, and we walked out with the situation entirely resolved. We left the meeting with best wishes for each other. In fact I hugged Rick and he hugged me back, and I don't get the feeling he's a natural hugger.

My legal person is involved in matters like this every day and he said he had never experienced a situation where a group of people were negotiating the parting of the ways when they obviously got on so well and respected each other so much.

We left through an exit not normally open on the weekend, and I slipped away while Rick faced an onslaught from his own and other journalists. To be honest, having gladly stood by TVNZ for seven years, I was surprised and a little disappointed that they could only stand by me for a few hours. Such is life.

I left for Napier and had hit Tokoroa when the 6pm news went to air and a tsunami of calls started. A cameraman working on *One News* that night was the first to ring. He was a freelancer who worked on *Breakfast*, and he left an amazing message, almost in tears. The phone continued vibrating until it ran out of battery.

I got a text from Lucy: 'I'm unbelievably proud of you, love Lucy.' Bella sent me a slightly more pragmatic text: 'As long as we're going to be OK for money I'm cool with this.' Sophie's message was: 'This is the only way a career like yours could end.'

John Key phoned me to check that I was okay. 'I feel really

bad about it,' he said. 'I know I shouldn't and I don't need to but I feel really bad about it and I hope you're okay.'

'John, what's happened to me will happen to you,' I said, 'because whether you're in politics or in the media, if you're in front of people, your achievements are singular, your failures are cumulative and sooner or later the people who thought they were going to get you last time and didn't will side with the people who want to get you this time, and the numbers will be against you.'

Although I had nothing but contempt for the people who were accusing me of being a racist when nothing could be further from the truth — I actually hold all races, genders, nationalities, sexualities, occupations and hobbies in equally low esteem — it is a nasty label to have flung at you. Even with a skin as thick as mine, it is not pleasant to be unable to turn on the radio or TV or open a newspaper without hearing that particular piece of misrepresentation.

There were, however, occasional compensations. One of these took place when I was test driving an Aston Martin for a magazine. Obviously this was during a time when I was trying to keep a low profile.

One of the keys to being a successful test driver is to keep the gas low because you don't want to be returning the car full of petrol that you've paid for. Sophie was with me when we needed to put $5 worth in the tank and pulled into a service station in Onehunga. Why we were in Onehunga I have no idea.

Sophie was cowering down in her seat long before we stopped. She predicted correctly that when we did heads would turn at the sight of this beautiful car. It was a bonus when people realised the Aston Martin contained me. It quickly became obvious that at least 90 per cent of the people on the forecourt and 100 per cent of the people inside were Indians.

Unusually for a service station, this one provided service,

and one of the staff approached me. 'Oh, Mr Henry, can I help you?' he said. And that was awkward because I have a small quirk when it comes to service stations, which is that I like to do everything myself because then you know it has been done properly. I have had a couple of instances a long time ago where expensive cars have been slightly scratched, not on purpose but because other people are never as careful as you. My problem was that if I said no he might take it as yet more proof of my notorious racist attitudes, especially when it came to Indians.

However, since this was a very expensive car, obviously brand new and not mine, I took the risk of damaging my reputation and declined his offer. Then I went inside where there were two people serving at the counter and two lines of customers, all of them, so far as I could tell, Indian. Finally, after what seemed like an inordinate amount of time standing there waiting to pay, I got to the head of the line.

'Can I just say, Mr Henry,' said the attendant, 'that it is a real sadness in our household that we can't wake up to you in the mornings and I feel ashamed for what's happened to you.'

And when he said that, it was as though everyone there had been given permission, and suddenly they were all saying how sorry they were and that they hoped what had happened hadn't in any way tarnished my feelings towards Indians.

It was very nice to hear, and it was also nice to have a chance to make the point if only to a select few that the whole fuss was about other people's prejudices, certainly not mine.

And very soon, the job offers started to come in. Tristram European, the VW dealer that I use, offered me a job as a car groomer and went so far as to guarantee me minimum wage before our negotiations even started.

There were calls from media organisations too. I wondered how they had come up with ideas so quickly. Had they known for months this was going to happen to me?

TV3, Radio Live, Newstalk ZB and so many others all contacted me. Some had firm offers; others sensed I was in no hurry and merely wanted to let me know that when I was ready to talk they would be ready to talk. The door at TVNZ too, it was quite clear, was pushed closed but certainly had not been locked or slammed. In talking to all those people I never got as far as asking what the hours would be or what the job would pay because this was like selling a roof — once I asked the price, the deal would have been as good as done.

I saw it as a great opportunity to spend a bit more time with the children and just live, to do stuff, to travel to places without being followed around by a film crew. I'm a traveller, both in mind and body, certainly in my business and in my goals and my aspirations. I don't look at anything as long term. When opportunities come up I take them or I move on to something else. When it became obvious I needed to leave TVNZ I was ready to leave, and then all of a sudden the excitement began. Did anyone really think I was going to stay on *Breakfast* for the rest of my life?

When I had toyed with the idea of leaving previously, people asked whether I wouldn't get bored and that had been one of the things that stopped me, because there is no way of knowing the answer to that until it happens.

'Won't you miss being a star?' was the other thing I used to get asked. That was much easier to answer. I'm not a star. Stars are visible, whereas I am a hermit and always have been. I don't like going out so I don't. At the same time I don't moan about being recognised. It's nice not to be and I enjoy that about being overseas, but you know when you go into television that it is part of the job. You even get paid extra to compensate for it and so you should.

There are good things about fame too. You often get better service from cringing toadies in restaurants. You also get bad service sometimes from people who have decided they know and despise you. You get free stuff, which is hardly ever anything you want. You get invited to events you would never dream of attending. All in all I knew I wouldn't miss being a star and getting all the benefits I didn't cash in anyway.

Once my hand was forced, those questions ceased to matter. Instead of boredom there was huge relief that I could move on with my life. A lot of time was spent mopping up — fielding job offers and ducking for cover. The *Herald* rang all the time. I never replied to their messages and if I picked up the phone by accident and it was them, I refused to say anything. So they ran stories suggesting I was desperate to have my say. I refused all interviews except for a story with *New Idea*, which was one of the few magazines not to have completely annoyed me with things they wrote over the years.

I was approached by an American production company who, unbeknownst to me, had been following my career for several years on YouTube. I had come to their attention originally via a *Breakfast* diatribe about obese Americans being sucked into Amtrak toilets. They had some programme ideas and wanted to represent me in what they considered, and at the time of writing still consider, my future career on television in the United States.

Since becoming unemployed I've spent many months in the US. I've always loved America and Bella does too. I bought a brand new 2011 Mustang which I keep at LA airport. I have had a lot of fun driving through umpteen of the states. Bella is on exchange in Colby, Kansas, for a year and this has tied in nicely with going to see her. I've had more studio executive meetings than a person of my short attention span can reasonably be expected to suffer and I'm told by my agents, production company and manager that my career — though non-existent — is stellar.

I confess to losing almost all of my interest in working in the

States given the amount of time it's taking for something to happen, which in the great scheme of things is no time at all, but if I've learnt anything from all of this it's that I need to work. I could retire but couldn't stand it. I need an outlet. Frequently I find myself thinking people need to hear my views on various subjects and I need to have them heard.

I have been putting off giving a definitive answer either to TVNZ or Mediaworks, who own TV3 and Radio Live, but recently decided it was not necessary to put it off any more so entered serious negotiations with both organisations. It's clear many people in TVNZ understood that my ability to be occasionally a liability was dramatically overshadowed by my ability to be an asset, and to their credit they wanted me back. But the approaches from Mediaworks' bosses and even the board chairman were consistently considerate, respectful and professional, and I signed a long-term commitment ensuring that when I'm broadcasting in New Zealand it will be with their organisations only. First up, the plan is I will be hosting the drive-time talk show on Radio Live, which means I get to go back to doing the kind of broadcasting I prefer to any other. My expectation is that I will appear regularly on TV3. I'm in discussions at the moment involving a range of projects, but I would like to think that at some point I'll have a weekly talk show.

But, as I put my pen down, (actually it's an iPad — dammit) sitting in the home I love in Albany, Auckland, surrounded by the knick-knacks and general detritus I've collected over the past 50 years, it is only my expectation.

Because you see, we're up to now. How much work I will actually be doing in the United States, exactly what I will actually be doing on TV3 and everything else that's going to happen is not entirely clear to me at this time. It will have to be part of my next book if I ever find the heartbeats to write again.

Some people might be a little disappointed that I haven't mercilessly slagged off the arseholes who have thwarted me over the years. After all, I am a particularly forthright person. In the last few pages alone I could have named some people I consider to be gutless wonders at Television New Zealand who don't understand, amongst other things, the meaning of loyalty. But the thing is this, I am not even remotely bitter about anything that has ever happened to me. I can't remember a time in my entire life when I haven't been ready to move on. So, no bitterness and only a few regrets, none of them relating to employment.

Partly for obvious reasons but also because these memoirs reveal only a few squares of the rich tapestry that is my life it's impossible for me to put myself in the position of someone reading this for the first time. But if I try very hard to do just that, I think I would want the book to end . . . now.